ISLAMIC MEDIA

ISLAMIC MEDIA

Dr P Quereshi

MD PUBLICATIONS PVT LTD
NEW DELHI
www.mdppl.com

Published by :

MD Publications Pvt Ltd
"MD House", 11, Darya Ganj,
New Delhi-110 002
Phone : +91-11-41563325 (Customer Service)
+91-11-41562846 (Editorial)
E-mail (orders) : order@mdppl.com
Website : www.mdppl.com

ISBN : 978-81-7533-231-7

Published and Printed by Mr. Pranav Gupta on behalf of **MD Publications Pvt Ltd** at Printext, New Delhi.

Preface

Islam is the fastest growing religion in the West. Nevertheless, the West has many stereotypes and misconceptions about Islam that are due to the media, prejudice, and ignorance. The Islamic world is poorly represented in the West in terms of press and media coverage. Not only are there just handfuls of news agencies in Muslim countries; there is the concern over the number of inexperienced reporters. Many reporters don't understand the local cultures nor speak the language, leaving them with access to only those English or French speaking Westernized elites.

A negative image of Islam is becoming more inherent in the Western culture from inaccurate media coverage. The media helps to make an image of Islam to unsuspecting audiences. The Western public often is misinformed about Muslims through the images on television, motion picture screens, magazines, radios, and comic strips in newspapers, which promote strong messages among their audiences. Western reporters often say that Muslims are terrorists. This becomes a common image to the general person that all Muslims are terrorists.

Aside from the fact that the media misrepresents Islam because of ignorance, the media is also a profit-seeking organization which often seeks to create a false image of reality. Islam is often news of an unpleasant sort for the general public of the United States. Islam has often been presented as a menace or a threat to the West. These negative images do not correspond to Islam, but are the belief of certain sectors of a particular society. These prominent sectors can propagate negative images of Islam, which sometimes influences people's views on Islam. The Western media actually poorly represents Islam.

Some biased reports come from negative images that have happened in the Muslim world in the past like the hijacking of airplanes by Palestinians, the occupation of the United States Embassy by students in Tehran, the fact that there are no democratic governments in most Islamic countries, and the Gulf War. For most of these events, the media has misinterpreted and misrepresented them. The media sometimes unintentionally blows things out of proportion, sometimes because of biased feelings toward Muslims. However, many positive developments in the Muslims world rarely go noticed. Some inaccurate representations of Islam are often due to the media's incorrect representations of Islamic countries, such as jihad, or Islam women's rights.

Today, the vast majority of Muslims - old and young, men and women, city-dweller or villager - are almost totally immune to the western media and, in some parts, hostile. To be honest, there is no basis here for any fight for hearts and minds. Today the western media is increasingly only influential within its own boundaries and among its own peoples. New technology means an even more disastrous consequence: the emergence of a media, particularly in the Arab Muslim world, which has far outstripped traditional opinion-makers and voices of influence such as the BBC or the Voice of America. Nowadays, the main source of all news, and of the truth, in most of the Arab Muslim world is al-Jazeera Satellite Station. The strength of al-Jazeera lies - in the eyes of its 35 million viewers - not only in its ability to provide alternative and relevant news, but also in its ability to master modern techniques for presenting that viewpoint.

I am very grateful to Mr. Pranav Gupta, Director of MD Publications Pvt Ltd, New Delhi, for his kind cooperation and support for this book.

Dr P Quereshi

CONTENTS

Contents

1

Structure of the Islamic Media

TELEVISION INDUSTRY AND THE RISE OF SATELLITE

The rise of technology and the constantly changing media landscape have been greatly affecting not only the Western civilizations but the Islam world as well. Since the beginning of the twenty-first century, with these technological and societal changes, more choices of mediums have been offered to cater to the commands and interests of Islam audiences. The rise of satellite broadcasting and the internet have especially been major factors in triggering new social and "power dynamics" in the Islam region, for with this wide array of informational sources, hegemonic messages are fading and public opinions are beginning to diversify.

With regard to ownership in the world of Arab media, many media sources either operate under the government or under a patron or "some rich owner who in many cases is associated, in one way or another, with the ruling elite". This is mainly due to the fact that the government is able to provide large sums of money and funding, as well as is capable of preserving a centralized government system over the people. However, while many fear of the manipulation of ideas and messages by the government over its audiences, satellite TV has in fact challenged the two main communication hindrances: government intervention and illiteracy. Although mediums in the Arab world are not fully independent from the government, satellite broadcasting nevertheless grants them a good amount of freedom from state control; major Arab countries can no longer effectively dominate smaller countries. Additionally, as a result of the introduction of satellite, audiences have transitioned from being passive and easily manipulated to being opinionated and more skeptical.

COMPETITION AND "THE WEAPONIZATION OF MEDIA"

The prevalence of satellite broadcasting is parallel to the competition amongst the channels in Arab media, especially in television, which, in most parts of the world is the most popular and public medium. With the growth of new technologies, there is now competition for digital media products, which in turn is giving television producers no choice but to "shift to free speech and interactive dialogue". Satellite has opened the doors for a diversity of critical perspectives and opinions from both the producers as well as the audience and has challenged behavioral codes and set different rules for religious and political minorities. This revolution of television has especially benefited the Arab world, for there has been an "explosion of online information sources, which not only created a new public sphere for the free exchange of views among Muslims around the world, but also enabled Islamists and other dissidents direct access to populations they would have been unable to reach through traditional media". Through this constant communication of satellite broadcasting, the Muslim dream is fulfilled, for "constant communication within the community is what enhances its dynamism".

Aware of the obvious power and effectiveness of the media as a "weapon," world leaders and influential figures are taking advantage of it, all struggling to spread their messages across expansive publics. This psychological warfare has been negatively termed the "Weaponization of Media" and specifically exists between the U.S. and terrorists such as the members of al-Qaeda and Hezbollah. Each is struggling to combat the other - the U.S. fighting against terrorism and the latter focusing on using the highly popular yet controversial news channel, Al-Jazeera, as its way to spread propaganda and reflect reality, including American policy. This ruthless competition amongst the groups of course leads to constant foreign involvement in the Arab world of media. Arab television, however, does not consist of solely anti-American propaganda.

ADVERTISING

As mentioned earlier, satellite broadcasting offers endless informational sources and challenges government control, intervention, and manipulation. With the encouragement of audiences to provide feedback and with the change of roles from "being manipulated pieces on the chess-board to becoming its major players", viewers in the audience are now less passive and are overall ideal targets for advertisers. Not only has the competition increased for audiences among all sectors but the prevalence of satellites has also made it "possible for smaller operators to compete" as well. Because of satellite, the fragmentation of audiences triggers the competition amongst advertisers in Arab media.

CURRENT PROGRAMMING TRENDS

Current programmatic trends in Arab television are associated with two significant factors: modernity and globalization, which have greatly contributed to its evolution. Much of what is seen today on Arab TV is not very different from what is seen in American TV programs. However, many of these Arab television programs often lead to strong criticisms and complaints, as they lead to debates about the importance of Islam in modern-day life.

Al-Jazeera

Al-Jazeera is a 24-hour pan-Arab satellite news channel headquartered in Qatar, a small emirate in the region of the Persian Gulf that seeks to achieve an image of a country that wants to modernize itself. Seen as the "trendsetter" in Arab news, Al-Jazeera has gained itself a permanent reputation as a revolutionary channel that offers rapid and honest news and is not afraid to cover social and political issues that most Arab governments prefer not to disclose. Al-Jazeera's main goal is to provide "food for an audience that is hungry for credible news and serious political analysis" (Zayani 5) and therefore has enjoyed its freedom of the press without any constraints. It has acquired respect - even by the US -for its aggressive news reporting and its call for Arab unity, as Arab viewers of all ages appreciate its graphic and disturbing images as a "viable alternative which offers coverage of the Arab world that has been distorted by the American news media" (Zayani 29). Al-Jazeera has transformed news reporting in the Arab world from simply transmitting messages to audience sharing, participation, and association. Below are charts of Al-Jazeera's demographics, specifically by age and area.

However, as much as Al-Jazeera is widely viewed as a leader in the Arab media, it also is extremely controversial to many, including Arab governments and to journalists and politicians of the West. Firstly, many Arab companies have boycotted the channel out of fear that associating with Al-Jazeera may lead to scorn from governments in the region. Also, others question whether or not Al-Jazeera is capable of reporting objectively about Arab issues - can it steer away from its biased perspective? Lastly, many Western journalists and politicians view Al-Jazeera as too critical of the US and of Israel. With its large audience of Muslims, many fear that the channel is "igniting the anger of Arabs and the fury of Muslims against the US" (Zayani 23), therefore causing even more hateful feelings towards Americans.

Women's Television

The number of women being represented and even working in the world of Arab media is increasing noticeably and such women are seeking to diminish negative attitudes and stereotypes of Muslim females. Heya TV is a Lebanese satellite broadcasting channel whose objective is to "cater to diverse tastes among diverse women" (Matar 514). Heya defines itself as the "platform for Arab women" and aims to portray women other than being completely liberated and lacking values or as being submissive and ultraconservative – this is rare in the Arab world, which typically lacks gender-sensitive perspectives and policies. Heya TV offers a myriad of programs, such as talk shows, cooking and sewing skills programs, educational programs, dramas, and even fashion programs. Rather than focusing on the topics such as violence against women, women in the economy, and even women and religious rulings, Heya simply deals with encouraging women to participate and discuss private topics publicly as women, apart from religion. Heya is distinct in the way that it follows a feminist agenda as well as an agreement between the presenter and the audience. This illustrates how the Arab media today truly is a public sphere for audiences to address and discuss controversial topics before they are dealt with by the government.

Islamic Pop Stars / Popularizing Islam

In the Arab world of television, pop stars and celebrities are just as cherished and influential as those in other modern countries. The "traditional" image and religion of Islam has somewhat eroded and as a result, pop stars such as singer Sami Yusuf are popularizing and redefining Islam. Yusuf, who is mostly revered by young, female audiences, sings about the possibility of being both a devout Muslim while living in a modern world. His music videos feature him walking through the streets of large international cities while fulfilling his duties as a devout Muslim. While he competes against Western pop stars, he is not against them; Yusuf solely aims to show that being Muslim in the modern world is possible and sings about religion in order for his audiences to see him as authentic and influential. Pop stars like Yusuf promote a diasporic Muslim community and the ability to live in a modern and public Islamic sphere. Despite these stars' good intentions, however, they are also highly criticized for being inauthentic Muslims and for taking the symbols of the West – such as modernity and globalization – and making them "Muslim." These pop stars' criticisms illustrate the ongoing disagreements between "modern" Muslims and "traditionalists."

ANALYSIS AND SUGGESTIONS

It is strongly believe that the current involvement of the United States in Arab television should be discontinued. The "Weaponization of Media" perfectly illustrates that there is strong hostility between the two sides and that they literally use the media merely as weapons to destroy each other. American viewpoints - such as the one found in The New York Times Magazine article, "What the Muslim World is Watching," which automatically assume that Arab news channels make names for themselves "through stridency and anti-Americanism" - must be avoided. As shown in this report, Arab TV is not anti-American; it seeks to build unity, a sense of community, and understanding in such a society that is difficult to find a balance between traditional and modern beliefs.

Instead, the media should be utilized in the way which they were originally intended: as educational sources. Rather than feeling threatened by Al-Jazeera's radical and aggressive news reporting, the U.S. should take the time and effort to understand why producers in Arab television feel the need to report such issues. The U.S. cannot make the same expensive and time-wasting mistake of creating advertising campaigns such as "Happy Muslims" to illustrate the "happy" lives of Muslim-Americans, all of whose stories do not apply to Muslims in the East. What the U.S. must do is research the underlying reasons as to why Arab TV is the way it is today, whether it involves delving into history, economic policies, and of course, religion. Assumptions must be avoided and each side should learn from each other's media sources.

ISLAM TELEVISION INDUSTRY

Up until the 1950's-60's the media landscape throughout the entire Middle East region was managed and profited by the colonizing powers. The advent of all Middle East television and Radio networks later introduced by those colonial powers fostered a shift from public broadcasting to national ownership. That shift from public to national control took place in 1948 in

Israel, 1952 in Egypt, and throughout the 1950's-70's to the rest of the region. According to the renowned media scholar Andrew Hummond, "it would be no exaggeration to say that the model for media as a weapon for state control in the Arab world was established by the Egyptians."

Egypt quickly became the transnational Arab media source creating and exporting the most programmatic content throughout the Arab World. However the significant shift in the landscape of the Arab Television Industry occurred in during the 1990's with the emergence of satellite technology. Prior to the satellite breakthrough Arab government monopolies operated and controlled the media outlets completely relying on national unity, political control, and the banning of private groups. Media monopolies dictated the landscape by 1954 in Morocco, 1956 in Iraq, and in additional countries such as Algeria and Lebanon.

The control was maintained using two power systems: one included the strict- control model where there was no criticism of the government policy where the state-owned media served as a mouthpiece to deliver the government's political platform; or the latter was a loyalist model where the media outlets were loyal to the monarchies and favored but not owned. Countries such as Morocco, Tunisia, Kuwait, and Qatar adopted the loyalist system while Israel and Lebanon served as the Middle East region exceptions, embracing the free media market. The four media systems adopted by countries in this region cover the entire spectrum of government-media-audience dynamics conveying the levels of journalistic autonomy, state-control, and media ownership. The four systems are: Nationalized: government controlled, funded, and filtered (ex. Syria, Libya, Sudan, and Algeria) Loyalist: independent but corresponds with government agenda (ex. UAE, Qatar, Oman) Diverse: free from government involvement, competitive open market (Kuwait, Morocco, Yemen + Israel, Lebanon) Transitional: undetermined fusion of government involvement and private control (Egypt).

The transnationalisation of the media landscape created divergence in broadcasting formats: between public service formats of top-down control, rooted in overtly political, ideological neutrality, and non-commercial incentives. The public service aims to educate the masses (such as the BBC) to commercial networks such as the (U.S Media Market) focused on commercial gains, entertainment, and presentation of a spectrum of perspectives. In 1991 MBC: the Middle East Broadcasting Center, currently a private Dubai operated network, started in London as the first satellite, free-to-air multichannel media group of its kind in the Arab world. MBC 1 took to the airwaves during the Gulf War in 1991 with the first-ever independent pan-Arab news. Over the past 15 years, MBC added five TV and two radio channels, a drama series and hit reality TV shows, with a strong commitment to local programming it continues to serve as the number one family viewing option in the region Middle East coverage. Other Arab nations quickly followed suit which the establishment of their own networks such as: Al Manar- meaning the "lighthouse," founded in 1991 as Hezbollah's resistance media network based in Lebanon.

Interestingly, the forces of deregulation and liberalization in the West have led to the transformation of broadcasting form mainly a cultural to an economic activity in the last few decades. Though in many Arab Nations the Media is still state regulated to some extent the process of 'setting the media free' has transformed broadcasting institutions based on notions of public service into ones concerned with commercial or quasi-commercial objectives. One would assume the arrival of commercialization would increase profits, but Al-Jazeera interestingly unlike some other Arab networks makes very little in profits as a result of not being supported by the Saudi Arabian government. Also it has "cut the umbilical cord to state funding in some regards.

The satellite revolution of the 1990's led by Saudis, Qataris, and the Lebanese infringed upon Egypt as the transnational Arab media hegemony. As the media infrastructure of the Arab world shifted in the 1990's with the introduction of satellite media networks, governments formerly controlling their national media coverage were suddenly challenged by borderless transmission. The first Arab satellite TV network to challenge the realm of individual Arab governments was Al-Jazeera, the first leading, 24 hour, Arabic-language news network delivering fair local coverage with exposure to the often under represented Arab perspective in global media of the Middle East. It was during the historical moment in which the United States invaded Afghanistan, in 2001, that the mapping of truly transnational Arab Media landscape commenced.

This transition in Arab Television, which began in 1996 with the establishment of the Al-Jazeera headquarters based in Doha, Qatar, changed the Middle Eastern Media Landscape forever. It can be argued that for the first time since the early 1970's Al-Jazeera managed to unite Arabs behind a single issue. With the Middle East population over 300 million, the majority of which is young and living in very strict societies ruled by governments who wish to stay in power and maintain control at any cost, it seems that with its launching, Al-Jazeera managed to target a previously untapped audience. Although half of the Middle East population is illiterate, filled with dreams of liberation and basic freedoms the network provides an interstate representation of civil rights and liberties.

Despite its leading ratings, being a global competitor to CNN many Arab governments have been highly critical of the media outlet blaming that its coverage of the Palestinian uprising "threatened the stability of their regimes and exposed them to criticism by their own people." Ironically, Egypt and Jordan have been more critical of Al-Jazeera than has Israel, which could theoretically ban Al-Jazeera correspondents from operating freely within its borders if it believed it helps incite Palestinians to riot. Today more than 350 channels exist, "free to air" on satellite television in the Arab world with no subscription necessary. Although many networks are deemed sensationalist or polarized, perhaps by western media critics, they aim to provide an authentic local perspective. Following Al-Jazeera's footsteps other stations surfaced, in 1996 the LBC:

Lebanese Broadcasting Corporation founded initially in 1985 went Global, generating most popular Lebanese programs and then in 2003 Press TV emerged, an Iranian Tehran based station generating what was often tagged as oppositional anti-American sentiment surfaced.

PROGRAMMATIC TRENDS

As Negrine and S. Papathanassopoulos discusses in *The Internationalisation of Television*: a "key indicator of internationalization is the degree of commonality of television programs across frontiers- the more programs are shared and exchanged the more television fare of different countries begins to look alike." Post 1990's the abundance and diversity of Arab Media Programs has spiked dramatically in addition to higher foreign programmatic imports. Lila Abu-Lughod exploration of Egyptian serials exemplifies one popular realm of Arab programmatic production and its effects. Her demonstration exemplifies how the serials produce a national community in Egypt. Because the television in Egypt is state-controlled, as is the case with many other Arab media outlets, Lila assesses how the entertainment in Egypt provided to these large audiences that cross boundaries of class, gender, and region, articulates with national politics, policies, and cultural identities.

In studies of media in the non-Western world alarms are often sounded about cultural imperialism in the domination of national culture and production by international imports, usually from the U.S. and Britain. But Egypt, much like India, Brazil, and Mexico, produces and even exports a healthy amount of film and television programming of its own. She demonstrates that within Egypt, local productions are often more popular and widely viewed than imported films and television serials, which are subtitled and therefore largely inaccessible to the non-literate population. Her analysis of the internal politics of these national productions alongside who controls these messages and who is excluded in the serials reveals a lot about Egyptian and Arab culture. While these Ramadan serials can range in topic and setting, the mini series air exclusively during the holy month of Ramadan, when most

Muslim families spend the day fasting and the evening watching television with their families. These shows "account for nearly a quarter of the years advertising revenues, the equivalent of American sweeps weeks combined with the Super Bowl," demonstrating how strong a presence the media and commerce are making in the Muslim world.

Another example of a program in the programmatic sphere of the Arab media landscape includes the hit show 'Star Academy.' Marwan M. Kraidy's research on the Star Academy, a programme launched by LBCI in December 2003, which quickly became the most controversial show in the history of Arab satellite television, depicts the pan-Arab media event as a platform for political discourse. Kraidy considers connections between the entertainment industry and politics and further narrows the case study to show links between reality TV and politics. The show thus became political as it "articulated an alternative view of public participation in the public process" and recognizably was a local format adaptation.

However despite the dramatic growth in the Arab Media landscape with programmes like Star Academy, some may still be inclined to apply the "media imperialism thesis" to the Middle East. Countries such as the USA dominate both national and international media structures and contents whereby they impose their cultures, values, and ideologies on the receiving nations. Some tag this as a process of domination that is intentional or part of a 'conspiracy' whereas some describe it as an imbalance of trade, dealing with imports and exports often with the west and 'developing countries' but the programmatic media development in the Arab region proves how its development. There are all these false notions of a supposed-backwards Arab world- when really most major leading Arab Nations are media producing nations, which have fully embraced modernity. The constant development and expansion of local Arab programs resulting in increased ratings, such as the case with these Ramadan Serials, proves that the Arab World wants and relates to its own cultural content. This notion is only further supported by Berlusconi's view 'that equal quality domestic product will always triumph over foreign product.' With that in mind the assessment of U.S involvement and future relationship with the Arab Media Landscape is more than necessary.

U.S INVOLVEMENT AND RELATIONSHIP WITH ARAB TELEVISION

Despite pluralistic representations in the Arab media and what many consider to be programmatic expression of modernity, the new public sphere created by the Arab Media has stirred much controversy, especially concerning U.S relations. Al Hurrah operated by The Middle East Television Network, Inc., a nonprofit corporation funded by the U.S. Congress through the Broadcasting Board of Governors (BBG) airs in 22 Arab nations via satellites. Its programming is reportedly often met with skepticism, being thought of as American propaganda although the Lebanese director, Muafac Harb, maintains that one of the missions of his network is to deliver accurate and balanced coverage. Anne Marie Baylouny discusses Al-Hurrah: "The U.S. station accused of preaching, condescension, and cultural inappropriateness. Its name, the "free one," assumes the traditional U.S. stance of representing the better society but contradicts its actual journalistic nature" Another news media network that has stirred much skepticism has been Al Arabiya, a Dubai based station, widely popular in the Arab world, that isn't owned or regulated by the U.S but rather harshly criticized. Al-Arabiya has been regularly critiqued by the U.S. government for its news coverage of Iraq, which allegedly incites violence against the U.S coalition there. After broadcasting footage of masked men inciting attacks against Iraqi Governing Council members as well as U.S. interests in Iraq, Al-Arabiya was banned several times.

Their Baghdad office was shut down and their equipment seized following the airing of an audiotape that claimed to be the voice of deposed Iraqi President Saddam Hussein calling on the Iraqi people to resist the U.S. - led forces. Though its coverage is sometimes viewed as provocative, founder Walid al Ibrahim, who reportedly views the work of the station as a step toward advancing the Arab World and freeing it from dictatorship and repression, promised that their coverage would be objective and accurate. The BBC reported, "Across the Arab world, Al-Arabiya probably has about 20 million viewers, as compared to Al-Jazeera's 35 million."

R.S Zaharna discusses how on the surface footage is very different, however below the surface the American networks and Al-Jazeera appear to share the same philosophy and approach, covering the story from a local angle and the audience's perspective. Hence you see, Americans focusing on the Military goals, weaponry and troops, whereas Al-Jazeera assesses Iraq from the personal up-close perspective, where many viewers have family members living in Iraq . Here we see to perspectives from opposite sides of the reporting spectrum providing to differing local angles. It is rather significant to note that Al-Jazeera English is censored in the United States, resulting from fears that it should be banned because Osama Bin Laden was using it for secret encoding or so-called terrorist goals. Donald Rumsfeld even went so far as to call it "the mouthpiece of terrorism." In the revolutionary documentary Control Room, created in 2003 about the Iraq War, the highly critical documentary of U.S incentives conveyed that American sentiments or approach should not be: "Democratize or I'll shoot you" or "bombing people into submission" (Control Room, 2003). The U.S involvement in the future landscape of the Arab Media has to be thoroughly revised.

THE FUTURE LANDSCAPE OF ARAB MEDIA

Mark Yudof put the role of the government well- "what seems as first blush a paradox or antinomy… may really be a question of balance" acquiring the balance between government power and media influence. The role of the media will have a lasting effect on the development of the relationship of these two international spheres of influence. What may at first appear to be mutual incompatibility between the Arab World and the West, can be mediated by the media and overcome? Is it true as Hussein Amin, a communications professor from the American University in Cairo suggests: "that in the new world of television, censorship basically does not exist?" One sociology professor disagreed claiming that the new freedom is "contrived at best" with "one step forward and two steps back" but with censorship only some of the "red lines are gone." In the coming years will new Arab media outlets that arise be able to challenge Al-Jazeera's credibility, audience size, and financial resources? As of right now no Arab Satellite TV network other than Al-Jazeera has ever attempted to present Arab views, opinions, and beliefs with such "vigor and legitimacy" even Al-Arabiya still lagging behind short of 15 million viewers. Perhaps as more Arab satellite channels and entertainment outlets spring up, while Al-Jazeera continues to develop its massive media enterprise, the polarizing notions of the "anti-Islam" U.S and the "anti-American" Arab world will fade. There exists a flourishing possibility that the evolution of Middle Eastern Media sphere will dissipate the perceived antinomy of the Arab world and modernization.

As progressive media centers such as Al-Jazeera and media networks like it continue to dominate news content in the Arab World and in the transnational media landscape, Arab television has a long road ahead. By offering unique coverage and transmitting news content across oceans, further dispelling stereotypical perceptions, U.S involvement in the Arab media production will perhaps be even more so less accepted and eventually terminated (as Al-Hurrah ratings are already alarmingly low). David Chambers for Middle Eastern Times OP-ED expressed: "Expect also to see Al-Hurrah TV drop from its average 1 percent rating to 0 percent" being state-sponsored channel of "retro-style propaganda." He advised the U.S. Government to "pull the plug" on al-Hurrah, hoping it will recognize ..."Democracy should mean first and foremost open access to information" (David Chambers). Despite some lash back from individuals highly critical of its "Arab agenda" the Arab Media will become more widely circulated in the international sphere in the coming decade. Will the U.S using "soft power" truly sway Muslim world public opinion but for news media content probably not. They don't fall for "Americanized propaganda" they read right through it. But in terms of entertainment media- with all of the U.S sought after programming, there's a good chance the demand for U.S Programme formats will only increase in the Arab media landscape.

Amahl Bishara, an assistant professor of anthropology at Tufts University, recently spent two years in the West Bank studying media, and observed that MBC2, which carries American movies, was particularly popular. "There's an acute understanding of the difference between the U.S. government and the American people," she said. "And they look at U.S. entertainment as just that, entertainment." It appears that demand for American-produced television shows is stronger than it has ever been as American culture is blossoming even in the Middle East despite polls consistently showing starkly negative views of the United States. Viacom started MTV Arabia last fall and introduced Nickelodeon Arabia in July on satellite services — endeavors that entail lessons in cultural sensitivity. Much of America's programming is beamed to Middle Eastern audiences from two satellite channels, MBC2 and MBC4, airing American shows such as ABC sitcom "8 Simple Rules," "Inside Edition" and the Oprah Winfrey show.

The increasing Arab audience proves there's more than enough demand for American entertainment programs. That is where America should get involved in Arab Television-predominantly in the entertainment sphere not with disseminating political agenda (though some do argue entertainment is fused with some subliminal political sway). The U.S must stop perpetuating this Arab propaganda and Islamic terrorism message to the West, so that the Arab World and the West finally overcome the "media terrorism relationship."

Many young Muslims in Britain are becoming more confident about asserting a specifically religious identity. This desire to be 'Muslim' is reflected in the social, cultural and educational activities they participate in and other aspects of their behaviour are strongly influenced by the increasing importance of Islam in their lives, including their consumption of media. The role of the media, especially Muslim media, in the development of Muslim identities and communities is increasingly evident. As this media form develops it provides a rich resource for the construction of British Muslim identities and presents Muslim communities with a platform from which to communicate amongst themselves and evolve as a minority population within Europe.

For young, second and third generation Muslims, these media forms can offer new ways of thinking about what it means to be Muslim and can help develop new cultures which combine parental traditions with norms from the host society. Muslim media also provides opportunities for dialogue with wider society, thus being one of the most potentially useful ways of building relations with other groups in society. The processes of globalisation have impacted on the development of media and the information available to young Muslims has become more varied in content, which influences how they see themselves not only as British Muslims but as part of a wider European and global umma.

In order to investigate the relationship between media culture, the social landscapes and changing concepts of 'community' in which Muslims find themselves and articulations of their identity, examines the lives of young Muslims in relation to their consumption of Muslim media, both traditional and those using new information technologies. To contextualise their media consumption and present real examples of Muslim media, an overview of Muslim publications (press and internet) will be given, offering a political economy of Muslim media in Britain. The aims and objectives of media editors are also presented giving an insight into how they see themselves as contributing to a knowledgeable society.

The role of media in contemporary society is increasingly evident. With advances in information and communication technologies, traditional sectors of media are being supplemented with new means of information production and dissemination. One of the most apparent developments in recent times has been the greater availability of alternative, community media sources. In addition, the development of media in a globalising world is presenting us with new ideas about community and identity, enabling diverse and dispersed people to build new contacts and redefine what it means to belong. These processes are undoubtedly affecting all populations around the world; however, studying their particular impact on Muslim communities is of importance in the current geopolitical climate.

By examining how a selected group of young Muslims in Britain are using and thinking about media, this paper examines the role of community media as a vehicle for change and development amongst a religious and ethnic minority in European society. It will be suggested that expanding the definition of media to include more than just press and electronic communication enables us to gain a better understanding of how young Muslims are expressing themselves, creating new cultural spaces and developing collective identities.

This paper consists of three sections; the first presents a brief history and current overview of Muslim publications in Britain (selected newspapers and magazines); the second focuses on the presence of Muslims in cyberspace and the third examines how various forms of expression are influencing what it means to be a young Muslim in Britain through social, cultural and educational practices (using two examples of new Muslim organisations).

MUSLIM PUBLICATIONS IN BRITAIN

The existence of Muslim press in Britain is a relatively recent phenomenon. Though a small number of publications have been in circulation for many years, the majority of publications have a shorter history. The events of late 1989 onwards with respect to the Muslim community, specifically the reaction to Salman Rushdie's book, *The Satanic Verses*, and the first military action in the Gulf, were the background events in which the beginnings of much of the Muslim press can be framed. The demand for media in English grew as this became the preferred language for a growing number of Muslims.

Newspapers had often previously been in the mother tongue (e.g. *The Jang* and *Awaz*), effectively cutting out many second generation Muslims who although had a basic command of spoken Urdu, Punjabi or Bengali, for example, were often not fluent in reading or writing it. As the Muslim communities developed a more distinctly religious identity, alternatives to mainstream media were sought through which to express this identity and Muslim media become an important means by which information was obtained and ideas developed. Those with a desire to maintain (and even strengthen) cultural and religious identities saw a strong and vibrant media as was one way to help achieve this. There was much encouragement from the community in the development of Muslim media at this early stage.

In expressing their aims and objectives for setting up publications, editors noted that the intention was to produce a publication - title, content, and outlook - that reflected strongly a Muslim or Islamic identity of both its producers and its readers. This took place in an environment that was also keen to promote a Muslim identity and editors were conscious about distinguishing themselves from the British Asian media. The nature of the British Muslim population meant that a large proportion of Muslims were South Asian but despite this fact the publications wanted a strictly Muslim identity. This was encouraged both from the readers and writers themselves. Certain aims and objectives for setting up their respective publications were shared by all editors, for example, the gap seen in mainstream media in reporting on Muslim issues and the need for a perspective more aware and sympathetic to Muslims. A combination of both the demand from within the Muslim community as well as editors' own conviction brought about the realisation of Muslim media.

Clearly the contents and outlook of each publication are determined by the background of the publications itself, the ideological or political stance it takes, its editor/writers and its expected readership. It is also determined by whether the producers' aim is to provide a current affairs (political) source of information or is more concerned with addressing social and cultural issues. All publications advertise events taking place around the country aimed at young Muslims have book reviews and also publicise charity appeals (mainly Muslim charity/relief organisations). As certain publications have arisen out of already established groups or movements, for example, Crescent International closely follows trends stimulated by the Iranian revolution; the ethos of the publication reflects this. Whereas The Invitation (The Family Magazine), as its subtitle indicates, is aimed at young families and the simpler writing style reflects this. For Q-News their niche market appears to be young, professional Muslims for whom they are providing a publication relating relevant social and cultural issues. The recent expansion of Q-News into the North American market also indicates they are targeting young Diasporas Muslims in the West, presumably having identified the commonality between the European and North American markets.

The variety of issues covered by the publications varies and like mainstream media they have regular features. Editorials, news, book and conference reviews, profiles, regular contributors, spiritual sections, question and answer, matrimonial, jobs and other advertising are amongst these. At this fairly early stage of development of Muslim media - not even 15 years for some publications - much of the focus is solely on Muslim issues. The editors themselves want to expand the topics they cover and almost be an Islamic version of a broadsheet so that they are not always tackling negative issues or issues of concern to the Muslim communities alone; to this extent the editors are conscious of their niche within the media environment. They are providing news from different sources and also topics which mainstream media would not cover or would do so in ways perceived to be inaccurate.

The diversity of Muslim media is illustrated by the different kinds of publications available. Most publications (excluding specialist ones) tend to have a combination of current affairs, social and 'religious' issues. The latter category comprised of faith or belief issues, explanations on the Qur'an and Hadith, 'how to' guides on certain practices in Islam and reminders of special dates in the Islamic calendar. Social and cultural matters relating to Muslims in Britain and dealing with problems in the community were also a focus. The target audience of many of the publications tends to be young Muslims; therefore it is common to find the types of issues affecting this age group in the pages of magazines. Frequency of publication (weekly, monthly, bi-monthly etc) automatically influenced the currency of topics.

Muslim media is certainly playing a key role in developing and disseminating Islamic knowledge to Muslims, particularly in Diaspora communities. Not only have young Muslims utilised Muslim media as an alternative to mainstream media but they are actively seeking out Muslim 'media' (used in the broadest sense to include audiovisual, electronic, print and social and cultural activities) to fulfil the requirement of obtaining religious knowledge. Disillusionment with reporting on Islam and Muslims in British mainstream media (and Western media in general) has been a specific reason for opting for Muslim media (see Table 1.0 for reasons cited for reading Muslim publications). For those particularly conscious of their religious obligation to seek useful Islamic knowledge, mainstream media has been of less significance, in fact to be avoided wherever possible. This focus on Islamic learning is also visible in academia, with organisations emerging to deal with the roles and responsibilities of Muslim academics, researchers and students.

Table 1.0: Reasons for Reading Publications

Reason	Frequency
Muslim current affairs (national and international)	47
Religious knowledge	21
Interesting news/articles	9
Supporting Muslim media	7
News from alternative perspective	5
Sense of community/unity	4
Disillusionment with mainstream media	3
Reviews	2
Academic study	2

RESPONDENTS OFTEN GAVE MORE THAN ONE REASON

In a way the diversity within Muslim media represents the variety of opinions, organisations and perspectives within the British Muslim population. Identifications with various ways of thinking and approaches to Islam such as different political inclinations, dawah oriented outlooks, academic or spiritual Islam, are facilitated and reinforced by different publications. Certain fundamental aspects of identifying oneself with Islam are shared by almost all groups of Muslims, but there is also diversity amongst them like in any other community.

THE MUSLIM PRESENCE IN CYBERSPACE

Whilst the older, more traditional sectors of the media such as the press are developing, Muslims are also familiarizing themselves with new technologies and means of disseminating information. One of the most significant of these is the Internet. The number and variety of internet pages relating to issues about Islam and Muslims is great. It would be difficult to mention all of these in any comprehensive way but the following can be noted from even a brief search of internet websites on Islam and Muslims:

Due to the structure and distribution of the internet and its users, many websites are based in Western countries and are in English;

There is diversity in the ideological or sectarian outlook of websites;

Various categories of website exist, for example, organisations' homepages, individual homepages, academic and research forums;

The contents range from dawah material, informative/ educational, political, current affairs, interfaith dialogue and indices of articles, as well as discussion lists. In addition it is interesting to highlight some of the most common themes found on websites. These are shown in Table 1.1.

Table 1.1: Internet WebPages Relating to Islam and/or Muslims

Fundamentals of Islam	The Holy Prophet (pbuh)
The Qur'an	Muslims in the West
How to pray	Events listings
Islamic articles	Women in Islam
Mosques listings	Pray times
Question and Answer	Qur'an and hadith browsers
News from the Muslim world	Political Islam
Dawah (invitation to Islam)	Rulings on various legal issues
Common misconceptions	Matrimonials
Charity appeals	Interfaith

Bunt (2000) explores the internet presence of Islam and Muslims using specific categories. He surveys the diversity of material available, for example, Qur'an and hadith literature (including various translations of the Qur'an available to search, download and listen to using audio technology), jurisprudence according to the four schools of thought, ideas of Muslim philosophers, Shi'a literature and 'converts' related literature. The diversity he finds is also along ideological lines with Sunni, Shi'a, Sufi and unorthodox groups all expressing themselves on-line. Political dimensions are explored by using the examples of several countries around the world where the internet is playing a part in articulating Islamic and Muslim discourses (Afghanistan, Pakistan, Kashmir, Malaysia, Singapore, Sudan and Saudi Arabia). He also demonstrates how 'political Islam' is manifesting itself with groups such as HAMAS and Hezbollah and what he classifies as dissident groups such as the Campaign for Democracy and Legal Rights (CDLR) also having a presence on the internet.

This diversity does not mean however that there are no common grounds between different websites. There is 'connectiveness' on certain issues such as the five pillars of Islam. Similar to Mandaville's (2001) analysis of how the internet and global technologies are affecting Muslims, Bunt (2000) sees the role of the internet as one of an authority dealing with people's questions and concerns about being a Muslim.

The servicing of Muslim websites has also developed with web designers, maintainers and navigators in place to help existing websites and create new ones. Some of these bigger 'gateway' sites provide links to further sites making navigation of the internet easier for users.

Baktiari's (2000) study of the 'Cyber Muslim and the Internet' also lists various websites relating to Islam and/or Muslims. He sees the net as having three consequences for Muslims; reducing geographical limitations, challenging traditional methods of learning and accelerating pluralism in Islamic political activity. Websites have also been useful channels for conversion to Islam, where ironically people who have been curious about negative media portrayal of Islam or have tried to convert Muslims, have themselves become Muslims (Winter, 1999). By presenting details about 100 converts to Islam, Winter notes that the internet plays a significant role in missionary activities.

The internet is certainly a medium of great importance to young Muslims in Britain. Whilst there have been positive aspects of coming on-line, there have also been conflicts between different Muslim website regulators, a proliferation of deviant sects, blatantly false information about Islam, unregulated chat rooms enabling un-Islamic behaviour and a very limited (if any) presence of scholars and sheikhs to act as proper authorities. So although these are issues which Muslims have to consider, the relatively cheap and easy access to the internet and the wide range of information available on millions of WebPages means that the Muslim presence in cyberspace is of increasing significance.

COMMUNITY 'MEDIA' - ACTIVE IDENTITY, SELF-EXPRESSIONS AND NEW CULTURES

The notion of community has gained much significance in recent years. Whilst on the one hand globalising forces appear to be fragmenting traditional community structures, on the other, revived and new ideas of community and identity are being formulated. For young Muslims in Britain their concerns about members of the Muslim umma in different parts of the world have enabled them to define and redefine the communities in which they live - be these real or virtual. Extensive reporting in the Muslim media of international conflicts, natural disasters, and political, economic and sociocultural issues covering the Muslim population from China to Alaska has increased awareness of a global Muslim community. At the same time, local structures and activities have realigned the associations and identifications of young Muslims. In avoiding mainstream social and cultural activities, including media, they are establishing new social spaces for themselves. Whilst not totally rejecting their parental and traditional community structures and customs, they are increasingly taking into consideration the British aspect of their lives and outlook. By breaking down and questioning some of the boundaries that exist within their own ethnic, class and gender groupings, they have used the idea of 'Muslimness' to redraw their own small communities. These smaller, localised associations often have links with movements or ideologies operating on a global scale.

Closely tied to the development of different ideas of community and these new social spaces is the role of Muslim media. The Muslim media have promoted the concept of a Muslim identity to a considerable degree and many pages are devoted to discussing this concept as well as advertising events which are related to it. One of the ways in which new concepts of community can be detected amongst young British Muslims is through their social, cultural and educational activities. Additionally, the structures and organisations which they are establishing give an indication of the focus of their social lives. Some of the activities are shown in Table 1.2.

Examining the wide range of activities that young Muslims are participating in demonstrates that the idea of 'media' consumption can be expanded to include less conventionally recognised media. Indeed the significance of these types of activities may surpass the importance of traditional print or electronic media. This may be especially the case if young Muslims are deliberately excluding or limiting their intake of mainstream media, though their attention may turn to Muslim media, which includes audio and video cassettes, websites and electronic mailing and discussion lists as well as publications.

Table 1.2: Activities Mentioned by Respondents

Activity	Females (12)	Males (6)
Study Circles	10	4
Lectures	3	4
Other Learning*	8	-
Family/Friends	10	4
Weddings, parties, events	3	1
Sport	-	4
Cinema	1	2
Camps	-	2
Non-Islamic learning	2	1
Conferences	1	-
Mosque	-	2
Dhikr	1	1
Yoga/Meditation	1	-

* This includes Arabic and tajweed classes.

Apart from reporting on events around the country and globally, Muslim media works to influence and shape the way Muslim communities themselves develop. For those readers who are actively looking to Muslim media as their main source of information and as a way through which to measure their own opinions, its presence is vital. Using the media as a stimulus for discussions with other Muslims is one way of developing concepts and issues in the community. As the concept of British Muslim identity is often discussed within the pages of Muslim media, readers are automatically focused on this issue.

By writing about experiences and possibilities of being a British Muslim, readers can relate to others in their community. Cases of discrimination, issues of education, employment and similar concerns are shared and the media highlights these experiences to reflect the reality of living in Britain as Muslims. The shared experiences portrayed in the media then lead to a perception of shared identity because Muslims in various parts of Britain are tackling similar issues and facing the same challenges. So whilst raising awareness amongst its readers, the Muslim media is also contributing to a sense of belonging to a particular community and therefore it has helped enhance a British Muslim identity, as illustrated by the following quotes:

"I get a feeling of belonging to the Muslim umma as I go through Muslim media - something that was not there before I started reading Muslim publications".

"The Muslim media has contributed greatly to my sense of belonging to a British Muslim community because it has made me aware of worldly issues that concern me as a Muslim. The Muslim media has greatly contributed with equipping me with the necessary knowledge of Islam to inform my non-Muslim friends what Islam is really all about and I can now also answer their questions about Islamic issues which I would otherwise have difficulty with".

British Muslims have recognised the importance of mediated communities in today's global setting. Media and technology have brought together seemingly dispersed communities (Mandaville, 2000) and this unification has found expression in local media. Not only has access to information increased the opportunities for learning about Islam but it has also developed a sense of belonging and identification with a local, national and global umma. The concept of identity links very strongly to knowing about other Muslims and their condition and being informed about Muslims around the world seems to have a direct link to how people identified themselves as Muslims. For many their identity has been influenced directly by the existence of Muslim media. This seems to have been done mainly through providing knowledge and information about Muslims and obtaining religious advice and instructions.

Establishing an infrastructure of Muslim institutions such as the media and social and cultural activities is helping to create an alternative social life for Muslims. At the same time there is an appreciation of these organisations and structures retaining an element of Britishness. Art and film exhibitions, promotion of Islamic calligraphy and music are all evidence of the development of a halal alternative to mainstream cultural activities. For second and subsequent generations of Muslims in Britain, the need to create these new social spaces is evident through the establishment of new organisations which reflect the idea of a British Muslim identity. Two such organisations are City Circle and ArRum. Both organisations point towards new ways in which Muslims are expressing aims and aspirations for themselves as citizens of Britain, playing a confident and fully inclusive role in society. These aims are expressed for those involved in the City Circle:

"For the organisers, the City Circle presents a pioneering opportunity to channel the dynamic talents and unique energies of young Muslim professionals into grassroots community activity. (e.g. education projects with youngsters in the inner city). By fulfilling their social and community responsibilities, these young men and women are applying the learning they take on board from the study circles and social forums. In this way the City Circle hopes that it can make a contribution to the betterment of civil society in the UK in the 21st century".

The second of the two organisations, ArRum, based in London, is a social club which opened in October 2001. Incorporating beautiful Islamic art and design into its surrounding, it is a space within which Muslims can interact with each other and develop their own social life. "Celebrating our cultural heritage, promoting a God-centred approach to life, asserting our Britishness and associating Islam with beauty" are amongst the aims of the founder for her club (Yaqub, 2001). Within the Club there are 'circles' for art, cultural knowledge, business and careers. Some of ArRum's activities include involvement in an anti-war movement through fundraising, organising an awareness campaign and housing a photographic exhibition of Afghanistan. ArRum's webpage carries comments from various members of the

Muslim community expressing their aspirations for the Club, for example;

"The establishment of ArRum can be taken as a sign of the coming of age of the Muslim community .... Islam does not isolate different aspects of life but tries to bring them together, so the Club will emphasise the splendour of Islamic art and culture while proving a venue for productive networking between Muslims who are active in public life, in industry or business".

Between March and August 2002 ArRum (in conjunction with IMAN, FAIR and Khayaal Theatre) hosted a Festival entitled 'Best of British Islam'. The festival, held at the ArRum premises, consisted of over 100 events (lectures, workshops, films, and theatre and musical performances) in visual, creative, performing and literary arts, faith and spirituality, Islamic thought, community affairs, business, gender dynamics, Islam and science, current affairs and Islam - past and future. The festival aimed to "reach out, inform, provoke, entertain but above all celebrate the depth and diversity of Islam in Britain". What does this type of activity demonstrate about the outlook of Muslims in Britain?

ArRum itself is an example of a new social, cultural and educational space for British Muslims and this Festival shares similar elements to some of the activities cited above, though its audience is perhaps more diverse than just university students or young Muslims. The title and presentation of the Festival can be seen as a positive and assertive manifestation of how Muslims see themselves in society. Rather than represent Islam as detached from British society, something sitting uncomfortably on the surface, they have presented it as in the grain of Britishness. 'Best of British Islam' gives a sense of permanency, like that of any British heritage, creating an alternative discourse to Islam being a foreign entity in Britain. As well as appealing to non-Muslims (whom probably form the minority of attendees) the Festival was a way of rescuing the image of Islam amongst Muslims. Where young Muslims may be presented with a contradiction between being

Muslim and being British, the Festival steers away from this dichotomy by showing that it is possible to be Muslim and British. It dispels fears that being Muslim means having no social life, no contact with arts or 'culture' and no capacity to develop intellectually, by offering entertainment and debate with an Islamic ethos.

Perhaps the people involved in the Festival, both organisers and visitors, are saying we want to be recognised as British Muslims, without compromising either our Islamic values or our affiliation to Britain. In addition the message that it appears to be presenting is that Islam can exist in Britain without posing a threat or being a danger, either to itself or to Britain. This is a prime example of how broader 'media' forms are being used to communicate with the host society in which British Muslims are now firmly established. It also paves the way for the development of new cultures that are absorbing elements of all the other cultures and discourses to which young Muslims are exposed.

An entire social, cultural and educational infrastructure appears to be developing amongst young Muslims which provide 'Islamic' alternatives in areas of entertainment and social life but more importantly in knowledge acquisition. By furnishing themselves with information about fellow Muslims, readers of Muslim media perceive a feeling of community or belonging created by this media (both through its production and consumption). This belonging includes local and national Muslim groups but also extends to the global Muslim umma, going beyond simple Diaspora connections (mainly to South Asia and other South Asian Muslims around the world). For Muslims in Britain it also takes into consideration their position as European Muslims. Asserting a more confident Britishness will no doubt extend to impact on the wider European identity of young Muslims. Ramadan (1999) sees media and social structures as being one of the most important elements through which Muslims will become inclusive European citizens. Developing Islamic entertainment and new European-Muslim cultures through their intellectual growth and activities is paramount for young Muslims. This will enable them to exist as a minority religious and ethnic group which is neither isolationist nor assimilations but one which merges surrounding cultures and values whilst retaining its own cultural and religious principles.

The main aim was to examine the lives of young British Muslims in relation to their media consumption and identify the role this media is playing in developing their ideas of self and community. Community media has grown out of a set of circumstances that have determined its progression and its overall focus has been on concerns and issues affecting British Muslims. The Muslim media serves a number of functions. It acts as a source of information on issues of relevance to British Muslim communities and from this British Muslims acquire knowledge which helps them to understand the situations affecting them and how to make informed decisions on relevant issues, such as, political representation, religious discrimination and education. Within the Muslim communities the Muslim media's functions include the creation and development of a knowledgeable society. As one editor commented Muslim media should be working towards creating "a better informed society, better informed Muslims" (Impact). Investing in Muslim media as well as keeping involved with mainstream media is important if Muslims are to develop and contribute in society.

The need for Muslims to express themselves and be represented has been partly fulfilled by the Muslim media and in this way media needs to be included in the broad socio-cultural and political infrastructure of representation. Having a platform on which to voice their opinions within the Muslim community is a positive step towards having greater representation in wider society. Muslim 'media' is also being used to reach out to host communities and develop positive relationships between different sections of society, particularly important in today's socio-political climate.

The numerous forms of community media, both new and old, are not only enabling Muslims to explore new ways of expressing their conviction to Islam and what it means to be

Muslim, but they are creating new hybrid cultures which merge together aspects of South Asian culture, Islam and British cultural norms. These in turn are being complemented by increasing information about Islam at a global level and giving rise to new relationships between young British Muslims and their environment. The emergence of a distinct Muslim media has provided a focal point through which Muslims, and particularly young Muslims, can find expression of their concerns and aspirations. Enthusiasm for Muslim media demonstrates the need for a public discourse on Islam and Muslims and Muslim media have articulated a British Muslimness which their readers find increasingly relevant to their lives.

2

The Mass Media in a Post-Communist Country

INTRODUCTION

The history of the free Polish mass media begins in the year 1989 with the lifting of the state censorship. From that time the Polish mass media have been allowed to write, show and say whatever they want. 1989 marked also a watershed for the manner of presenting the image of Islam and Muslims in the Polish media. Because the Islamic countries belonged to the so-called Third World, which was treated by the Polish Communist regime as a friend and ally, it was forbidden to present them in an unfavourable light. The situation changed at the beginning of the 1990s with the freedom of speech and the development of private newspapers, magazines and TV programmes.

Another factor also has to be considered. After 1989 the private Polish mass media had to earn money. Consequently many journalists were made to write, for example, about Muslim women one day and about a flood in India the next day. They were expected to attract the attention of the audience, to prepare sharp 'news' and catchy texts or programmes.

After 1989 the image of Islam and Muslims begun to differ from the one prescribed by the communist leaders and authorities. From that time on all typical themes, motives and attitudes towards Islam and Muslims found in the world mass media, i.e., the tragic fate of women in the Muslim world, alleged Muslims' inclination for cruelty and quick resort to violence, their supposed hate for Christianity and Europe (the famous Islamic threat), to mention only a few, have found their place in the media reports. The news and reports were moulded into well- selling sensations and very often contained a lot of mistakes and misunderstandings. From the beginning of the time of freedom of speech we could observe a kind of reaction to the past with its prescribed positive image of Arabs and Arab countries, Islam and Muslims, of the Third World in general. Some of the specialists in Arabic and Islamic studies were surprised by the anti-Islamic attitude of the Polish media.

However, until 11 September 2001 Muslim issues appeared in the Polish mass media rather incidentally. The frequency grew, of course, in the time of important international affairs and events linked directly or indirectly with Islam, such as the Rushdie affair or the wars, especially the Gulf War, the war in former Yugoslavia or the revolution in Afghanistan.

During this time we could observe the same main subjects and tendencies in writing about Islam as found in the media of other European countries: the alleged inclination of Muslims for violence and their tendency for spreading their faith by the use of force ("the sword") - all kinds of fanaticism and terrorism; especially these two words were used together very often; writing about Muslim fundamentalism the media has hardly ever compared the fanatical behaviour or opinions of Muslim fundamentalists to similar behaviour or opinions of fanatical members of other religious groups, for example, in Northern Ireland, India, or Israel; the word jihad or "holy war" has been used very often as specific only for Muslims, as if there were no "holy wars" waged by the Christians against members of other religious or ethnic groups.

The tendency for confrontation and clashes with Christianity (nowadays the West, Western world and culture) - the myth of an Islamic threat, the hate towards Christianity from the beginning of Islam: "extermination of Christians in the Near East began already at the beginning of the Muslim faith"; report about the year 2000: "During this year Christians were killed in the holy war - jihad - in most Muslim countries", then the details are given only about the situation in Indonesia (generalization); "It is forbidden to Christians to teach Arabic, because it is the language of the Prophet"; there is no response from Muslims for the Christian initiatives of interreligious dialogue, and there are no Muslim initiatives concerning this dialogue.

The position of Muslim women in the Islamic society and all prejudices about this issue: a Muslim woman is intimidated, made submissive, browbeaten, with her face hidden behind a veil (always; even in Iran or in Syria all women have to cover their faces when they are in public, in the streets!), she has no rights (there is no law in Islam, or in Islam religion replaces the law); religion is always accused of every inconvenience in the life situation of Muslim women and of inequality between a man and a woman. Meanwhile, the problem of women in Islam is not only a religious issue, but also above all a social one. Religion is used by the patriarchal society (by the men) in order to keep women away from the real life, its dangers and surprises.

The unity of the Islamic world - the journalists treat the Islamic World as a monolith, with religion playing the main role in it; in fact we know that a unified Islamic World does not exist! This world consists of many different countries and nations or population groups living on five continents, representing various religious streams, law schools and different levels of education.

The backwardness of the Muslim World and Islam; this conviction is expressed in words like: "the muezzin croons", men drinking tea lap, praying men have socks with holes in them, there has not been even a single successful country in the Muslim world.

The attempt to explain all developments and circumstances in the Muslim World as signals and consequences of extreme religiosity and not of politics or social matters - for example, journalists see in the religion the only reason for the inequality of women or the lack of democracy in the Muslim world (the specification about the observance of human rights in Muslim countries did not contain any statement that most of them are governed by military dictatorships or totalitarian regimes).

The tendency to present the views of any given person as being formally representative of the religion as such, assuming wrongly that such a person possesses sufficient knowledge of or expresses representative views about this religion - another example of the tendency to generalize.

Unlike in Western Europe before 11 September 2001, the Muslim migration to Europe and the growing number of Muslims on our continent was not the issue for the Polish mass media. At that time Poland did not seem very attractive to immigrants from the Muslim world, so the increase of Muslim immigration did not concern our country. There had been a tiny Muslim minority (10,000-13,000) in Poland that did not draw public attention. That minority consisted basically of two groups: well-organized, Polish traditional Muslims, the Tartars (about 3,000-5,000 people, residing in Poland for the last 600 years), and the immigrants (former or actual students, refugees and traders - mostly Arabs, but also Bosnians, Chechens, Turks, Afghanis, Pakistanis, etc.). The debate by the French (hijab, the Islamic headscarf in public schools in 1989) or by the British (state funding of Islamic schools in 1990) seemed to belong to a distant world.

Poland has a long tradition of wars with Muslims, Turks and Tatars. We read about them in novels, watch them in our films and learn about them from our school-books. Everybody knows Islam; everybody could be a specialist in this matter, even after a two-week journey to one Muslim country. It is easy to write about the Islamic threat, harems, and the position of Muslim women, cruelty of Muslim warriors, and the role of "the sword" in spreading the Islamic religion - in Poland we all know it.

A Muslim is the "other", but this "other" is not so distant and unknown. The Polish people had to deal and fight with

Islam and Muslims for centuries, even on Polish ground, so the problem of coexisting with Islam is not new. However, it belongs to the past and is seen from another perspective than in the Western Europe. Unlike Western Europeans, the Poles have no experience of colonial contacts with Muslims. The appearance of Muslim immigrants in Poland in the 20th century has another connotation altogether, because the Western European countries are for the first time confronted with significant Muslim minorities on their own, European, territories.

There were numerous mistakes in the texts or programs about Islam, e.g. Muslims pray four times during the day, temporary marriages were invented by the ayatollahs at the end of the 20th century in Iran, Mecca is the holy place only for Sunnis, there is no law in Islam, it is forbidden for all Muslims to marry Christians. Journalists quote passages from the Qur'an concerning pagans and apply them to Christians. The lack of knowledge in these matters is concealed by the repetition and reduplication of already existing stereotypes and prejudices. Not knowing the subject properly, journalists quite often omitted consulting the most suitable experts on the topic, and consequently they gathered only negative and inaccurate information. The time pressure under which journalists constantly have to operate quite often forces them to turn to the most accessible, mostly secondary sources, which are already replete with prejudices about the Muslims.

It is interesting that most of the subjects and themes presented above were already present in the writings of the early Christian theologians, who were engaged in polemics with Islam and Muslims, and also in the works of the early Orientalists and Romantic writers, poets, painters and sculptors. For the early Christian theologians sexuality and violence were the basic characteristics of Islam (fornications et furta).

For example, they viewed the use of force as the predominant constituent of the Islamic religion and, of course, as an evident sign of its error. Christians propagated this view in Europe, but at the same time they praised with enthusiasm almost identical doctrines of the Crusades. Muslim morality and social life were examined by Western theologians and writers almost invariably with the closest attention, especially sexual morality (Muhammad taught a 'new licence of promiscuous intercourse', as revealed in order to gain more believers).

The life of the Prophet was also examined from this point of view. It was felt that this subject was very stimulating to the imagination of the writers (e.g. they wondered how many wives and concubines were allowed for a Muslim - 4, 10, 100? - it was generally implied, that the Muslims would always enjoy in practice as many women as they could by law). The Romantic writers or artists used Islamic background to express their imagination (women in harems, waiting naked for the sultan, moving ponderously and lustfully or lazily lying on a bed etc.).

The tragic events of 11 September 2001 influenced the image and especially the method of the presentation of Islam and Muslims in the Polish media. After this day there was an influx of texts, TV and radio broadcasts about Islam and Muslims. Of course everywhere the agglomeration of (the connection between) "Islam", "fundamentalism" and "terrorism" was repeated time and again. However, when the first wave of fear and hate passed, a lot of decent texts were published and many good programmes broadcasted. Every journal or a magazine presented material about Islam as a religion, described its history and characteristics. Knowledge about Islam has become more widespread. One observes fewer mistakes or misunderstandings concerning Islam and the Muslims in the Polish mass media nowadays.

We could say that after the 11 September 2001 journalists paradoxically know more about Muslims and their religion and so does their audience. And when they write about Muslims they do it with more respect. They try more to examine all socio-economic circumstances and to ask opinions of the specialists. As a matter of fact the specialists have been asked so often, that almost everybody knows their names and faces. It is impossible or at least less possible to write improperly researched texts or fabrications based only on stereotypes and prejudices; if such things happen, they are rare.

Of course, among Polish journalists there have always been those who do make efforts to understand the culture, religion and people they write about and to present them with respect. But they first have to learn a great deal and approach another culture, while leaving behind the values and images of their own culture - a very difficult but not impossible task, as evidenced by writers like Ryszard Kapuscinski, Wojciech Jagielski, and Olga Stanislawska, to mention only a few names.

In order to avoid the development of new prejudices about Islam and Muslims, especially after 11 September 2001, it is necessary for the media to adjust their existing incorrect views and procedures and adopt a preventive strategy, i.e., a well-balanced and prejudice-sensitive approach. Also, oversimplification and generalization should be avoided as much as possible, while at the same time the stress should be put on the socio-economic and religious diversity within as well as between the groups and countries concerned.

Writing about a real terrorist threat, a journalist must not forget that terrorists constitute but a small part of all Muslims. Most Muslims are ordinary people like us. The media should start differentiating in their texts between various Muslim movements and groups/trends, and empathies the existing diversity of opinions in the Muslim world. Improving the knowledge of reporters on this topic during their vocational training would greatly help this process.

The stereotypical image of Islam and Muslims is particularly dangerous nowadays. People start hating "others" just because they are differently dressed, have a different appearance and have different beliefs. This distorted image of Islam and Muslims could be even more dangerous in the future, when more Muslims choose Poland, the new member state of the EU, as the country of their residence.

As stated above, the image of Islam in the Polish media after 11 September 2001 has become better, more accurate and more real. Some of the journalists have also discovered that there cannot be any dialogue between cultures and religions without respect shown to each other and without deepening the knowledge about the other. Dialogue is the only lasting solution to the problems emerging from the meeting of cultures and civilizations in the globalized world.

TRANSNATIONAL BROADCASTING AND ITS IMPACT ON PEACE IN THE MIDDLE EAST

At the beginning of the 21st century, shifts in global economics and the communications revolution have initiated a new collective experience in dialogue, bringing the hope of a better level of mutual knowledge and understanding. Cyberspace technologies now being introduced have brought the global community into a state of rapid mutation. These changes will undoubtedly alter the way humanity interacts and communicates in the future. As a result of these new developments in information and communication technology, the world is facing an unprecedented fusion and opening of cultures and economies that will impact cross cultural dialogues and relationships as well as stimulate development in cultural, social, economic, and educational arenas.

Mainstream media in the region – and the governments that control them – have steadfastly tried to maintain the appearance of continuity, hanging on to old formulas, even after years of momentous change that have catapulted the rest of the world into the information age. The Arab world has been largely insensible to the implications of this change, but it has not been immune to all its manifestations. However, the recent changes throughout the Middle East in the last 20 years compel us to try to envision the possible transformational effects of these changes on different fields and the resulting impact on the media. These possibilities include changes in areas such as electoral politics, democracy, professional associations, civil society, human rights, pluralism, accountability, privatization and others. Already some leaders and governments throughout the region are showing signs of steady liberalization, modernization, and democratization.

The Middle East is a diverse region that has been a challenge to generalization. Ranging from southwestern Asia to northeastern Africa, today the term Middle East refers to the area extending from Egypt in the west to Iran in the east, including Israel and Turkey. A broader, more cultural definition might also include the Muslim countries of Morocco, Algeria, Tunisia, Libya and Sudan and the Asian countries Afghanistan and Pakistan. The "Arab World" is a concept frequently discussed in the Middle East region. Arabs appear to share a common language, culture, religion and geography, but there are many social differences and diverse political ideologies. There are numerous formal communication activities that articulate the Arab World. These include events such as conferences among religious and civil organizations across Arab countries, political communication among leaders, and participation of individuals in associations offering Arab news services, tourism councils, and cultural exchanges. In politics, there have been many attempts to create a bloc of Arab countries, speaking with one voice and acting in concert for the benefit of the region as a whole. In reality, these alignments, both legal and ideological, have been difficult to achieve, with national concerns and interests superceding regional alliances.

Globalisation forces in general and transnationalisation movements in particular illustrate the new model for media economies, which depend on the following processes: privatization of culture; deregulation; and mergers across industries and nations for global penetration and commercialization. These global forces now challenge Middle East societies. Countries in the Middle East have begun to sense the dangers of global communication as well as the opportunities. Critics have stated that these media messages hurled from space bring social complications, engender cultural disputes and erode their identity as coherent cultural and religious groups.

The mass media need to be considered in terms of the economic conditions, cultural environments, and political realities of the societies they serve in the region. Since the introduction of mass media in the Middle East more than a century ago, the media have been dealt with as a Western phenomenon. The media and political regimes enjoy a very close relationship in most of the countries in the region. Since the time these countries gained their independence, most have used the mass media as a device to promote nationalism or Islamic universalism. In most cases, a powerful executive branch exercises a strong control of the state, including the media, and freedom of expression is repeatedly curtailed. The media have traditionally been seen as a propaganda tool, whereby many voices would confuse and divide rather than create consensus.

Media in the Middle East in general are tightly regulated by a combination of structural arrangements, whereby governments monopolize the press and broadcasting, and legal controls, with all but the bravest deterred from reporting freely on sensitive domestic issues or deviating from official foreign policy when reporting on international affairs. The political power systems in the Middle East utilize the broadcast media as a tool promoting public mobilization. They have, therefore, a strong interest in keeping them out of hostile hands.

Because of the high rate of illiteracy in the Middle East, broadcast media have been very popular and more influential than other forms of media; for this reason, most audiences in the Middle East rely on radio and television for information (Boyd 1998). Although the primary function of broadcast media in many countries in the region is to convey news and information of general interest, interpreting and commenting on events as well as providing opinion and perspectives, the media is also used as a tool to reinforce social norms, cultural identity and cultural awareness through the dissemination of information. Promoting Arab culture, Arab unity and Arabism were the main aims for many of the electronic media systems of the region after the wars with Israel. This is one main reason why radio and television broadcasting in these countries were centralized, and to a large extent, absolute monopolies under direct government supervision. Other reasons include preservation of national unity, protection of national security and centralization in government and administration.

On the other hand, Israeli media is considered more dynamic media. Although they face many restrictions, electronic media in general and television broadcasting in particular are powerful media. Since its start in 1967, Israel Television has been the state's principal and most influential medium, however, Radio and television news is entirely a government-sponsored affair.

The Middle East is witnessing a wave that is transforming broadcasting from a monopolistic system in which few diverse voices are heard to a diverse platform where freedom of speech is a requirement. Transnational broadcasting has the ability to circumvent severe censorship laws, marking the end of the censorial culture. It is becoming clear that the more the Arab media continues to present heavily controlled news and entertainment, the more likely Arab audiences are seeking better content from transnational media that are freer than their local systems.

Transnational broadcasting began to evolve in the 1980s, with the introduction of multi-channel delivery environments that reaped the benefits of the lowered costs of launching communications satellites. Furthermore, miniaturization enabled individuals with small dishes and signal decoders to pick up signals directly from satellites. With the introduction of direct broadcast satellites (DBS), broadcasters could reach worldwide audiences directly, without interference from government censors.

The Middle East has at least five competing digital television platforms battling for audience loyalty: ART/1st Net, Nile Package, Orbit, Star Select, and Gulf DTH/Showtime (Forrester, 1999). Al-Jazeera, CNN, Fox News, BBC, ANN, Al Arabia, and Nile News are a sample of the competing transnational television news programs now available in the Middle East. A few years ago, transnational television services posed little threat to the monopoly state-run national television. Although they were introduced to the region when the Gulf war started at the beginning of the nineties, their fast development and pan-Arab impact is by far greater than national television in any of the Middle Eastern countries. For example, the coverage of the second Intifada since October 2000 has attracted perhaps the largest audience for uncensored coverage in the history of Arab broadcasting. Television viewers from Rabat in Morocco to Riyadh in Saudi Arabia share the news experience from their living rooms or coffee shops. The Palestinian uprising was made available to the world through the many correspondents working for Arab and non Arab trans-national broadcast services, causing Israeli officials to conclude that the "media war" wasn't going their way. Furthermore, transnational broadcast services were responsible for the creation of a strong pan-Arab public opinion, when millions of people demonstrated in the streets of Arab capitals in support of the Palestinians Intifada. The strong coverage of the event from transnational broadcast media such as Al-Jazeera and other Arabic language channels created a regional pan-Arab movement out of what started as a local protest in Jerusalem.

Transnational media are forums of free public discourse and can set agendas of public debates on national, regional and international issues ranging from political democratization, to intellectual freedom, to understanding about peace in the Middle East. Not only does transnational broadcasting affect all walks of public life in the Middle East, but it also affects the individual citizen in his different roles in a wide variety of ways. The medium can take on certain important functions in the Middle East society. These include its role as a forum for the exchange of thoughts and ideas between citizens or the different social groups of a democratic community; its function as an integrating influence upon children and young people; its importance as a platform and agent for all kinds of cultural forms and expressions; its function to advance understanding, speed recognition and enhance development, and finally, and perhaps most importantly, its function to promote peace, as only in peace can the enormous potential of the Middle East be realized.

Today, the transnational multi-channel broadcasting environment created by the satellite television channels offers a new horizon of excellent programming that targets a wide variety of audiences in the region. Transnational broadcasting currently provides educational, entertainment, and cultural and artistic services. It has also begun to play a part in enhancing the information flow as a comprehensive program provider. In addition, it reaches a good part of the region and does away with the isolation of deserted and rural areas. Because of the multi-channel environment it creates, it invites people to take the opportunity for fair and equitable access to local and global resources and offers facilities for conventional and advanced channels of communication; to receive opinions, information and ideas; to receive a range of cultural products designed for a wide variety of tastes and interests; and to have easy access to facts about the world.

This ease of access has created a lot of potential roles for non-governmental, syndicated, civil and partisan organizations. Now is the time for such institutions to realize the magnitude of the medium and concentrate on forming a solid ground for a regional society. Signals from different countries in the world, in Arabic, Hebrew and other languages, can be pulled in throughout the region, carrying content that is completely different in terms of freedom and diversity from what is offered on the national services.

Transnational broadcast media are also having an impact on the presentation of news. The accelerating pace of transnational news networks in the region turning to 24-hour news formats removes the barriers of time and space between broadcasters and information consumers. It also obviates attempts by governments to control and manipulate information for its own purposes. Audiences are often dependent, directly or indirectly, on transnational media for their information because their own national media lack resources to access information and often present a simplified coverage of conflict that is not perceived by the public as being credible and reliable. Another critical factor is the abundance of international broadcasting in Arabic; most Arab media were traditionally focused on domestic audiences, who were subjected to a daily diet of protocol news, state directed programming, and in many cases direct propaganda. Transnational broadcasts, in contrast, include a wide mix of the above as well as free-ranging and often provocative debates and talk shows, controversial interviews, and news coverage meeting international standards in Arabic and from an Arab perspective.

Transnational broadcast news coverage about the Middle East conflict has a tremendous appeal to Arab audiences, since unlike print, it favors movements over stillness, simplification over complexity, specificity over abstraction and the present over the past or the future. National news networks are usually state-controlled and selective in the news they present, lacking the visual content that involves graphics, illustrations, still photos, maps, charts and video clips that are available on the transnational news networks. Pictures are extremely suggestive. Audiences in the Middle East generally give more credence to what is shown and presented on transnational media, since they have the benefit of visual information as well as a reputation for relative objectivity, which does not exist in the national media.

The transfer of news values and presentation from global networks such as Cable News Network (CNN) and the British Broadcasting Corporation's World Service (BBC) to transnational broadcast media in the region is affecting broadcasting values throughout the region. Transnational Arab television news covering the Middle East conflict utilizes international standards in terms of quality programs and presentation through Arab news networks such as the Arab News Network (ANN), Al-Jazeera, and Nile News and the new channel from MBC, Al Arabia.

Because the global nature of satellites limits governments' ability to control domestic usage of these technologies, some governments in the Middle East have begun taking tentative steps to deregulate their broadcasting policies and liberalize their content. Many governments have found themselves unable to cover the cost of infrastructure, and have chosen to let private investors enter the market. Some societies regard pluralism a matter of public interest, but this has not been a prevalent view in the Middle East. It is important to remember that since broadcasting and media services in the Arab World are state-run activities, the misuse of these technologies during times of conflict may result in a form of communication warfare. Governments are concerned that communication warfare in the Middle East could polarize societies, provoke conflict, create misperceptions and mistaken ideas about others, and cultivate fear and mistrust, making people vulnerable and dependent. In addition, officials of the media institutions, because they are still largely inspired by old media models, do not know how to handle the tension that is created by transnational broadcasting between the dynamic openness of the new media and the protective isolation of the old and still govern the current media environments.

The most important events that have influenced the development of mass media in the Middle East have been the Islamic revolution in Iran; the collapse of the Soviet Union; the Gulf War; and the decades-long Arab–Israeli conflict. Media has long played an important role in political discourse in the Middle East, especially in the Arab-Israeli conflict. Since the start of the conflict between the Arabs and Israelis around the turn of the 20th century, the mass media began mirroring the conflict. In 1948, the area that both Arab and Israeli claimed was known internationally as Palestine, and this conflict was marked by heavy reporting and analysis in both in print media and radio. But following the war of 1948-49, the land was divided into three parts: the state of Israel, the West Bank (of the Jordan River) and the Gaza Strip, and Arab media in the Middle East and Islamic media in particular dealt heavily with the conflict, telling the story from their governments' perspectives.

In May 1967, when Egyptian troops entered the Sinai Peninsula bordering Israel, Egyptian president Gamal Abdel-

Nasser, an Arab leader who utilized the media to serve his political goals, mobilized the Egyptian public through print and broadcast services and asked the UN observer forces stationed between Israel and Egypt to evacuate their positions, preparing the country for war. At that time radio Sout Al Arab (Voice of the Arabs) was the main transnational service influencing the Arab world and was empowered by the transistor revolution that made the service available even to mobile societies. In 1967, Israel preemptively attacked Egypt and Syria, destroying their air forces. Jordan joined in, but consequently was attacked by Israel as well. The Egyptian, Syrian and Jordanian armies were defeated, and Israel captured the West Bank from Jordan, the Gaza Strip and the Sinai Peninsula from Egypt, and the Golan Heights from Syria. All this occurred within a very short period of time, but the Voice of the Arabs continued for days after the war promising victory, an unsuccessful strategy that cost the radio service its credibility afterwards.

The power of the "free" transnational broadcast media attracting and influencing hundreds of millions in the Middle East was clearly documented during the second Intifada. Visual information that was presented through transnational broadcast services provided a wealth of infor-mation that in many cases circumvented long oral messages in the news and had a great impact on Middle Eastern viewers. The media started to focus heavily on the Arab-Israeli conflict with the start of the first Intifada. In December 1987, the Palestinians in the West Bank and Gaza started a mass uprising against the Israeli occupation. The second Intifada is widely regarded as beginning in the last year of the millennium. The Intifada has involved hundreds of thousands of people, many with no previous resistance experience, including children, teenagers and women. For the first few years, it included many forms of civil disobedience, including massive demonstrations and general strikes, later evolving to include both small and large acts of violence, from rock-throwing children to suicide bombings. The active periods of the first and the second Intifada were overwhelmingly the focus of all the Arab and transnational media, causing the Israelis to block media coverage. Since then, both Israel and the Arab countries have traded accusations of biased coverage by the transnational media.

Israel on the other hand started an Arabic-language satellite channel beamed to the Middle East with programmes to explain the government position. The main goal of the station is to try to gain regional public opinion inflamed against the Jewish state by a Palestinian uprising. Many Israeli media experts believe Israel is lagging behind in what they defined as a "Cold War"-style propaganda war being waged on state-owned Arab satellite television.

Half a century of Arab-Israeli conflict has cost the Middle East region six major wars and the loss of thousands of lives, leaving both Israelis and Arabs frustrated and angry, and creating rage and hostility that escalated tension in the region and complicated geopolitical alliances around the world. Some have lost hope, but many still believe that peace will finally prevail in this region. Yet almost quarter of a century after the Camp David accords that established hope for peace in the Middle East, a comprehensive peace is still a dream, and Arab Israeli relations are at a peak in terms of conflict and disagreement. Israel and Arab countries that have formed peace agreements with Israel continue to honor the provisions of their treaties; however, suspicions about the future of peace are growing daily. These suspicions were projected and enhanced by the transnational broadcast media that have developed in the countries in the region during the last ten years.

Some media experts had hopes that the introduction of transnational broadcast media in the region would help to establish peace or at least have a positive impact on the Middle East peace process. Media experts in the Middle East have also argued that the broadcasting of violent images has a negative impact on the ability of their governments to work for peace. The public's access to a continuous barrage of disturbing images and uncensored news, particularly in regard to the Intifada and more recently the Iraq war; have raised the emotional stakes of public discourse. National news, to a large extent, still involves official lines, biased information and censored reports that contribute to the "information warfare" in the region. It is critical now that researchers in the field of transnational broadcasting examine the performance of these services and their relation to political power and to ask questions about the applicability of media content.

Since their introduction, transnational broadcast services in the Middle East have fought for greater market share. This usually means that they look for issues that appeal to their audience and are different from what is currently available from their national services. In this sense, their target broadcast audiences are not individual national audiences but the general Arab audience. The Middle East conflict was, and still remains, the most attractive item in news broadcasts because of its relative importance to many viewers in the region.

Coverage of the recent Palestinian-Israeli violence and the war in Iraq is demonstrating the power of the transnational media to cut out the government middleman by reaching viewers directly in their households. Before, news about the conflict came to the Middle East through the state broadcast media with the official line, suppressed or exaggerated depending on whether a particular government supported peace with Israel and its relationship with that country. This time, Arab TV viewers are getting the picture, to a large extent, uncensored, direct from the scene, and sometimes taking to the streets in protest at what they see.

Both Western and Arab governments are seemingly at a loss as to how to deal with incendiary broadcasts, such as the broadcasting of messages purported to be from Osama Bin Laden or Saddam Hussein and the images of war, including video of US prisoners of war and war casualties from both sides. The content of transnational media broadcasts has become the topic of diplomatic rows, and the willingness of governments to attempt to control these broadcasts has been elevated from accusations of censorship to support for diplomatic alliances and even patriotism. Journalists and their transnational media organizations reporting on the various conflicts in the region have been detained, accused of supporting terrorism, fired upon, accused of willful bias, and, most recently, imprisoned. Governments not only in the Arab region but also around the world have begun to recognize the power of transnational media to impact foreign relations, set public policy, and form public opinion, and they are still finding their way in the murky region between supporting freedom and wanting to control content.

Transnational broadcasting is seen now by many to have the potential to act as a social engineer in the Middle East, including facilitating domestic understanding of regional conflict; providing new neutral perspectives to the general and target audiences; linking the region together and also with the rest of the world; increasing government awareness of other governments' performance in the region and shaping government effectiveness; promoting human rights; advancing formal and informal education; broadcasting news and information about the region and the people and finally familiarizing the region with other cultures, values, traditions and religions, all aspects that work to enhance the culture for peace. However, with respect to coverage of the Intifada, transnational broadcasting in the region did not effectively clarify the different standpoints of Arabs and Israelis. It did not recognize the gravity of the situation until demonstrations extended everywhere, broadcasting and replaying negative images and using value-laden language to heighten regional passions. This did not enhance the culture of peace but rather magnified the march to war and significantly elevated the level of emotion in public discourse.

On the positive side, transnational broadcasting paved the way for more a collective aspect of Arab identity. Cable News Network (CNN) helped introduce the region to the concepts of freedom of expression and freedom of the press during its coverage of the Gulf War. The Gulf crisis marked a turning point not only in establishing the genre of 24-hour satellite television news but also in bringing to light Middle Eastern viewers' dissatisfaction with terrestrial television news coverage. New Arabic transnational television services such as MBC, Al-Jazeera, Nile News and the Arab News network have been trying to imitate program formats from CNN. These new networks, particularly Orbit Networks, MBC and Al-Jazeera, have brought these values home to the Middle East. With this in mind, whatever is defined as the journalism culture in the Middle East is now challenged. Many journalists as well as people living in the Middle East now have access to international television networks without any kind of control, censorship, or government approval of content.

Governments have not yet thrown in the towel, however. While some of the new transnational services have not lived up to the promise of providing reliable and unbiased coverage, they are still educating governments and their audiences about the benefits and challenges of an uncensored press. Restrictions on the freedom of the national press and on the flow of news must be counted among the bitter harvests of the Middle East conflict. Coverage of activities of many of the peace movements and groups of people in the Middle East was limited if reported at all. The media scene has been particularly discouraging until now, as some of the most popular transnational broadcast services were often biased and failed to present well-rounded views in their coverage of the conflict in the Middle East. In this overheated environment of hate and revenge, unsympathetic public opinion was enhanced and boosted. The overwhelming majority of transnational media in the region have reported on the Palestinian-Israeli conflict through the Palestinian lens. They have presented the conventional wisdom, the dominant interpretation, or the story line. Any presentation that does not take the Palestinian side is colored with many accusations and labeled biased, yet in many cases, these services invited Israelis to comment and explain. Surprisingly, some people called for Arab public opinion to remain hostage to traditional national one-sided views, to turn away from transnational media sources. These voices are frustrated by the transnational media raising issues and presenting views that are uncomfortable, both to a public used to hearing affirmations of what they already believe and to governments used to controlling news broadcasts.

Transnational broadcasting is providing the region with an unprecedented opportunity to share the thoughts and worries of the people in the region without fear. Transnational media are providing the world with a tremendous chance for developing the foundation of peace, an unprecedented forum for the exchange of views. Arab television stations are having secularists debating Islamists, Iraqis debating Kuwaitis and Israelis debating Palestinians. Although the Arab public never before had a chance to watch an Israeli leader speaking in Arabic, they recently watched a number of Israeli political leaders debating in Arabic on an Arab satellite television network during the Israeli election. Arabs can watch the AlSharq AlAwsat (Middle East) network broadcast in Arabic by the Israeli government, watch the new Hebrew service that is being broadcast by Nile TV International, an Egyptian transnational broadcasting channel, and listen to Sawa (Together), the new Arabic-language radio station broadcast to the region by the US government.

By bypassing government gatekeepers, transnational broadcast services have the opportunity to free themselves from the political agenda of Middle East governments and broadcast well rounded news reports that include Israeli views on the conflict. Orbit network was among the first transnational broadcast media to introduce Israeli officials to the Arab viewers. The Middle East Broadcasting Center (MBC) was first to have news coming from AlAqsa mosque in their main news bulletin and interviewed many Arab and Israelis. Al-Jazeera network, which is based in Qatar, took full advantage of freedom of expression and direct delivery to Arab viewers, airing outspoken commentary that has angered several Arab governments. Jordan closed down Al-Jazeera's office recently. Kuwait temporarily shut the network's offices there after it broadcast a caller's insult of its leader. Egypt threatened similar reprisals when one of its commentators accused it of not doing enough to support the Palestinians.

The station is funded by the Qatari government but is editorially independent. Most recently, media experts have stated that the Saudi recall of its ambassador to Qatar was the result of Al-Jazeera's broadcast of criticism of the Saudi royal family's role in the peace process. Al-Jazeera delivered another striking example of the Middle East's new journalism: it broadcast interviews with former Israeli Prime Minister Ehud Barak and his Palestinian adversaries.

Various scientists' of Middle Eastern politics have indicated that media performance is tied to the political culture. They describe the term "political culture" as the values, norms, beliefs, sentiments and understanding of how power and authority operate within a particular political system. Generally it sets unrecorded ground rules as to how the political process is to be performed. It is understood that a particular political culture grows as a result of historical development and that it contributes to the reproduction of the system or the processes that supports such a culture. The majority of discussions on domestic political culture go back to the features of traditional heritage, religion, and political history of the region. Authoritarian press systems in the region started to realize that media wars in the Middle East has could polarize societies, provoke conflict, create misperceptions and mistaken ideas about the others and cultivate fear and mistrust, making people vulnerable and dependent. Stereotypical portrayals misrepresent all of us and stigmatize those who are the most vulnerable. Conflict situations in the Middle East raise in the most intense way many questions on professional standards and ethics – objectivity, accuracy, independence, the need for the understanding of the subject, and public duty. Many journalists in the region have little professional training to help them deal with these issues. In many countries in the Middle East low standards pertain throughout the media for various historic and systematic reasons, and in conflict situations the pressures to ignore professional standards are intense. Responsible freedom is a concept that must be a reference for the many media outlets that still carry messages that encourage violence and provoke fury, dividing people and creating clashes and public disorder in the region. New independent transnational broadcast systems, built on a culture of professional broadcasting ethics, are needed to maintain the national differences of multiple voices.

In today's world, whoever can effectively use transnational media to communicate their messages can have an immense impact on world opinion. No longer are we talking about city newspapers and national networks. Today, images and stories can be transmitted to hundred of millions of viewers in the blink of an eye. Those organizations and governments who refuse to acknowledge the ascendancy of this technology in forming world opinion and affecting national and international policy stand to lose a great deal. The shortcomings of the national media have led those who can afford it to obtain access to foreign satellite television, but such access is still only for a small minority representing mainly decision makers and elite from the different fields.

The challenge for the region at this point in time is to recapture its drive by examining the structure of the mass media and its relation with the state as well as rethinking the role of media in general and transnational media, in particular a global society. Transnational broadcasting reintroduced and strengthened the concept of Arabism to the Middle East after a decline of some decades. Satellite broadcasting through the transnational multi-channel environment has brought the people of the region together, deepened the dialogue between nations, crystallized the thoughts of social classes, strengthened the traditions and customs in the region, established the interactivity between its organizations, blessed its values and formed a unified public opinion toward the new challenges of the millennium

Although many people of the Middle East started to refrain from their national and traditional media systems that constructed and maintained a national identity, the region is hampered by the economic and political realities of central authorities and leadership that are unwilling to change. However, it is equally important for transnational broadcasting in the region to find a language and pictures suited to enhance tolerance, reconciliation and understanding in the midst of the overflow of information about violence. They can broadcast news about crises but it is equally important for transnational broadcast media to insist on dialogue and compromise to provide a well- rounded approach to preserve an open and unbiased exchange among the two parties. Governments are finding it increasingly difficult to block the flow of information. Transnational broadcasting is now challenging the local/ traditional broadcasting and government in the Middle East not only by providing access to its own transnational media, but also by posting official documents, judicial proceedings, parliamentary actions and legal notices bypassing interpretation or alteration and potential misunderstanding or misrepresentation by news media by going directly to the public. As a consequent democratic model transplantable around the world, governments would be held accountable by the news media, and the news media would be accountable to a public operating in a market-oriented, transparent society.

Transnational broadcasting in the Middle East has had an impact on expanding public access, strengthening international understanding, and encouraging a free flow and a wider and better balanced dissemination of information. Nevertheless, at present, the Middle East conflict continues to involve whole societies in the region, while with increasing wealth and developments in the industry, more information, of different perspectives, reaches deeper into the Middle East communities and individuals.

Middle Eastern society is slow to change, and the media reflect of the political, cultural and social backgrounds of the people of Middle East. This is perhaps why the first generation of transnational broadcast media did not fully utilize its power to be a key player in the peace process. Only time will reveal if the second generation of trans-national broadcast services to and within the Middle East will have a better impact on peace in the region. A better understanding between peoples and between cultures will result in building a better understanding between the Arabs and the Israelis. Propaganda has less power when there is access to alternative sources of information. It is now the new millennium, the time for peace and the time for freedom and democracy, prosperity and opportunities. Media organizations and institutions in many parts of the Middle East are just beginning to understand the great possibilities that lie in the future. Transnational broadcast media are a crucial determining factor in how we perceive other continents and peoples. Now, that we can see the passion, the pride, and the heartbreak of "the other,"

Transnational broadcast media have the potential to foster movement towards peace, democracy, tolerance, and awareness the shared experience of humanity.

RELIGIOUS MEDIA, DEVOTIONAL ISLAM, AND THE MORALITY OF ETHNIC PLURALISM

Focusing on the circulation of religious media and their emphasis on religiously grounded notions of the common good, this paper addresses the importance of a media-sustained public sphere for the modalities of ethnic pluralism in Mauritius. I contextualize uses of religious media against the background of a dominant discourse of pluralism, which identifies successful coexistence with moral and social values emerging from the negotiation of orthodoxy and authenticity in religious traditions. The media-driven dynamics of ethnic and religious pluralism also highlight the affective and emotional dimensions of the public sphere, as they are evident in Mauritian engagements with religious media.

Recent comparative work on Muslim publics has emphasized the significance of new media in shaping public spheres. The main stress has been on a democratisation and fragmentation of such publics engendered through the capacity of new media to undercut the dominance of established powerful players, such as the state and the 'ulema. Eickelman and Anderson, for example, claim that the rise of a new class of "interpreters of Islam" throughout the Muslim world has gone hand in hand with the spread of new information technologies, such as audiocassettes, audio-CDs, satellite television and the internet. These new participants in public debates about Islam and the "common good" often lack traditional or other formal credentials as interpreters of Islam in exchanges about public morality. Because such media circulate discourse and images in different ways, they create new media producers and audiences and therefore have a fundamentally transforming impact on the shape of the public and its limits. They have the potential to empower previously disenfranchised actors and enable interventions in public exchange on their part while largely evading the control of the state and established religious authorities.

A second, primarily anthropological focus on new media in Muslim publics is the intersection between media practices and personal piety. Here the emphasis is on how uses of electronic media become part of the work of subject making, in particular regimes of pious discipline. Electronically mediated sound and images have recently been described as playing an increasingly important role in the production of religious sensibilities and sentiments within the context of turning embodied listeners and viewers into religious subjects. Highlighting the performavit and visceral dimensions of religious experience, this strand of research asks how uses of electronic media have shaped or have even become constitutive of these aspects of religious practice and belonging. Coinciding with a growing interest in sensory experience in media studies, the intersection of electronic media practices with embodied religious subjectivity has therefore emerged as a second site in which media practices articulate both with the making of Muslim subjects and debates about the common good.

The main aim in section is to draw these fields of inquiry on the production of piety and conceptions of the common good together. Recent work on Muslim publics above all poses the question of how uses of electronic media impact Islam as a religious tradition and Muslim notions of personal piety. However, such processes also have important consequences for the dynamics of ethnicity in plural societies, especially where there is a strong correlation between religious and ethnic identities. In Mauritius the morality of ethnic and religious pluralism and piety often converge in notions of peaceful coexistence. The latter is seen as a supreme common good, which many Mauritians in turn associate with moral conduct conforming to religious values.

Moral values and sensibilities influence how subjects participate in publics, thus shaping the very sense and limits of the public sphere (LeVine and Salvatore 2005). Moreover, the reproduction of pious dispositions in the contemporary world depends to a considerable degree on the public circulation of discourse and images. Electronic media practices intervening in this interrelationship between pious subjectivities and public spheres concerned with notions of the common good are therefore highly significant for questions of ethnic and religious pluralism.

COEXISTENCE AND PIETY AS COMMON GOOD

Mauritius is a former plantation society in which almost 70% of the approximately 1.2 million populations are of Indian origin. Members of the middle class among Hindus, 52% of the population, in particular those of north Indian background (approximately 41% of the total population) have dominated the Mauritian government and state institutions since independence from Britain in 1968. They have established the hegemony of a notion of cultural citizenship according to which Mauritians are subjects with origins in other parts of the world and ongoing commitments to diasporic "ancestral cultures". These ancestral traditions are in turn largely identified with different religious traditions, as religious difference is of supreme importance in the making of boundaries between the "communities" distinguished both by the Mauritian constitution and the larger public. The cultivation of officially recognized ancestral cultures with religious biases is strongly encouraged and supported by Mauritian state institutions, and for Mauritian Muslims who constitute 17% of the population and who are like Hindus also of Indian origin, Islamic traditions represent their official "ancestral culture." The management of religious pluralism is one of the chief public concerns in Mauritius, as much fear that political competition and power struggles could quickly slide into destructive religious "communalism" between members of different ethno-religious communities, a worry heightened by violence between Hindus and (Christian) Creoles in 1999.

Mauritian politics of "ancestral culture" and ancestral religious tradition are officially presented as engaged in a combat against "communalism," as they emphasize a normative contrast between destructive religious communalism and "true" religiosity. While the former is the curse of a plural society, encouraging violence and intolerance, the latter makes citizens capable of coexistence and respect for the other, enabled by the moral guidance of "genuine" moral values. According to Mauritian state institutions and many Mauritians in everyday contexts, authentic ancestral cultures with their religious traditions are the chief source of such moral values. In this, the Mauritian politics of coexistence through promotion of ancestral religious traditions resembles aspects of Indian debates about secularism, in particular a Gandhian critique of modernization according to which the destruction of "authentic" religious traditions of coexistence among the populace in a process of modernization and secularization are the principal culprits for the recent rise of violent Hindu nationalism in India.

RELIGIOUS PLURALISM AND SECULARISM IN INDIA AND MAURITIUS

In some countries, such as France and Turkey, secularism has involved separation of state from religious institutions seeking to confine religious practices and identifications to a sphere of the "private," thus creating a secular public sphere. Indeed, it can be argued that the modern category of "religion" as a area of life distinct from politics, society and law, and the emergence of the "secular" as a particular type of public sphere or as new techniques of social transformation have emerged simultaneously and are mutually dependent. However, this separation is not the only way in which the problem of equitable coexistence under conditions of religious pluralism has been approached. In India, for example, the postcolonial state has heavily intervened in religious institutions with the aim to suppress practices deemed as "backward" and to ensure that religion does not interfere with the production of modern, progressively minded citizens. Indeed, a discursive distinction between secular elites and masses easily consumed by religious passions is fundamental for understandings of secularism in India. The latter also helps to explain why the state seeks to regulate religious tradition in order to foster the emergence of rational citizens inclined towards coexistence with others. The creation of a public sphere from which religious symbols and identifications are absent is not considered a feasible project, as the latter are expected to be very visible in the political process and in the public sphere. As they cannot be eradicated from a public sphere of political discourse and performance, still less from popular culture, and constitute a danger for peaceful coexistence in the form of uncontrollable religious passions, control and regulation of the religious by a secular elite dominating state institutions is essential. Closely related to the distinction between regulated and enlightened religion and backward and violent religious passions mentioned above, another key theme in discourses of Indian secularism is the Gandhian opposition between "true" religiosity and violent religious communalism. While the former fosters nonviolent coexistence and mutual respect among followers of different religious traditions, the latter is the product of a cynical instrumentalization of religion for political gains, encouraging violence and intolerance. Accordingly, those favoring this vision of Gandhian coexistence and nonviolence do not favor a politics free from the use of religious images and discourse but have appealed to Gandhian nonviolent and "true" religiosity supposedly inherent in Indian popular religious traditions in order to fight violent Hindu nationalism.

Understandings of the secular in Mauritius share several of these themes prominent in Indian politics. In particular the theme of "true" religiosity as an antidote to dangerous "communalism" is of supreme importance in Mauritius, where the citizenry is not only officially differentiated in terms of religious identification, but where the public salience of such identifications is also encouraged in the context of a state-sponsored policy of "ancestral cultures" above all equated with different religious traditions. In comparison to Indian discourses of secularism with their suspicion of religious passions among the masses, religious values and identifications feature as more positively valued elements of a politics of secularism. Instead of being concerned about an excess of religious passion among the populace, Mauritian state authorities appear to be more apprehensive of a decline of religious values among citizens in a process of modernization and rapid economic transformation.

While recent economic success and relative prosperity in Mauritius is of course welcomed, these economic transformations are also accompanied by a concern about unbridled competition and moral corruption that many believe have accompanied the "economic miracle" since the early 1980s. As a consequence, Mauritian state institutions have sought to mobilize "ancestral cultures" and the religious values presumed to be inherent in them in order to combat social anomie and moral decline. Mauritian politicians have also invoked these ancestral traditions in order to foster peaceful coexistence among Mauritians of different religious communities, while conversely the recent changes in Mauritian society and economy are portrayed as undermining "true" religiosity ensuring nonviolent coexistence and mutual respect among Mauritians. Both Mauritian state institutions and many Mauritians in everyday contexts cast secularism understood as equitable and peaceful coexistence in an officially multi-religious polity as a moral problem. In this, secularism becomes a field of values and dispositions conducive to coexistence and to be inculcated into citizens, and these dispositions are in turn inseparable from religious themes and discourses.

One way in which this identification of religious values and traditions with the common good is manifest in mediatized political performances on state-controlled Mauritius

Broadcasting Corporation (MBC) television. On occasions such as the numerous official religious holidays, or inaugurations or anniversaries of religious centers, representatives of the Mauritian state frequently make this connection explicit. For example, the annual Hindu pilgrimage to the temples surrounding Grand Bassin, a mountain lake, on the occasion of the festival of Shivratri is also major political event during which the prime minister and other senior dignitaries give speeches centered on religious themes, and take part in ritual. State television coverage of such events is extensive and demonstrates quite clearly that a separation of state from religious institutions and relegating religious practices and identifications to a sphere of the "private" is not the way religious pluralism is accommodated in Mauritius.

There is, however, another level on which the intersection of the common good and religious tradition is manifest. Media practices intervene in this issue not only because they circulate images and discourse demonstrating how Mauritian secularism and religion are not in an antagonistic zero-sum relationship, even though this aspect may be the most obvious. This is because the use of electronic media has also become part of religious practices. Such uses of media have turned into one of the chief battlegrounds on which contests over authority and authenticity in religious tradition have played themselves out.

For my purposes here, the most significant aspect of this Mauritian politics of coexistence through the proportion of presumably genuine and authentic ancestral religious traditions is that this notion of the common good ultimately locates the task for ensuring successful coexistence in the formation of piety among Mauritian citizens. It does so by placing particular stress on the authenticity and validity of religious traditions, as only they can shape Mauritian citizens in a spirit of moral virtue and rectitude, and thus enable successful coexistence in an officially multi-religious polity. For Mauritian Muslims, Islamic traditions represent their officially recognized ancestral culture. Therefore the cultivation of "genuine" Islam and the shaping of pious Muslims are of supreme importance in their claims to be good citizens who contribute to the task of coexistence and the fight against "communalism" as the central notion of the common good in Mauritius.

DEVOTIONAL GENRES AND ELECTRONICALLY MEDIATED AFFECT

In contemporary Mauritius the audition of cassette and audio-CD devotional discourse and poetry is one of the key ways in which electronic media practices and the formation of Muslim piety intersect. The particular genre I am concerned with is na'*t*, devotional hymns and poetry in praise of the Prophet Muhammad, and also of other Muslim authorities such as the prominent Sufi teachers Mu'inuddin Chishti (d. 1235, popularly known as Khwaja Gharib Nawaz), 'Abd al-Qadir Jilani (d.1166), and even in praise of members of the ahl-e bayt (the family of the Prophet and their descendants) such as the Prophet's son-in-law 'Ali and his grandson Husayn, a practice recalling Shi'ite traditions.

Na't is usually performed in Urdu and is very popular among Muslims in South Asia and its diasporas. In Mauritius, as in also often the case in South Asia, the performance of this poetic genre takes place in religious speech events known as mahfil-e mawlûd on auspicious occasions, such as the birthday of the Prophet and prominent saint teachers, as well as key events in life such as weddings or moving into a new home. Performing na't has been an established practice usually confined to these performative occasions, but starting in the 1980s, the circulation of cassette and later audio-CD recordings of this genre has not only extended the practice to new contexts of audition, but has also begun to shape how na't is performed in mahfil-e mawlûd. Cassettes na't from India and Pakistan, as well as live recordings of visiting na't khwân (accomplished performers of na't) from both countries have emerged as authoritative models for local performances of the genre. At the same time, a few Mauritian na't khwân who received training from Indian and Pakistani Imams have also started to produce recordings of the genre, and their cassettes and audio-CDs are now the most commonly used in Mauritius.

Na't is a key practice in a larger complex of spiritual mediation characteristic of some South Asian traditions of Islam. In particular the Ahl-e Sunnat va Jama'at (Barelwi) tradition emphasizes the role of the Prophet as a mediator between Muslims and God. According to this tradition the Prophet continues to have a spiritual presence of his own manifest as pure light (nûr-e Muhammadî) and his powers of intercession can be appealed by the performance of na't poetry in praise of the prophet. The performative dimensions of the recital are of supreme importance for the act of spiritual mediation. This is because in reciting the poetry, the performer becomes immersed in love for the Prophet and a better Muslim. Given the transformative qualities of practicing na't, its adherents consider that enormous spiritual benefits derive from the act of reciting and listening to this genre of praise poetry. In other words, na't is a performative technique creating pious dispositions in its practitioners. More in particular, it is a technique for producing certain pious affective stances, especially deep affection and love for the Prophet, resulting in a sense of visceral closeness to him.

Na't is a controversial genre, because for some the exuberant praise and description of the Prophet's attributes is going too far, approximating the Prophet Muhammad to a Godlike figure. Practitioners of na't are keenly aware of the delicate status of the genre, which in the eyes of most Muslims should never suggest equivalence between the Prophet and God. Therefore the authoritative status and the authenticity of the recited poetry, ideally traceable to scholars and poets of repute, is of great importance for the performative efficaciousness of na't. Performing poetry that steps over the acceptable boundaries of praising the Prophet would turn the perceived benefits of na't into their opposite, instead of enacting a pious transformation of the self or the successful enactment of spiritual intercession.

Against the background of controversy around na't, uses of electronically mediated na't have interacted with Mauritian Muslims' practice of the genre in shaping notions of textual and performative authenticity. Concern about the correctness and faithful reproduction of na't has invested na't recordings from South Asia or those of local performers trained by South Asian Imams with particular authority. From the perspective of many of its users, electronic reproduction of voice facilitates authentic textual transmission. Audition of cassette or audio-CD na't is thereby domesticated into an established tradition of recitational logo centrism also attested for other Islamic traditions. Even if recitation of scripture directly summoning the presence of the divine is not at issue here, the concern for the authentic presence of the "correct" text through long chains of interlocutors is also important in other engagements with Islamic traditions in Mauritius and elsewhere, such as in the faithful transmission of Hadith, the record of the words and deeds of the Prophet and his companions, or as in the case here, the authentic transmission of na't.

But the faithful transmission of text through long chains of interlocutors and performers is not the only aspect addressed by media practices such as cassette and audio-CD na't. Equally important is the safeguarding of a particular performative style, which is as decisive for the pious transformations sought in the practice of na't as the "correctness" of the textual dimension. The affective dimension of the practice of na't is at the forefront of concerns about the faithful transmission of a particular performative style, which is as significant for the efficaciousness of na't as the authoritative transmission of texts. According to my interlocutors, the recitational style in the expression of love and affection for the Prophet should never remind one of Hindi film songs in a setting such as Mauritius where the consumption of Bollywood entertainment is extremely popular. There is no use of musical instruments and there are no female voices. Also, unlike in Hindi film songs, recitational qualities should be emphasized, with moderate speed and rhythm. The expression of overwhelming affection should be balanced with the decorum, the restrained conduct and absence of agitation many conceive as iconic characteristics of a pious Muslim. Unlike the transmission of the "correct" text, this performative dimension cannot be effectively mediated by print, but by techniques of sound reproduction. There are only a few accomplished na't khwân in Mauritius to serve as examples in live performances. However, in the eyes of many Mauritian Muslims, circulating audiocassette and audio-CD recordings can provide the guidance necessary for the successful performance of na't.

The successful performance of na't with its production of the "right" kinds of affect within a framework of spiritual mediation depends on the "right" way of performing, and also listening to na't. This entails the ability of the performer to move his audience towards the experience of strong love and affection for the prophet, and for the audience the capacity to hear in the right way, against a background of shared knowledge of spiritual mediation and of the generic conventions of na't. Cassette and audio-CD na't are treated as enhancing this process, as for many Mauritian Muslims listening to na't recordings ensures not only the faithful transmission of text, but above all provides guidance in matters of performative style.

Despite the popularity of cassette and audio-CD na't, many reject the practice of this devotional genre. This is related to the antagonism between adherents of the Sunnat Jama'at, as the Mauritian followers of the Ahl-e Sunnat are locally known, and the local representatives of the Deobandi tradition. The latter, in Mauritius above all the followers of the Deobandi-connected global missionizing movement Tablighi Jama'at, reject the former's openness to Sufism as well as their veneration of saints and their perspective on the Prophet as a mediating figure that can be appealed to for intercession. They regard these practices as illegitimate innovations that they attribute to the Indian environment in which they arose, and seek a "return" to the original society of the Prophet.

The collective recitation of na't as an invocation of the Prophet and saint-teachers is part of this complex of spiritual mediation the Deobandis reject from their purist perspective. As such, the differences between Deobandis and the Ahl-e Sunnat or Barelwi tradition has so far been above all understood as a matter of different philosophies of spiritual mediation and different understandings of what the original society of the Prophet was like. But disagreements about na‘t among Mauritian Muslims show that these differences are not only a matter of different theologies or conflicting perspectives on the authenticity of certain Prophetic traditions. They are also concerned with the role of affect in devotional practice. This in turn has also led Mauritian Muslims to develop different perspectives on the electronic medium in this devotional practice, the one more optimistic, and the other more skeptical.

AFFECT, PIOUS PERSUASION, AND COEXISTENCE

So far the Mauritian Muslims domesticate the electronic medium into a paradigm of authoritative devotional discourse. Cassette and audio-CD na‘t both fit into the concern for safeguarding the transmission of authentic religious discourse through long chains of interlocutors, while also intervening in support of the transmission of a particular performative style. I have sought to emphasize how the interplay between the textual and the performative dimensions in the practice of na‘t address both the conceptual underpinnings of the act of intercession the practice of na‘t aims at, as well as its affective dimensions. Mauritian Muslims treat techniques of sound reproduction as largely supportive of the processes of spiritual mediation and pious transformation the performance of na‘t seeks to bring about.

These considerations also have important implications for the question of pluralism. In fact, many would regard the role of the affective dimensions of religion in equitable and peaceful coexistence with a large measure of suspicion. Have religious passions not been driving forces of hatred, intolerance and violence against perceived others in a considerable range of regional and historical contexts? How can one be sure that the mobilization of religious affect does not exceed its normative purposes and be destructive to the practice of religious pluralism instead?

In our case here, this raises the following questions about

the production of pious, "truly" religious Muslims through electronic media practices. Does the electronic mediation of the affective dimensions of the religious heighten a disjuncture between the affective and the conceptual-ideological? Is the worry of the detractors of na't, of strong affect moving into wrong directions, towards improper objects of desire, not also reinforced by the practice of electronic mediation? Is the demarcation of na't from Hindi films songs with their aesthetics of romantic love and sensual dance, which the proponents of na't seek to further by giving guidance in matters of performative style through the use of techniques of sound reproduction, not also blurred by the use of cassettes and audio-CDs? In short, is the production of pious Muslims with its affective and sensual dimensions only facilitated by media practices, or do they not also destabilize this process, highlighting gaps between affective engagement and the normative spiritual relationships between God, the Prophet Muhammad, and Muslims? Mauritian Muslim's uses and evaluations of sound reproduction in the context of religious tradition suggest that there is no perfect fit between the affective and the conceptual dimensions of the circulation of electronically mediated devotional discourse.

At first glance, the connection between these very particular internal Muslim debates about orthopraxy and "true" Islam with the question of pluralism and coexistence between the different ethno-religious communities of Mauritius may not be immediately obvious. Nevertheless, such internal debates are intimately linked to the question of pluralism because they address the authenticity of ancestral religious traditions as representatives of presumably benign religiosity. Many Mauritian Muslims connect the struggle over religious authority and the contest between rival South Asian traditions of Islam to the making of pious Muslims, whose morally fortified character also enables them to be exemplary and tolerant citizens of Mauritius as an officially religiously plural polity. In fact, opponents in these debates not only denounce their adversaries' claims on authentic Islam, but also their moral competence for coexistence with others. The adherents of the Ahl-e Sunnat, who also promote the practice of na't, often criticize their purist Deo-bandi opponents as too "fanatic" to coexist with others. The latter in turn argue that their reformist project is more "modern" and contributes to educational enlightenment among Mauritian Muslims. They consider their project of purifying Islam in Mauritius not only compatible with religious pluralism but as actually supporting the building of authentic "ancestral cultures" inhabited by moral values.

The area where concerns about affects that go against the larger conceptual framework of spiritual mediation invoked in the practice of na't most frequently araise is the perceived danger of Hindi film music and aesthetics influencing na't performances. Sharif Chady, currently the best-known Mauritian na't khwân (accomplished performer of na't) regards the dissemination and use of cassette and audio-CD na't as useful guidance against the negative effects of Hindi film music. The consumption of Hindi film entertainment is very popular in Mauritius and Chady and others are worried that Mauritian Muslims recite na't poetry to the tunes of films songs they hear in their everyday lives, thereby endangering the spiritual benefits derived from this act. In their eyes, Hindi film music and aesthetics carries with it the sensuality of dance and romantic love and not only detracts from the love to the prophet both expressed and motivated by na't poetry, but dangerously blends this affection with the sensuality of illegitimate forms of attraction prevalent in Hindi films. The fact that a few Hindi films do feature na't makes this perceived danger even more acute in the eyes of the advocates of na't, and lends additional justification to the detractors of the practice. Therefore many Mauritian Muslims describe the characteristics of a "good" na't recited appropriately and effectively in negative contrast to Hindi film music and aesthetics.

Otherwise, my Mauritian interlocutors stressed how the production of the "right" affective stances not only dovetails with the relationships of spiritual mediation evoked in the practice of na't, but also actively constitutes them. As a civil servant in his thirties put it: "You can feel the love for the prophet in the voice of a good na't khwân. If his voice is clean and beautiful, it will make others feel the same way." The moving expression of love and attachment for the prophet in the performance of an accomplished na't khwân represents the ideal to be aspired to- a complete overlap between the affective stance inhabited and communicated to others and the normative relationships between Muslims, the Prophet Muhammad and God invoked in this particular tradition of spiritual mediation. Since such a successful performance of spiritual mediation with its transformative qualities depends not only on the authenticity of the recited text, but also on the appropriateness of the performative style, cassette and audio-CD na't provides important orientation in ensuring this normative overlap between affect and spiritual relationships. This circumstance is even more important in a diasporic location like Mauritius, where Muslims are a minority who often see themselves as not only living far removed from South Asian centers of Islamic authority, but also on the periphery of the Muslim world in general. In the words of an Urdu teacher: "There are not enough good na't khwân in Mauritius. It is not possible for Muslims in all the communities of Mauritius to listen to a fine na't performance in person. But people listen to the cassettes to learn. When they do this they can lean about the teachings and the poetry of great scholars in India and Pakistan directly." According to many Mauritian Muslims this perceived closeness to Islamic authorities is facilitated by the circulation of cassette and audio-CD na't. Electronic reproduction of voice provides Mauritian Muslims with a performative model to be emulated, which most of them could not experience through face-to-face interaction. In this it also provides a model for the appropriate production of affects, which are part of a normative vision of spiritual mediation in which the continued presence of the prophet Muhammad plays a key role.

The Deobandi-linked critics pay particular attention to a problem also acknowledged by some advocates of performing na't- the possibility of affect going in "wrong" directions. They have little sympathy for the production of overwhelming emotions of attachment to the Prophet, which they think should be exclusively focused on God. At the same time, they also note what they consider a fluid boundary between na't and musical entertainment genres. As I have mentioned above, the concerns of na't being influenced by Hindi films songs, thereby not only crossing over into the category of "music" but also into a sphere saturated with illegitimate affect, are even shared by some proponents of this devotional practice. From the perspective of such critics there is no privileged relationship between qualities understood to be characteristic of the electronic medium and the ideal relationships between Muslims, the Prophet and God the practice of na't aims at. For them, the perceived fact that techniques of voice reproduction enable the authentic transmission of not only devotional text, but also performative style, is no safeguard against affect going in "wrong" directions, such as in the intense veneration of the Prophet, which in their view detracts from the oneness of God.

To sum up, Mauritian Muslims are acutely aware that affective stances produced in the audition of electronically mediated na't may exceed the normative limits set by the theology of intercession presupposed in the performance of this genre. They especially point to the powerful influence of Hindi film music they think as influencing local engagements with this devotional genre. On the other hand, the role of cassette and audio-CD na't as a means of ensuring faithful transmission of na't in a diasporic location clearly seems to outweigh the perceived dangers that come with the association of these media with the world of Hindi films. In other words, the affective and conceptual dimensions in the audition of cassette and audio-CD na't are more seen as mutually constitutive rather than latently at odds with each other. Nevertheless, the interplay is not always a seamless one as the concerns about Hindi film music and aesthetics testify.

To sum up, the emphasis on the importance of religious media for the making of public spheres in which citizens engage with notions of the "common good" under conditions of ethnic pluralism. At the same time, I have asked how affective and corporeal dimensions of electronically mediated religious experience relate to questions of ethnic pluralism, secularism and nonviolent coexistence.

In highlighting the affective and corporeal aspects of the nexus of public culture and religious experience, scholars have provided a much-needed critique of the idea of publics as primarily deliberative and ideological spheres. But a neovitalist privileging of the affective over the deliberative in the name of an autonomous sensory sphere that is primary to and constantly excessive of the conceptual-ideological runs the danger of merely inverting the established Platonic-Christian opposition between the spirit and the flesh that continues to dog much work on religion, media and the public sphere. Rather, it is necessary to pay attention to the complex interplay of affect and the conceptual-ideological dimensions of the public circulation of religious discourse and images. It is in this way that previous work on the deliberative aspects of publics can be fruitfully brought in relation with the affective and somatic experiences animating the circulation of discourse and images, as both constitute the possible "common good" in plural societies.

3

Islamic Television

Private Ownership vs State Control

The most general trend in this respect in Arab TV shows a move toward private ownership and control. Before 1990, television stations were structured as a strict control system monopolized by the government, a loyalist system which was loyal to government but not necessarily owned by them, or a freer system which only Lebanon and Israel allowed. These government relationships attempted to use their control to use TV to spread national unity or as a medium for propaganda and to keep control out of marginal groups. Egypt was the first to create a private satellite TV station, Nilesat, in December of 1990. Other countries immediately followed Egypt's lead (Middle Eastern Broadcasting Corporation, MBC, in 1991 was the next). By now, nearly all Arab countries have their own satellite transmissions and there is a growing diversity in the kind of shows that are produced. With the trend leaning toward private ownership, much of the constraints previously encountered with government control and political censorship are gone and channels are much freer to expand the kind of content they produce. For instance, in 1995, Sheikh Hamad bin Khalifa al-Thani of Qatar announced an end to the prior administration's censorship office, and while he still funded certain projects, Qatari-based Al-Jazeera satellite news station is a breakthrough news source in the Arab world, whose journalistic freedom will be discussed later in the report.

COMPETITION

As satellite opened the playing field in Arab countries, a few things happened. First of all, compared with the slow rise of channels in America, Arab countries experienced a period of skyrocketing creation of new channels. This in part has to do with creating niche channels for distinct members of the TV audience, but is also representative of the kind of competition that exists and thus creates the impetus for more improvement. Second, as state revenue for satellite dries up in some Arab countries, competition between channels has increased and caused a much more commercial environment (Sakr). This can be seen in an American context with the advent of all different kinds of dancing or singing reality shows; while the format is not the most innovative or hard-hitting, multiple networks pick it up because it draws a big audience and can help them compete.

COMMERCIALISM

As stated in the section above, increased commercialism appeared in Arab satellite TV as a result of growing competition. This growing commercialism is received in an interesting way in the Arab world. Whereas in the US market, commercialism is often seen as something that reduces the value of a piece of art in the hierarchy of culture that exists, in the Arab world, commercialism has been seen as a good thing. Since commercialism has grown as TV broadcasters have become more open (by open, I refer to the absence of state control), this commercialism exemplifies a gateway to new and different ideas. Also, as Marwan Kraidy describes, reality TV (perhaps the most commercial of all TV) has often led to substantial political debates and activism.

ROLE OF ADVERTISING

With the advent of satellite television, advertisers found themselves in unfamiliar territory. Their products would now be displayed in a much larger geographic area reaching a more diverse group of potential consumers. However, they did recognize the importance of advertising on satellite almost immediately and began allocating almost as much money to the medium as to terrestrial television by 1997 (Sakr). The uncertainty was trying to understand how people from such disparate places would react to the same message. Answers to these questions have still not been fully addressed in the Arab TV landscape and thus is one area that definitely still deserves more development as Arab satellite TV matures.

PROGRAMMATIC TRENDS

News

With the arrival of Al-Jazeera in Qatar in 1996, the Arab world found itself with a very capable competitor to American 24-hour news stations. (Saudi-backed, London-based Middle East Broadcasting, MBC, was the first news network of this style, but Al-Jazeera is a more iconic example to consider.) The news station has experienced both praise and criticism from around the world. The positive remarks applaud the station's wide array of topics covered and its willingness to show multiple opinions. Its criticism ranges from not covering Qatari issues to expressing anti-west or anti-American propaganda. Many countries have followed Qatar's lead, so it would seem Al-Jazeera is doing something right. Saudi-run Al-Arabiya and Iranian-run Al-Alam are examples of Al-Jazeera's simultaneous protégé-competitors. The advent of these kinds of news sources, modeled after CNN and BBC, are also frequently discussed as a notable step toward democracy: with less state control, viewers receive more objective information. Before satellite and the appearance of these news networks, "news" was simply recorded and transmitted political hearings or ceremonies. There was no place for questioning, explanation or criticism.

Reality TV

Arabic reality TV looks just about the same as American reality TV. Following the tradition of the Netherlands (the first country that produced reality TV) and later the British and American format for reality programming, this type of TV is popular for its low production costs and wide appeal. The general term, "reality" can mean several kinds of shows: dating shows, game shows, confessional situations, and hidden camera tricks, all of which exist in the Arab market. And even in the Arab world, where one stereo-typically thinks of a male-dominated or repressive society, there have been reality programs that place men and women together in progressive situations such as communal living.

Ramadan Serials

An interesting phenomenon in the landscape of Arab television is the emergence of Ramadan serials. During what is supposed to be the holy month of renewal for Muslims, most Muslim households wait until sundown to binge eat and then watch the next installment of these soap opera-like miniseries (Hammond). Evidence of the Arab world's growing involvement in the evermore commercialized global community, the month of Ramadan serials is comparable to the advertising frenzy of the Superbowl here in America.

Women's Programming

Lebanese broadcaster Heya is an interesting case study to consider in this section on women's programming. Heya was the first pan-Arab broadcaster to offer over 200 channels geared directly to women (Matar). It represents the first pan-Arab women's platform and also encourages the integration of women into all roles in TV production. The politics of gender-specific programming aside, the growing prominence of women on Arab TV stations is a positive development. One might compare it to reprsenting the marginalized minority voice in America; historically, women have not experienced nearly as much freedom of expression in the Arab world as men, so giving them more opportunity to have a public voice is definitely progressive. Women's programming in the Arab world, just as the news stations and reality TV, resemble American women's programming. There are talk shows, cooking shows, and advice shows. Something to appreciate about these women's shows, as with much of the programming in the Arab world, is the wide range of diversity that exists, both in terms of religion and home country.

Religious Material

Evidenced by Amr Khaled, the Arab world is catching up to the US in its attempts to popularize religion. However, religious counseling shows like Khaled's seem to be a little less ostentatious than Billy Graham, who Khaled has been compared to. In most Arab shows that talk about religion, there is a genuine understanding and reckoning with the Koran. And oftentimes, more prominent in these messages are broad lessons about morality than specific instructions (Khaled might find more comparison with Graham in this aspect, as he has been known to advise very certain tasks to bring one closer to God). The advent of shows that deal with religion could almost be seen as inevitable; with the lightning speed arrival of so many options on satellite TV, some viewers understandably felt unsure of how to navigate the growing modernization and/or globalization of their community. Religious programming can help navigate these uncertainties. Another important factor in the rise in this kind of religious programming is the type of scrutiny Islam faced after the 9/11 attacks. Khaled markets himself as the "anti-bin laden," trying to "turn around a generation of lost Muslim youth".

THE NEEDS IN ISLAMIC MEDIA

Islam is the fastest growing religion in the West. Nevertheless, the West has many stereotypes and misconceptions about Islam that are due to the media, prejudice, and ignorance. Islam is often looked upon as "extremist", "terrorist", or "fundamental" religion. Many people hate Islam and do not want to acknowledge its true teachings. In many cases, the media's reports about Islam are incorrect due to ignorance. This is one of the reasons why the West often hates Islam. In contrast to what many Westerners think of Islam, Islam is a peaceful religion, which does not promote any forms of uncalled for fighting or "terrorist" actions.

Stereotypes about Islam are not new to Western culture. Problems can be traced back 1400 years. At that time, Islam and Christianity were involved in the Crusades in the 1100's and in the Ottoman and Moorish control in Europe. Islam spread quickly to the West, and started to threaten the position of the Christian Church and the ruling class. The Western elites, mainly the governments and the churches, then became highly involved in seeing that negative images were presented about Islam. As a result, not only were battles fought against Islam, but also a war of words was initiated to make sure that Islam would not have any converts or sympathizers in the West. These kinds of actions and feelings that the West had long ago still seem to be the case in the West today.

Today, the West, with little or no understanding of Islamic history, has identified a new enemy, "a new demon that has replaced the Red menace of the Cold war, i.e., radical Islam". This "radical Islam", a stereotype common to Western thought, portrays Muslims as fundamentalists or potential terrorists. Some of these ideas that the Western people have about Islam are due to the mass media of the West. Reporters who cover the Muslim world often know very little details about it. The media then develops a distorted image of Islam that Western culture adopts.

A major factor which contributes to Islamic stereotyping in the West is due to the media's ignorance of selecting their words that describe Muslims. Some common names heard or seen in the news about Muslims are "extremist" or "terrorist". These words are misleading and are mainly anti-Islamic. The media rarely uses more neutral terms such as "revivalist" or "progressives".

The Western media also creates the idea that Muslims are "returning" to Islam. This is not true in most cases, because most Muslims have never left Islam in the first place. Islam has always been a big part of their lives. A more accurate and just way to describe this idea is to say that there is a revival of Islam and it is becoming more and more influential to everyone.

Adding to the fact that the media creates inaccurate ideas about Islam, the Western media is also very influential to its audiences in making negative Islamic stereotypes, such as the assertion that all Muslims are fundamentalists. The term "fundamentalist" is actually a term that is interpreted by the media. A fundamentalist, in fact, only represents a normal Muslim who follows his or her religion. Fundamentalism means an attitude, an effort, or a movement that an ideology, group, or religion tries to promote in its fundamental beliefs.

The "fundamental" beliefs of a Muslim is to believe in only one God (Allah) and the Prophet Mohammed is His messenger (PBUH), pray five times a day, fast the month of Ramadan, give alms to the poor, and make a pilgrimage to Mecca. This means that all Muslims are fundamentalists if they believe in their own religion's fundamentals. Although the media is uncomfortable with religious groups, it focuses heavily on "Islamic fundamentalism". A majority of the media's reports that talk about Islamic fundamentalism usually describes most Muslims as extremists. This shows how the media is ignorant, because Islam specifically prohibits any forms of extremism. The Prophet Mohammed said, "Those persons who go to extremes (in practicing their religion) were cursed (by God)". The media most often portrays Muslim "fundamentalists" prostrating themselves before God in prayer. For example, in the October 4 issue of Time, Muslims soldiers were shown performing prayers with guns. The caption on the bottom of the picture said, "Guns and prayer go together in the fundamentalist battle". The part that the reporters omitted or failed to state was that the Muslim soldiers were praying on a battlefield in Afghanistan. Common sense of the situation meant that the soldiers had to remain armed at all times in case of an ambush at any time. This is a clear example of the media's biased and inaccurate reporting.

With regard to the soldiers, another great misconception that exists is the truth about Jihad or "holy war" in Islam. The ideas of war and violence have become related to the Islamic religion from the media. Jihad is so often apparent in the news because the media thinks it is Islam's justification for war and violence. The Quran (Muslim Holy Book) says "Fight for the sake of Allah those that fight against you, but do not attack them first. Allah (God) does not love aggression". A Muslim is permitted to take up arms only as an act of self-defense. A

Muslim has the right to defend his life, and his property.

Jihad literally means "The struggle in the path of God", or "holy war". However, the Western media often abuses the meaning of jihad by referring to it as a holy war where Muslims unreasonably kill non-believers. But the fact is, is that jihad can mean a numbers of things that a Muslim does for the sake of God. Rarely has the Western media used this kind of a definition in their reports. The way the media represents jihad is wrong. The media often takes the word "jihad" out of context to propagate negative views on Islam. A student striving for top grades, individuals pursuing for equality and justice for all people, honoring your parents, a mother giving birth to a child, eating, and even simply sleeping can all be considered jihad.

The association of Islam and violence is a common misconception that the general Western public has developed about Islam. An example of this kind of misconception is that the Western media and some historians often say that Islam was a religion spread by the sword, meaning that Muslims went from one end of the world to the other forcing people to either convert or die. Islam spread by people learning about it and some by holy wars, but they did not force people to convert or die. Since a majority of the American public only gets their information about Islam through the media, they believe this wrong idea. The media's reports about Arab or "Islamic" events, such as the Gulf War, are often misunderstood. The media usually fails to give background information about these Islamic events that it reports on. The media infrequently distinguishes between the religion Islam and the political affairs that occur in most Islamic countries.

For instance, what Saddam Hussein, the president of Iraq, did in the Gulf War was not Islamic and totally wrong (to attack other people for no reason, especially Muslims). But the media still makes reports about Islam and how Islam is made of war-crazed people. For example, to help put things into perspective, Hitler was a person of the Christian faith. This does not mean that all of his actions were consistent with the Christian beliefs. Likewise, Saddam Hussein is of the Islamic faith, but all of his actions do not necessarily represent Islam. So you can see that the media's reports about "war-crazed Muslims" are incorrect. The notion of associating of Islam and Muslims with the terms Arabs and Middle East are in fact misleading. Arabs only account for 18% of the Muslim population across the world.

Aside from the fact that the media misrepresents Islam because of ignorance, the media is also a profit-seeking organization which often seeks to create a false image of reality. Islam is often news of an unpleasant sort for the general public of the United States. Islam has often been presented as a menace or a threat to the West. These negative images do not correspond to Islam, but are the belief of certain sectors of a particular society. These prominent sectors can propagate negative images of Islam, which sometimes influences people's views on Islam. The Western media actually poorly represents Islam. Most of these problems of poor representations come from poor language translations, the absence of developed news agencies with international networks and native reporters, and biased reporting by many Western reporters.

Some biased reports come from negative images that have happened in the Muslim world in the past like the hijacking of airplanes by Palestinians, the occupation of the United States Embassy by students in Tehran, the fact that there are no democratic governments in most Islamic countries, and the Gulf War. For most of these events, the media has misinterpreted and misrepresented them. The media sometimes unintentionally blows things out of proportion, sometimes because of biased feelings toward Muslims. However, many positive developments in the Muslims world rarely go noticed. Some inaccurate representations of Islam are often due to the media's incorrect representations of Islamic countries, such as jihad, or Islam women's rights. Waseem Sajjad, former Chairman of the Senate of Pakistan explains the situation of Islam and the media:

The Islamic world is poorly represented in the West in

terms of press and media coverage. Not only are there just handfuls of news agencies in Muslim countries; there is the concern over the number of inexperienced reporters. Many reporters don't understand the local cultures nor speak the language, leaving them with access to only those English or French speaking Westernized elites. Thus their representation is often a biased account of the political and social events from the point of view of the ruling minority in Muslim countries.

A negative image of Islam is becoming more inherent in the Western culture from inaccurate media coverage. The media helps to make an image of Islam to unsuspecting audiences. The Western public often is misinformed about Muslims through the images on television, motion picture screens, magazines, radios, and comic strips in newspapers, which promote strong messages among their audiences. Western reporters often say that Muslims are terrorists. This becomes a common image to the general person that all Muslims are terrorists. Edward Said's book, *Covering Islam,* talks about how the media and experts determine how we see the rest of the world. He says that:

> The term Islam as it is used today seems to mean one simple thing, but in fact is part fiction, part ideological label, part minimal designation of a religion called Islam. Today Islam is peculiarly traumatic news in the West. During the past few years, especially since events in Iran caught European and American attention so strongly, the media have therefore covered Islam: they have portrayed it, characterized it, analyzed it, given instant courses on it, and consequently they have made it known. But this coverage is misleadingly full, and a great deal in this energetic coverage is based on far from objective material. In many instances Islam has licensed not only patent inaccuracy, but also expressions of unrestrained ethnocentrism, cultural, and even racial hatred, deep yet paradoxically free-floating hostility.

As well as creating inaccurate images about Islam, the Western media usually identifies Islam in Muslim conflicts. The media hardly points other religions out in their conflicts.

For example, the news would say, "Five Israelis may have been shot, but they were shot by five Muslims", instead of saying "Five Israelis were shot by five Palestinians". The media often reverses this action when a conflict is against Muslims, for example the news would usually say "Bosnians are being killed by Serbians", but instead rarely says, "Muslims are being killed by Christians". In addition to the media's inaccurate representations about Islamic conflicts, human rights of women in Islam, such as women veiling and women authority are big topics that Western media often confuses and misinterprets. The media often represents Islam as a male dominant religion where Muslim men have complete authority over all groups of people. The media often says that Islam discriminates against women, and that women have no power or authority. However, it is ironic of what the media represents, that the Prophet Mohammed was one the greatest reformers for women. In fact, Islam probably is the only religion that formally teaches women's rights and finds ways to protect them. When Islam is practiced correctly, it becomes the best example of an equal gender society.

As Islam came around, traditional pre-Islamic roles of women were replaced by new Islamic roles that women followed. Islam allowed women to have the right to be educated and the right to participate in political, economical, and social activities in their community. This created upward mobility in their communities. Women were also given the right to vote, something the U.S. did not allow until 1919. Women were given the right to inherit property and take charge of their possessions. While most of these rights are denied to Muslim women today as a result of cultural tradition, one should not associate this with Islam, because they do not correlate with it.

Islamic women wearing veils is a commonly misunderstood concept in the West. Westerners often think that this is a harsh custom that Islam requires of women. Westerners often say these women have no freedom or dignity for wearing these veils. But in fact, these veils actually help protect women and help them remain in chastity. In Islamic societies there are very few rape cases and AIDS victims as opposed to the Western societies, were there are thousands of rape cases and AIDS infected victims a year. But in some countries, like Saudi Arabia, women are forced to wear abbayyas (floor length veils). Such excessive forms of these kinds of dress are not mentioned in Islam. Islam requires women to wear a veil for their own safety, but if a woman chooses not to wear it, it is her choice and it is between her and her God. God will do anything He wants to her in this world and the after.

Islamic women are indeed supposed to be granted these rights, but the media often fails to inform its audiences about this fact. The media also fails to report that most of the Islamic countries have a high illiteracy rate. This means that it is "virtually impossible for many Muslim women to challenge cultural male authority when the women themselves do not know the difference between village customs and actual Islamic law". The Western media would be able to better represent women's issues in Islamic countries if they identified how and why governments have limited women's rights that are guaranteed to them by the Quran (Muslim Holy Book). Most so-called Islamic countries such as Syria are corrupt (according to Islam) in their religion and should be addressed in the media's reports. But instead "the media falsely portrays Muslim women as victims of a harsh and suppressive religion". While the media is so concerned about negative and discriminatory images about Islamic women, it fails to remind their audiences that there are three Islamic countries (Bangladesh, Pakistan, and Turkey) that have had female heads of states. In contrast, most Westerns nations such as the United States, "who condemn Islamic countries for their oppression of women, have yet to see a non-white, male president, let alone a female".

With regard to Islamic women's rights, Islam is also a hot topic of Western governments. Western powers do not usually easily tolerate Islamic movements or governments. One main reason is that in an Islamic government, in contrast to Western governments, there is no separation of church and state. Judith

Miller states in her book Challenge of Radical Islam, "that anyone who believes in universal human rights, democratic governments, political tolerance, and peace between the Arabs and the Israelis cannot be complacent about the growing strength of Islamic militant movements in most Middle Eastern countries". Miller says that the Western governments should oppose these kinds of Islamic movements. This statement shows one Western's views about how the West opposes Islamic movements.

Observers often say that the goal of Islamic fundamentalism is to wage a holy war against the West. These observers believe the idea that Islamic leaders only wanting the redress legitimate political grievances is totally nonsense. They think that even if Israel or any other opposing regime in the Middle East would disappear, "the appetite of the Islamic fundamentalists would only have been whetted". These ideas are false and also misleading.

The Western media often portrays Islam as a "militant Islam" or a "fundamental Islam" threat to the West. Edward Said states that: For the general public in America and Europe today, Islam is "news" of a particularly unpleasant sort. The media, the government, the geopolitical strategists, and although they are marginal to the culture at large - the academic experts on Islam are all in concert: Islam is a threat to Western civilization. Now this is by no means the same as saying that only derogatory or racist caricatures of Islam are to be found in the West...What I am saying is that negative images of Islam are very much more prevalent than any others, and that such images correspond, not to what Islam "is"...but to what prominent sectors of a particular society take it to be: Those sectors have the power and the will to propagate that particular image of Islam, and this image therefore becomes more prevalent, more present, than all others.

John L. Esposito's book, The Islamic Threat: Myth or Reality, states the question, is Islam a threat to the West? He tells us that the answer lies in the West's views. He says that if the Western powers continue to defend the unjust status of the Middle East in the name of an illusory or fleeting stability,

Islam will be a threat. "But if the Western powers begin to appreciate the legitimacy of grievances in the Middle East, the West and Islamic movements will get along peacefully".

With the Western media's spotlight and some Western governmental attitudes, the West is a place where Islam is a name of negativity. The Western media has contributed a great deal to this negative image of Islam. The media often misrepresents and inaccurately explains Islam and its manifestations. Sometimes the media seems to be biased against Islam. When the media distorts the image of Islam, the general public tends to believe it, because the media is a major source of information that the public gets about Islam.

This ignorance that the West accumulates from the media leads them into making stereotypes about Islam and associating all Muslims and Arabs together. The West often times views Islam as "fundamental" "extremist" or "discriminatory", but all of these terms have been manipulated, purposely because of biased feelings and accidentally because of ignorance, by the media to present a negative image about Islam. Islam is actually a peaceful and fair religion that most often does not correspond to the media's reports. As Islam grows more and more in the West, Westerners will eventually learn the truth about Islam and find out that these negative stereotypes are incorrect. It is possible that Islam will become one of the biggest religions in the United States. As more people follow Islam, the media will start to learn about it, understand it, and report about it in positive ways. As long as the Westerners are educated about Islam, they will probably learn to accept it as well.

THE MEDIA AND ITS REPRESENTATION OF ISLAM AND MUSLIM WOMEN

In June of 1995 an event seen as an international tragedy took place in an American government building in Oklahoma City was bombed. This atrocious act of terrorism killed many innocent people, including children. The following day a British newspaper, *Today*, carried the headline "In the name of Islam", accompanied by a picture of a fireman carrying the charred remains of a dead baby. It was then very quickly established that the bombing had, in fact, been carried out by Christian militants. This incident illustrates a trend which has emerged in the media - the demonisation of Islam and Muslims. The word 'Islam' means 'Peace', and also 'Submission to the will of God'. The Islamic religion and way of life is essentially one which provides total harmony and fulfillment to its followers, yet the media does not portray this image. In television, films, books, newspapers and magazines Islam is presented as being a backward and barbaric religion. It is seen as oppressive and unjust; and more than this it is seen as being most oppressive to women. These various forms of media misrepresent Islam in different ways, but overall achieve the same negative result - the creation of 'otherness' and from this a growing barrier of misunderstanding and hostility between Islam and its followers, and the West.

The form of media which reaches most people in Britain on a daily basis is television. It therefore has the power to communicate with and influence people at all levels of society. Television offers a source of information which viewers often accept as being factual, and thus use as a basis to form their own ideas. Therefore it should provide an accurate picture of what it seeks to portray. With regards to Islam this is rarely the case, instead only two stereotypical images of Muslims are offered. On the one hand we have characters from films and dramas, such as BBC 1's 'Eastenders' and BBC 2's 'This Life', who are Muslim, though only by name. These characters are Western conformists, totally adopting Western values and culture. There remains no sign of their religious or ethnic identity, and should the issue of their cultural background be mentioned it is treated as a cause for embarrassment. The other and more common stereotype is that of the violent religious fanatic. In current affairs programmes we are constantly offered the image of Muslims as savage terrorists, killing innocent people with no remorse. No insight is given as to why some Muslim organisations carry out acts of violence. What results from this is that the common people, the viewers of these programmes, recognise and accept only the labels - and therefore with 'Islam' they immediately associate negative images. As can be seen, two extremes emerge, and with this the question arises of whether these are the only types of Muslims that are acceptable to the Western media. One upholds the status quo while the other provides sensationalism, neither being a true reflection of the majority of Muslims. Myself as an example, I am a practising Muslim with all my values stemming from Islam, yet I also adopt some Western ideas and institutions, having been born and brought up in the West. I therefore represent many Muslims who are rarely depicted in the media; proud of my Islamic identity though aware of my position in the West. Directly related to this, an issue which is close to my heart, is how the media depicts Muslim.

Rana Kabbani, in the introduction to Imperial Fictions: Europe's Myths of the Orient, discusses how a journalist from the magazine Vanity Fair came to her for material on an article about Islam. When this article was published Kabbani was disappointed to say the least: "It was one more unrelieved catalogue of horrors about Islam ... it ignored any of the important debate within Islam about the rights of women. It distorted every sentence I had uttered ..."

She concludes that the article was "intellectually dishonest", but that "the whole Western debate about Muslim women is a dishonest one". Being Muslim, it is this misrepresentation that hurts me the most. With no insight into Islam, journalists and writers condemn the religions attitude to women. Only recently, an article in the newspaper The Telegraph claimed that an Islamic school of great influence in Deoband, India believed and taught that women are the source of evil. I am acquainted with the ideas of this school, and know that it does not make such a claim - to the contrary it teaches men to respect women, and to know their rights. In newspaper and magazine articles and on television in general, we are portrayed as being weak and submissive to a religion which seeks to oppress and dominate. Muslim women who choose to cover themselves are pitied, and are thought the victims of a patriarchal and misogynistic religion. However, for a large proportion of women this simply is not the case. In Islam there is a place for respect and equality and despite the beliefs advocated by the Media, our religion does not offer women a lower status than men, as the Noble Qur'an clearly illustrates: "And for women are rights over men / similar to those of men over women."

And as the Prophet Mohammed (peace be upon him) stated, "Women are the twin halves of men". Over fourteen hundred years ago Islam gave women rights which women in the West have only been given during this century, such as the right to own property, the right to inherit and the right to make a contract in ones own name. Annie Besant, who was writing in the 1930's, observed that, "It is only in the last twenty years that Christian England has recognised the right of woman to property, while Islam has allowed this right from all times. It is a slander to say that Islam preaches that women have no souls". Women are seen as the spiritual and intellectual equals of men, though again this is not the image presented. The hijab (the garment worn by Muslim women to cover the hair), is another issue of contention. The media presents it as being an enforced condition, though for most Muslim women it is a voluntary act which signifies their allegiance to Islam, as well acting as a symbol of their faith.

Islam is the fastest growing religion in the world. To this fact the media has again managed to attach a negative stigma. It claims that this spread has taken place in the Third World, and in deprived communities in the West, such as the black people in the inner-city areas of Britain and the USA (documentaries have been made in Brixton and the Bronx following this theme). It is therefore, according to them, isolated phenomena amongst people of lower standing in the larger community, which does not affect the majority of those in the West. Such a presentation is again untrue. Although it does appeal to the sections of the community mentioned above (who are just as important as any other section), Islam appeals to many different people from many different walks of life.

Islam is able to provide satisfactory answers to every question posed by the individual, and thus provides them with total peace of mind; something which many Muslims would argue no other religion can provide. Islam's appeal is universal, illustrated by the book Islam - Our Choice, in which testaments are given by people of many different professions (Lords and Barons, statesman, diplomats, scientists, doctors, scholars, writers, social workers, preachers) from all over the World (England, the USA, Austria, Germany, Hungary, Holland, Australia, Japan, Poland, Canada, Ireland, Sweden) as to why they chose to convert to Islam. Importantly, within these people are also women. If Islam is the misogynistic religion which the media claims it is, then this conversion to Islam by women brought up in the West would not make any sense. This supports my claim that the debate within the media regarding Muslim women is indeed an unfair one.

In the past some influential figures of the West have attempted to provide an account of Islam without prejudice.. In his writings in the 1770s the great German writer and philosopher Goethe concluded that "If this be Islam, do we not all live in Islam?" Another authority in the literary field, Thomas Carlyle, gave a lecture in 1840 to the "intellectual elite" of London entitled "The Hero as Prophet. Mohomet: Islam", this also did a lot to dispel myths associated with Islam, in an age where the religion was thought of as savage and barbaric. Countless other less influential figures within the West have also documented fair and unbiased presentations of Islam, yet in the current climate such open minded investigation seemingly no longer exists. Many young British Muslims are coming to the conclusion that Western discourse, of which they believe the Media to be a large player, is set against them, only satisfied when documenting them in a distorted light. The term 'Islamo-phobia' has emerged within these circles, and can be used to summarise the collective feeling of rejection and alienation that is being experienced by Muslims within Britain. At the hands of the Western media British Muslims face marginalisation, having their believes and practices ridiculed and degraded on a regular basis.

Salman Rushdie's novel, *The Satanic Verses*, and the Rushdie Affair that followed its publication demonstrates this marginalisation. Rushdie's novel makes a crude play with the sacred beliefs of Muslims; in effect he laughs at what he considers an irrational and ignorant people. Muslims worldwide were unsurprisingly deeply shocked, insulted and angered by the novel. In London a peaceful march in protest took place, in which many of my close friends participated - however, a small handful of youths became unruly, resulting in clashes with the police. Again the media chose to give the event a negative image, with news programmes giving coverage only to the small minority who became violent. The focus also turned to Ayatollah Komeini's *fatwa* (simply translated as 'ruling', and not as the 'death sentence' as the media has claimed) for Rushdie to be executed. The idea of Muslims as an irrationally violent people was again put across by the media, yet no mention was made of the fact that Khomeini's fatwa only applied to Shi'ite Muslims, who make up less then twenty percent of the Muslim population in the World. Throughout the Rushdie Affair the media came down heavily against Muslims; journalists and writers spoke out in support of Rushdie, and his right to freedom of expression. No voices lent support to the hurt suffered by the Muslims - to my memory only one writer, Roald Dahl, spoke out against Rushdie, and his insensitivity in insulting the beliefs of Muslims. Another sharp lesson was also learnt by Muslims within Britain due to the Affair; the limitations of the law in providing them with protection, and therefore the limitations of equality for all in Britain. When Abdul Husain Choudary attempted to bring summonses against Rushdie and his publishers, the Chief Metropolitan Magistrate in London ruled that the law of blasphemy in England and Wales protected only the Christian religion.

Why do the media choose to misrepresent Islam and Muslims in such a manner? The question is one with no defined answer. Many, included me, may first consider that ignorance is at its roots - that those in control of the media simply are not well informed on Islam, and that this comes through in the articles and programmes they produce. However, on further reflection this argument can easily be dismissed. There are too many good sources from which the true Islam can be researched, and found. There are books written within the West by Muslims, by converts to Islam, even some by non-Muslims that reflect fairly on the religion. There are monthly magazines published by Muslim organisations in Britain, and now there are even web-sites and CD-ROMs available with Islamic themes, and these show what Islam really is. With all this information it would be impossible to simply believe that the researchers are ignorant with regards to Islam. Many Muslims now have an alternative and more skeptical answer, that the media purposely misrepresents Islam as it challenges the order of the West. It commands an allegiance which goes beyond boundaries of wealth, nationality, sex, race or culture. It is a threat, and as such, it is treated as the enemy. Many have associated the rise of anti-Islamic sentiments in the media to the end of the Cold War - Muslims will now argue that with the fall of the USSR, Islam is the new common enemy of the West. Such ideas reflect the extent of the damage done to the Muslim community. The media has a great power, and how it chooses to exercise this power directly affects people. It is a propaganda machine of the highest order. The way in which this powerful organisation has mistreated and misrepresented Islam and Muslims is unjust, but furthermore dangerous. This subject warrants and desperately deserves further debate and investigation, which I sincerely hope it will receive in the near future.

4

Islam and Western Media

By the end of the 1980s the world had changed dramatically. And the causes of change crept up on us quietly, almost without our noticing. The main developments concern widespread use of the audio-visual media. These include video, fax and satellite communications technology. In the context of the global political situation, in which the USA has emerged as the master of the age, these developments assume a special cultural significance.

ISLAM AND THE WEST: CONFRONTATION OR CONSENSUS?

In the 1990s America and its cultural allies (like the countries of Europe) appear to dominate the world. They do so through the media. That is why the media is seen as hostile by the Muslim world. Anything from the West is regarded as potentially threatening; this creates neurosis and suspicion. Anyone associating with the West is seen as an agent, a representative of the CIA. It is the gut reaction and bizarre response of a people repeatedly humiliated and let down by the West. It is not the response of Islamic civilization which has survived over a millennium and produced some of the most enduring cultural systems ever seen.

The West, dominated by North America and Western Europe but also including countries such as Japan, is the driving force in the new global culture. The standards of living of many of their citizens have never been so high in history. But they have little to offer those outside their borders. Indeed, they would close their borders to outsiders. The notions of 'fortress USA' and 'fortress Europe' are just beginning to develop and will certainly grow in the coming time. Strong notions of race and social superiority are embedded in these countries and can very easily translate into dangerous political philosophies. We see the Nazi salute and ideology openly displayed in Germany once again. This was unthinkable even a few years ago. Once again the cries against Jews and foreigners are thick in the air, as crude racism re-emerges in Europe, including France and Britain. Once again immigration laws are debated and are being made stricter. So into the next millennium the dominant Western nations will wish to maintain a tightly run island of prosperity to be protected from the hordes of the hungry and restless wishing to join them.

Then there is the Islamic world. In its population and its resources it is potentially capable of forming a major world presence. Its politics, however, remain volatile. Its leadership still requires vision and stability. Its own thinkers still require clarity. It is for this reason that Western journalists find it easy to label groups of Muslim countries as an arc of crisis, or an Islamic crescent of crisis, and dismiss them. They take some Muslim countries and connect them across Asia or Africa; so Central Asia, Afghanistan, Iran, Iraq and Turkey form a crescent. This is a journalistic cliché.

Correctly or not, Muslims perceive the Western media as hostile. Many factors explain this sense of discomfort. The general attitude of hostility is largely true. Western programmes about Muslims are often slanted to suggest negative images of Muslims. Many carry messages of political instability and the poor treatment of women - the two notorious Orientalist prejudices against Islam.

The restless generation coming of age in Muslim societies is another factor. It has grown up with the media and feels familiar with American culture. It is ambiguous about what it sees: it cannot live by the American standards it observes, yet paradoxically it wants them. It also feels contempt for much of what it sees on television (particularly sex and violence) and believes it to be representative of American society. Frustrated, it finds its only legitimate sense of identity in its own traditional civilization, which is Islam. This generation therefore emphasizes its Islamic identity by rejecting the West.

Islam is not the only religion experiencing resurgence but there has been a rise of religious revivalism throughout the world. This has often taken new expressions, sometimes aggressive ones. Whether evangelical Christianity in the USA or Hinduism in India is the phenomenon of revivalism is peculiar to our age. Notions of the secular, of progress and of science which many took for granted generations ago are being challenged.

Another factor is that Muslim societies appear to be experiencing problems with the contemporary world and its ethos based on speed, cynicism and disbelief. Islam recommends balance and a steady pace. There is also the noise and dazzle of the media. Again, Islam emphasizes quiet, meditation and simplicity. The family itself is under attack in today's world. Islam emphasizes the family as the key unit of society and would safeguard it at all costs. Most important, Muslims believe in God in an age dominated by materialism and agnosticism or atheism.

Further, people have already been predicting that after the collapse of communism the West's next enemy would be Islam. Now that there are no more powerful enemies for the West to conquer since the break-up of its main adversary, the USSR, Islam alone remains in its path, preventing final world supremacy. There is a growing feeling among writers and commentators that the world is heading for a final showdown, a final crusade, between Islam and the West.

Because there is so much anger and frustration, there is little analytic or objective thought around Islam; there is little sense of working out solutions, of pondering on problems, in a global context. There is sometimes despair and at other times a wild attempt at striking at the enemy. Not unnaturally, this prevents understanding, analysis or communication.

THE MUSLIM FAILURE WITH THE MEDIA

Anyone today with access to a television, radio or newspaper will have been recently inundated with negative images of Muslims. The controversy regarding The Satanic Verses, the Gulf War and the collapse of the BCCI are three examples of the media focusing attention on Muslims and causing heated argument. Through the drama that surrounded the author and the novel, the way the Gulf War developed and was fought, and the story of the bank, Muslims all over the world were forced to engage in a debate with non-Muslims and indeed with other Muslims. With media descriptions of a 'criminal culture,' to many in the West Islam appeared to be a force for anarchy and disorder.

Some of the main questions in the media about Muslims that related to the above examples were: Is the burning of books a standard Muslim response to literature they don't approve of? Does this mean Muslims do not prize knowledge and learning? Are Muslim leaders merely dictators who invade and occupy smaller neighbours forcibly? Are Muslim businessmen only capable of fraud? What are Muslims really like? Muslims themselves were angry and bewildered by the extent and intensity of the criticism. While they did not approve of The Satanic Verses, most did not wish to kill the author; while many did not support the invasion of Kuwait by Iraq, they felt it was high time someone challenged the bullying attitude of the West; and while they were shocked at the extent of corruption in the BCCI, and many lost their deposits, they nevertheless felt that the manner of its public exposure was partly motivated by a deliberate attempt to humiliate Islam.

In the age of the media, of the sound bite, of television images, Muslims have not yet found a way of expressing themselves adequately. Their leaders - whether Gaddafi or

Saddam - rely too much on mob oratory and controlled television appearances which appear artificial and ineffective in the West. Besides, the vernacular translates poorly. Hyperbole may be thought appropriate for the mob gathered in the Muslim city - wiping the enemy from the face of the earth, the mother of battles which would claim thousands of lives, and so on - but it translates badly in the international press. Muslim leaders either appear as military dictators ordering the chopping of hands and the whipping of the poor (Zia in Pakistan and Nimeiri in Sudan) or as tribal tyrants (Arab rulers) or as socialist dictators (Saddam in Iraq and Assad in Syria).

There seem to be two distinct Muslim responses to the Western media in the 1990s. I will give two examples from Pakistan. One response is mimicry, to accept Western culture, indeed to reflect and further it, often unthinkingly. The weekly paper, Friday Times (Lahore), and the monthly magazine, Herald (Karachi), both in English, are edited by Oxbridge/London University journalists who provide useful and often penetrating political commentary. But they also faithfully echo Western jargon and ideas. Even the word 'fundamentalist' is used, without a trace of self-consciousness, to describe fellow Pakistanis; indeed it is often abbreviated to 'fundo'. Both carry detailed and regular commentary on the latest videos and pop songs coming from America. Pop stars like Madonna are frequently featured. The other response, also from Pakistan, is that of the Jamaat-i-Islami political party. A member announced in public that if Madonna or Michael Jackson were to be invited to Pakistan the party would not only agitate against the government for allowing the invitations but ensure that the functions were disrupted. More zealous members promised to break the legs of those who participated.

While one reaction was to absorb without thought what was coming from the West, the other was total rejection. But are these really well-thought out, balanced and serious responses? Will they be long-term? Do they solve anything?

Do they help us to understand better the relationship between Islam and the West?

Muslims have yet to discover how to use the media to project ideas and images of their own culture and civilization. A perfect example comes from Muslim Spain. Although the King of Spain has dutifully apologized to Jews for what his ancestors did to them in the fifteenth century with the fall of Granada, he has not apologized to Muslims. It is known that he is keen to build bridges but still awaits a Muslim initiative on the matter. From this it appears that Muslims who are so acutely aware of the loss of Andalusia in their popular literary culture find it difficult to translate this into realpolitik and international diplomacy. The failure to do so has cost them heavy. They are always lagging behind in the world, and the injustices inflicted on them are barely mentioned.

Another example comes from Afghanistan. We have discussed the mujahid as the equivalent of a Muslim Zorro figure. But in the Western media the word means different things in different times and places. Mujahid in the Middle Eastern context is a young man with a Kalashnikov wearing battle fatigues, his face covered by a Palestinian scarf, taking a Western hostage. A mujahid in Afghanistan was a heroic tribesman fighting the Soviets. There were thus different interpretations, different responses to the same person fighting for the same cause: the right to self-determination and dignity.

But the media is fickle. Once hailed as the giant-killers, those that successfully fought a superpower, the Afghan mujahidin in the wake of the new world order find themselves discarded. The Americans now see little need for them. Afghanistan is still in a state of turmoil, one-third of the population wiped out and the remaining scarred physically and mentally by one of the most savage confrontations in modern times. The Afghans find them-selves at a loss.

THE GULF WAR AND THE MEDIA

When they came out of the Arabian Desert in the seventh century, Muslims had little besides horses and faith. It was this faith that scattered the more established and powerful armies before them. It was a time when faith could sweep all before it, and that lesson was never forgotten. In 1991 in the Gulf War we saw how things had changed. The Iraqis could not even come near the enemy as death rained down from the skies thousands of feet above. It was impossible even to hold one's own against a superior technological force. It was a pitiful spectacle, a massacre.

It is a truism that the media are used as a weapon in today's world. I was in Britain during the war and I watched television and read the newspapers closely. In the first few days there was a complete blackout of news reported from the Arab side. Television channels broadcast a number of discussion programmes with some very distinguished participants. Because the Western media had built up the war as a major conflict between two largely balanced forces it was difficult to separate reality from illusion. Saddam's army (the fourth largest in the world), Saddam's nuclear potential, Saddam's Scud missiles and Saddam's super-gun were constantly paraded before us. It was going to be a bloody and prolonged fight.

The reality was totally different. Some of the most powerful nations in the world had combined their forces to lure, fight and destroy a Third World power. And at best Iraq was nothing more than a Third World power. Its armies had not even succeeded in penetrating beyond the borders into Iran in the long war in the 1980s. This was in spite of the full backing of the West and indeed the Arabs who wished to prevent the Iranian revolution from spilling into their areas.

However, watching the war on television one had the impression that this was going to be a repeat of the Second World War. Saddam had been elevated to the rank of a Hitler - indeed the word was commonly bandied around. Then there was the completely one sided nature of the commentary and analysis. No brown or black faces were to be seen on the discussion - panels in the early days. Furthermore, not only Iraqis but Arabs by extension became the enemy. It became the war of the white man against the brown one, the European and American against the Arab. By further extension it soon became the war of the West against Muslims.

This equation, looking back coldly now, appears astonishing. And yet it happened and is true. Because of this identification of Muslims as the enemy, numerous incidents were reported of Muslims being taunted, beaten and abused in the UK. The irony of picking on a Bangladeshi in the London Underground, a man who had nothing to do with Saddam and his politics or indeed the Middle East, did not strike those who vented their anger against Muslims. Even Indians were not spared. The further irony of an Indian - perhaps a Hindu - being taunted as a Saddam supporter strikes us as ludicrous now but created an uncomfortable atmosphere during the war. I was aware of the seriousness of the situation because my friend was part of a group of Muslims invited to call on the junior Foreign Minister, Douglas Hogg, at the Foreign Office. The delegation conveyed some of the apprehensions of the beleaguered Muslim community in the UK at the height of the war. A long list of incidents that had taken place over the last few days was presented to the minister. This included women being spat at, pushed and abused because they were easily identified as Muslim (wearing a hijab or shalwar-kameez). In the public mind anyone who even looked remotely Muslim was supposed to be a supporter of Saddam.

This atmosphere created a siege mentality within the Muslim community. Muslims began to feel their loyalty was on test. Many opposed Saddam and his policies, but there were many others who did not necessarily approve of him yet saw in him a man who had the courage to stand up to the West. The television discussion programmes in the West at first did not allow the opposite point of view. Not only were there very few speakers who could represent the Muslim point of view but they were rarely given a chance. Those that did appear sympathetic to Muslims were dismissed as the loony left or romantics who knew nothing of political reality. There was no doubt that the Muslim point of view was not only marginalised but was not allowed to be represented. On

Channel 4's Midnight Special programme, I found that positions were often firmly taken before discussions and then firmly held. There was little attempt at exchange of ideas or even dialogue; and these were extremely distinguished people: MPs, air marshals and experts. However, I also found that some of the famous names showed unexpected sympathy for the suffering of the Iraqi people. Harold Pinter, for example, spoke strongly in support of the underdog. He was, of course, roundly attacked by most members of the panel.

It was quite clear that whoever controlled the media could project how the war was being fought. More important, they could project why the war was being fought. The other side was simply not given a chance. Even untrue stories could be cooked up or true stories be presented in a manner that blurred reality. We were shown the savage bombing of a building in Baghdad that killed hundreds of civilians in the basement. We were not sure what happened. We were told that this was a military target. It was only through the emotional voice and the disturbed eyes of the British television reporter who went in and saw the carnage that we were aware that something terrible had happened. Hospitals, bridges, homes - the very fabric of society was being demolished. For each news item we had to use a method of calculation, to make adjustments, to arrive at the truth.

But there were other extraordinary developments in the Muslim world itself that needed to be explained. Although many Muslim governments supported the West against Saddam, the people were with him. It was a strange phenomenon, this support for Saddam. Muslims were aware that he was far from the ideal Muslim ruler - that, in fact, he was a tyrant created by the West and supported in the 1980s to stem Iran's Islamic revolution. Yet in Pakistan and Egypt, although the governments sided with the Western allies, the people took to the streets in support of Saddam. The Supreme Council of British Muslims met in Bradford and unanimously supported Saddam. His posters became the most popular item throughout the Muslim world. Suddenly Saddam was being seen as another Nasser, even another Saladin, who stood up to the West. Although Saddam was neither of these, he had assumed an almost mythical status. So intense was the sense of humiliation and anger among Muslims that they would even rally behind the devil himself if he stood up to the West. This is not only a disturbing explanation but an uncomfortable reality.

MEDIA ENCOURAGEMENT OF MUSLIM ORTHODOXY

There is a causal relationship between the Western media and the orthodox position in Islam. Ironically, the media encourage what they set out to deflate. Let me explain. Until the availability of modern technology which would link distant parts of the world, Muslim societies were culturally diverse. The Qur'an and the Shar'iah provided guidelines but local practice often varied. So the most colourful syntheses of cultures are recorded from one end of the Muslim world to the other. In due course these became part of Islamic observance. Unchallenged, they were accepted as custom.

Today, however, nothing can go unchallenged because everything is public. Within minutes, accounts of the behaviour of a Muslim group in one part of the world can be flashed to another. This has given the main centres of orthodoxy unimaginable powder and has allowed them to act and behave as the guardians of orthodoxy in a manner unthinkable and practically impossible only a few years ago.

Looking at South Asian Muslim customs, we observe that many of them are derived from Islam's close contact with Hinduism. Over the centuries these have become part of Muslim custom. But their absorption into Islam alarmed Muslim scholars. In the eighteenth century the Muslim scholar and reformer Shah Waliullah, emphasized the need for Muslims to reject these customs. But his voice, although powerful and respected, was nonetheless a single voice. His following and his writing had an impact, but it was limited to the literate. Today the power of the media is such that any custom which is deemed to be abhorrent or unorthodox can be exposed to literally millions of people through the media. It is therefore much more difficult to practise something that is not officially sanctioned or accepted by the orthodox. Sufism provides an interesting example. It is increasingly under attack by the orthodox. The media images of Sufism as a corrupt, decadent cult attracting hippy figures do not help. Sufism has already been under attack over the last century by modernizing Muslims who absorbed Western scientific and enlightenment concepts. Arab leaders with socialist ideas, like Nasser, have also attempted to suppress it.

Although Sufism in its purest forms is traced directly to the Prophet himself, and some of the greatest Muslim figures have been inclined towards Sufism, the more distorted forms attracted much contemporary criticism. Tomb worship, saint worship and stories of miraculous powers have contributed to the disrepute that Sufism now seems to have fallen into. However, this does not mean that Sufism is to be rejected in its entirety. It is one of the most endearing faces of Islam. Its philosophy of universal love, of universal peace, sulh-i-kul, is one of the most powerful and attractive messages it has for our age. Besides, its orthodoxy cannot be challenged. The Sufi's first task is to master the Shar'iah; a Sufi must first be orthodox before he can go on to the stage of mystical achievement.

Yet Sufism stands as a discredited force particularly among the younger generation. This is for several reasons. The strictly orthodox Wahabis of Saudi Arabia believe that much of Sufism is little more than mumbo-jumbo, a deviance from the straight path. They are especially critical of the notion of intermediaries between man and God. They believe that power attaches to God alone and not to human beings. Not even the holy Prophet has any special status apart from the fact that he is the last messenger of God. Some extreme sections of the Wahabis would even go as far as discouraging visitors to the tomb of the Prophet because it attracts worshippers who in turn begin to worship the tomb rather than God.

This is logical and correct. But, like all philosophies carried to an extreme, it can create problems on the ground. It produces a rigidity which does not allow for alternative explanations. Backed by the power of scholarship, funding and propaganda, it can easily convince the younger generation that anyone accused of being a Sufi is little short of indulging in shirk, attributing a partner to God, one of the most serious crimes in Islam. I have heard accusations against some of the most respected and saintly figures in contemporary Islam who were suspected of having Sufistic leanings. These people would in turn chuckle and say, 'May God give Muslims better understanding.

The media play their part in discouraging Sufism. It is not easy to convey the Sufistic message in the media. The hidden meanings of the saints, mystical powers and esoteric images do not translate easily. The image is far more powerful than the message. A Sufi is easily reduced to a Hollywood caricature.

The other Muslim position, the more formal and orthodox, is paradoxically enough boosted by the Western media. Images of crowds yelling anti-Western slogans and pictures of militant young men capturing embassies or blowing up planes do not discourage other young Muslims. On the contrary they attract them. It gives them a sense of identity, a pride in their cause. They are striking a blow for Islam, for the glory of their religion. They are prepared to make any kind of sacrifice and indeed it is on the news all over the world. This is acknowledgement. So the media play a role in assisting one form of Islam as against another, however unwittingly.

THE WESTERN BOGEYMAN: ISLAMIC FUNDAMENTALISM

What is this so-called Islamic fundamentalism? Why is it becoming such a force in world politics today? Islamic fundamentalism is an imprecise and elusive term which attempts to convey contemporary Islamic revivalism and resurgence.

Certain features of this phenomenon can be identified. There is a belief that Islam is a comprehensive way of life, that it includes society, politics and economics. There is also a belief that the failure of Muslims is due to their departure from the straight path of Islam and their infatuation with Western secularism and its materialist ideology. Then it is felt that the renewal of society necessitates a return to Islam, which draws its inspiration directly from the Qur'an and the Prophet. Many Muslims also believe that, in order to create a truly Islamic order, the present Western-inspired civil and criminal codes must be replaced by more Islamic ones. Westernization is condemned but modernization is not; science and technology are therefore accepted, but they need to be subordinated to Islamic belief.

The process of Islamisation itself requires organization and association of dedicated and trained Muslims who will struggle in jihad against corruption and social injustice. However, some go beyond this set of beliefs. They see the West as continuing the Crusades against Muslims with the Crusader mentality. They reject even their own Muslim governments because they are not inspired by the Shar'iah. While accepting that the Christians and Jews are people of the Book, their links with Western colonialism and Zionism make them unbelievers.

Many factors feed into this Islamic revivalism. Most significant are the rapid developments in communications which link up Bradford with Islamabad, Washington with Cairo, connecting Muslims living in the West to their own societies. There are also visiting scholars, diplomats and travellers. This is why when the explosion took place around The Satanic Verses in Bradford a movement developed rapidly among Muslims all over the world. In Bombay and in Islamabad Muslims were killed protesting against the book. Never before in history could the problems of an author living across the world have had such an effect on the politics of a country like Pakistan.

There is also a sociological factor. We note a polarization in Muslim society which often leads to conflict. Neither extreme is desirable: neither integration, for it implies the blurring of borders which would in the end deny a separate Muslim identity; nor isolation, for Islam is not and cannot be isolationist with its emphasis on the universal and the global. But the tensions of the times have created the crisis of polarization, and the lack of leadership among Muslims has allowed it to grow to the point of mutual incomprehension.

World politics have also contributed to the growth of the phenomenon. From the Muslim perspective it is important to understand that during the Cold War both the USA and the USSR were equally suspect in their dealings with the Muslim world. The Muslim perspective was best summed up by Khomeini's dictum na sharq na gharb, neither East nor West. During the 1950s and 1960s the USSR threatened Muslims. One of my memories as a young undergraduate in Pakistan is Khrushchev's drawing a circle around Peshawar in Pakistan threatening to wipe it out with a nuclear attack. Syria and Iraq fell to a local variant of communism and the results were disastrous. It was feared that if the USA removed its protection many other Muslim countries would fall to the Soviet Union. Then, in the 1970s, things began to change.

When the Soviets invaded Afghanistan in 1979, it was expected that like so many dominoes the surrounding states of Iran and Pakistan would be the next to fall. But the Afghans stood their ground, and eventually the USSR packed up and went home. This was followed by the complete break-up of the USSR, which in turn led to the emergence of six new Muslim states. Not unnaturally, this sequence of events was linked by Muslims to their own vision of Islamic destiny. For Muslims it was the triumph of their faith against Godless Russia; the inevitable victory of good over evil. - With the collapse of the USSR, Muslims believed that the USA alone remained as the major force hostile to Muslims. However, we must emphasize that not all Muslims accept conflict with the USA as inevitable. Many nations have close ties with the USA, including Egypt, Saudi Arabia and Pakistan.

In considering why Islam is becoming more of a world force today, we need to explain what is happening to make countries like Algeria - once firmly secular - turn to Islam. Algeria itself is an interesting example because it was one of the first Muslim countries to achieve independence from a European colonial power. After a heroic struggle which cost millions of lives, it then set itself on the path to secular democracy. Having rid itself of the French it would try to become as far as possible French. The paradox was not resolved. It was simply frozen.

All this, however, did not meet the economic and political aspirations of the ordinary Algerian. A generation later Algeria seemed to have got nowhere. Worse: in the process it began to lose its own sense of identity. Horror stories of the treatment of Arabs in France further alienated Algerians from the French model. Questions were raised: if we are to be totally French and yet the French despise us there must be something wrong? Where do we look for another identity? Is the answer in our own culture and religion? The alternative source of identity was, of course, Islam. It was always there. Earlier it had simply been assumed. Now the present generation of Algerian leaders began to examine it seriously and discovered in the process that there were many Algerians thinking along these lines.

"Islamic revivalism,' 'Islamic resurgence,' 'Islamic movement' - we imagine these are new and peculiar to our age. We think we understand something happening in the world by labelling Muslim expressions thus. In fact these very terms are as old as Islam itself. Islam is nothing short of an endless revolution, the eternal quest to reach out to God. It is the universal desire of human beings to pose the eternal questions and attempt their answers in our brief span here on earth.

A hundred years ago Muslim lands were under the European colonial powers. Muslim capitals such as Algiers and Cairo were occupied. Those that were not, like Kabul and Tehran, were under the influence of one or other power. It was the nadir of Muslim political fortunes. Today, a hundred years later, there are about fifty Muslim states, almost a billion Muslims in the world (with, significantly, about ten million Muslims in the West).

Islamic symbolism remains high among Muslims. Constitutions are declared Islamic and flags bear an Islamic star or crescent. Airlines like Pakistan International and Gulf Air say a prayer before the flight when announcing take-off. Major hotels indicate the direction of Mecca for those of the faithful who wish to pray in their rooms.

Perhaps because of the global Islamic position that is forming, there is also a feeling among non-Muslims that Islam is a threat. Throughout the world there is confrontation between Muslims and people of other religions: in South Asia between Hindus and Muslims (India and Pakistan), in the Middle East between Jews and Muslims (Israel and the Arabs), in Africa between Christians and Muslims (Nigeria and Sudan). Even the disintegration of the communist states shows how deep-rooted these divisions are in history. In Bosnia Muslims once again confront Christians, and in Azerbaijan Azeri Muslims fight it out with Christian Armenians.

The Andalus syndrome is never far from the Muslim mind. The sense of injustice, of loss, of the cruelty of the world is sharp. It is captured by a South Asian Muslim character in an Urdu novel commenting on Muslim losses which fuse in his mind and cause confusion: The bearded man tried hard to recollect: after a while, he said, 'all I can remember is that as I was leaving Granada ...

Granada!' the rest looked up at the bearded man with a start . . . And the poor old bearded man, already shocked at their mocking disbelief, felt utterly distraught at the laughter . . . 'I've been uprooted,' he remarked dolefully, 'and that's what matters. What difference does it make now for me to remember whether it's Granada that I've been thrown out of, or Bait-al-Muqaddis [Jerusalem], or Jahanabad, or Kashmir . . .?' The depth of sadness in his voice had an intensely melancholy impact on all the men. They drifted into silence. After a while the bearded man said tearfully, 'Friends, we left behind all that was once ours, and now it seems we've even left behind our memories. '

Andalusia, Kashmir, Jerusalem and now Bosnia - the list

of Muslim losses is long. It brings together the past and the present. It acts as an open wound. Political injustices, deep-rooted hatreds, disintegrating empires and overzealous reformers explain some of the confrontation between Muslims and non-Muslims today. But it is also to be explained by the ethnic and religious revivalism all over the world. It is a revivalism that is still to be understood in its present global context. We must therefore attempt to explain the differences that exist between Muslims and non-Muslims. By doing so we will make some sense of our different positions by avoiding it we will perpetuate the stereotypes and misunderstandings. There is no reason to assume that differences in themselves set different civilizations on a collision course. Indeed, in the plural world that we live in the differences must be not only tolerated but also understood.

5

Islam and Muslims in the Media

Global and regional political, economic and social development, in recent years, has troubled the relationship between Western, European and Islamic societies strongly and manifold. Throughout the world, people are witnessing unsettling changes. Non-Muslims and Muslims alike became victims of terror and violence by people pretending to act "in the name of Islam". Misunderstanding and prejudice seem to grow on both sides even though information systems and means of communication are highly sophisticated. In the era of communication, wars begin, continue and end with media war. The Media shapes public opinion and covers realities by their censorship. The mass media are used as the most important weapon. There is a connection between the role of media and post-modernity. The media shapes the world how we see it.

It is a common observation that crisis such as wars, recessions, stock market meltdowns, ethic scandals, and natural catastrophes often drive the public policy making process. A crisis reveals a problem and then a public consensus emerges that policy makers must do something about it (Snider 2006:1). These crisis reveal broadcasters' important role in communicating crisis information. They provide emerging information to the public in times of crisis. But choosing negative and frightening names for people or groups that powerful policymakers dislike, or using positive names for describing wildly acts - are parts of media tricks. Nowadays, numerous media campaigns are going on against Islam and Muslims. Most Western media with considerable financial resources and multiple channels try to show a rough picture of Islam to their public.

At the same time Muslim groups through various media outlets are trying to convey their messages, but in comparison to the global dominance of the western media, their efforts are somehow in vain. In this regard you can visit the website of the Islamic community in Croatia and many others. Most western media are using the September 11th event to capitalize its political gain. These media depict Islam as "fundamentalism", "extremism" and "radicalism". Of course, in the modern world where the role of media is central, the image of reality can be manipulated to misrepresent the actual facts. The media have tried to represent Muslims as "terrorists" posing a threat to the western security. By doing so, they try to justify the wars in Afghanistan and Iraq. In recent years, this approach has led to the emergence of "Islamophobia". However, little effort has been made to respond to these negative campaigns.

On the contrary, the act of terrorist groups who kill people, especially western hostages, help their media to show that they are collectively victims of terrorism. Despite the explosion of media coverage and publications on Islam and Muslims, the major challenge today involves getting accurate and verified information. The politicization of scholars, experts and media commentators in the post 9/11 period has created a minefield for policymakers and the general public as they search for answers to questions like: "What are the causes of radicalism and anti-Americanism?", "Why do they hate us?", "What do Muslim women think about their status in Islam?" "Is Islam compatible with democracy?", "What are the causes of global terrorism?" and many others. Too often, a reader is caught between the contending positions of seemingly qualified experts as well as a new cadre of Islamophobic authors who engage in a revisionist reading of Islam and Islamic history.

So, what we should do? Suddenly a new empirically

grounded tool emerged to get us beyond the limited interpretations and opinions of experts when answering the question: What do Muslims think and what do they care about? The sense of threat to the Muslim cultural identity is enhanced by a predominant feeling that a secular and powerful West imposes its values upon the Muslim world. When asked the open- ended question, "In your own words, what do you resent most about the West?", the most frequent response across all Islamic countries for both moderates and political radicals was "sexual and cultural promiscuity"; followed by "ethical and moral corruption" and "hatred of Muslims". Another source of resentment comes from the depiction of Muslims in the Western media.

A survey by Jack Shaheen in his book, *Reel Bad Arabs: How Hollywood Vilifies a People*, found that the vast majority of Arab characters in 900 American films were outright racist characters. Images of common day life and ordinary Muslims in their countries are almost non-existent or distorted in the western media. Moreover, the western media which are most popular in the Muslim world encourage emulation of Western fashion, personalities and values. TV news is the most important source of public knowledge about world events. Approximately 80 percent of population relies on it as their main source of news (Philo and Berry 2006:199). Western media with considerable financial resources try to show a rough picture of Islam to their public. Some scholars believe that there is a direct connection between terrorism and modern global communication. Their studies show that most terrorists' acts are propaganda.

Terrorism is an indirect psychological strategy which avoids direct contact with opponents. So, without media coverage terrorism disappears. After 9/11 the terms "Muslim" and "Terrorist" became synonymous in many western countries. Since this event, many experts and activists in the field of human rights have warned of the escalation of Islamophobia and racism against Muslims in many western countries. The representation of Muslims in the media relates to the lack of acceptance of differences.

The media creates public panic around the terrorist threat. As one scholar said the War on Terrorism is a war of images, and the most effective images are those of terrorists' victims. But on the other side we see discrimination associated with "Islamophobia". This phenomenon tries to show that Muslims are a threat to security. The focus on terrorism unifies TV coverage of Muslim news and the dominant image is "Islamic Terrorism". This belief leads to the production of anti-islamic films like "Fitna" by Dutch parliamentarian Geert Wilders. What is clear is that after the September 11th attacks, most experts talked about security matters, while the social and political causes of the attacks were forgotten. This stream continues in the Iraq war. Here too, the economic and political causes of the invasion were forgotten. It is obvious that the West has to review the idea of its own "Self" and the "Other". The representation of Muslims in the western media has to change and Interculturalism has to replace Islamophobia. To improve the image of Islam in the West it requires a strong and persistent effort from Muslims themselves, both in the Islamic world and in the Muslim communities in the West.

These efforts should include a comprehensive process of reforms. Muslims will never be able to improve their image in the world if they fail to appear as a nation of culture and civilization. Effective initiatives must also be undertaken to educate non-Muslims concerning correct Islamic concepts of peace and tolerance and to clarify the incorrect views of Islam held by some.

Tensions between Muslim immigrant communities and the majority populations are increasing in many European countries. Muslim immigrants are faced with discrimination and intolerance, wherever their identity became affiliated with their religion. It is certain that the political, economic and social challenges of integration can only be met by efforts on both sides and that these challenges are not necessarily linked to religion in the first place.

Another challenge can be seen in the prevention of young people becoming radicalized. For many young Muslims, Islam seems to have become a substitute for their homeland which they can not find in the societies they live in. Non-Muslims and Muslims alike, state and religious organizations are equally challenged by these developments. Pluralism and the opportunity to develop and live multiple identities are an essential characteristic of the European model of life.

The starting point of our dialogue initiatives is the conviction that although religion and religious identity have increasingly gained importance, regional conflicts must not be understood simply as culturally or religiously motivated. Lack of mutual understanding must be overcome by dialogue. Strengthening pluralism within societies and reducing prejudices and foe images be it in Europe or in Muslim countries - also play a crucial role.

Dialogue, therefore, must not refrain from controversies, must endure open debates in order to make the complexity of the issue at stake transparent and enable different perceptions still safeguarding the universal acceptance of human rights and fundamental freedoms. Real dialogue is possible only in the presence of mutual knowledge and acceptance of cultural and religious values. Accepting others must mean more than tolerance—it should mean accepting them as members of the community without necessarily any loss of their unique identity. Such mutual acceptance should integrate both sides' values into a culturally richer community. Where there is respect, there will be willingness and even readiness to integrate some of those values to enrich one's own cultural and religious values. Such respect for others requires certain knowledge of the others' history and culture, ways of life, and other factors.

Thanks to developments in communication technology, such knowledge is now easily available. Interfaith and intercultural dialogues seek to reach a better mutual understanding and to engage in common activities. Its main attitude is reconciliation in order to create a better and more peaceful world, to share the world's resources more equally, and to help the underprivileged. Doctrinal, communal, or religious union should not be the real aim; rather, we should work for union in collaboration to do something together, to rise above discussions on doctrinal and ceremonial similarities and differences. Such union in collaboration is possible only in diversity and in conserving as much as possible of our own identity in an increasingly homogeneous world. These are converging not contradictory developments.

This is true for nations and countries where borders are becoming less important or even disappearing, and also for religions. It seems evident that such a union can be realized only by collaborating with each other in a common global range of activities.

Some scholars say that intercultural dialogue is one of the major medicines to overcome humanity's common ills. Our world's durability depends, to a great extent, on the promotion of intercultural dialogue. The Islamic Community in Croatia also believe that establishment of dialog environments is a means to appreciate diverse opinions and eliminate the stereotypes often assigned to "Others". In that respect, we need to educate non-Muslims about Islam and Muslims about other faiths to establish mutual understanding and tolerance. To achieve this end, we invite and encourage sharing of various perspectives, partnership with other religious and cultural organizations and we organize educational activities such as seminars, lectures and discussion panels, all of which inspire and illuminate us in our endeavor to fulfill our mission.

FOREIGN POLICY, THE MEDIA, AND WESTERN PERCEPTION OF THE MIDDLE EAST

It is the mightiest power in the Levant and North Africa. Governments tremble before it. Arabs everywhere turn to it for salvation from their various miseries. This power is not Egypt, Iraq or indeed any nation, but the humble mosque. Over the past year or so, for the first time in a decade, Islamic fundamentalism has become the principal threat to the survival of regimes throughout the Arab world. Because this is an argument about how people think and live, not merely about lines on maps, its outcome may do much more than either the old conflict with Israel or the new one between Iraq and its neighbours to shape the Arab future. Like most big social movements, the expanding power of the mosque is a complicated affair. It takes different forms in different countries and its consequences are graver in some places than in others. But the threat is real enough."

This description of the political situation in the Middle East is illustrative of the view many foreign policy analysts, politicians and journalists hold in Europe and North America. It has been formulated by The Economist magazine, which on most topics of international relations expresses positions of an enlightened mainstream of thought. The Economist generally is not into alarmism, but takes its pride from being sober and analytical. Others have been using much stronger terminology when discussing the same topic: "The Gulf War was just one paragraph in the long conflict between the West and radical Islam; the World Trade Center bombing, just a sentence. We are in for a long struggle not amenable to reasoned dialogue. We will need to nurture our own faith and resolution."

Not just journalists, but also researchers and academics have recently emphasized dangers coming out of the Middle East. One of the best-known examples has been Samuel Huntington of Harvard University, who postulated an "Islamic-Confucian connection" threatening the West, its power and its identity. Others agree with Huntington's statement that "Islam has bloody borders" by making a strong connection between regional conflicts in the Middle East (and beyond) and "Islam". One of them is the German Member of Parliament and Vice President of OSCE, Willy Wimmer: "Between Algeria, the Balkans, the Chinese province of Singhiang and Indian Kashmir there currently is no trouble spot in which the conflict potential of the Muslim World is not fanning the flames of conflict and war."

This article will analyze to what degree and how the Western perception of Islam is influencing Western foreign polity towards the Middle East. It will try to assess the link between foreign policy and media reporting, as far as the Middle East is concerned and discuss the structure of mutual influencing each other. Is the political sector more successful in "managing" the media, or is it basically driven by newspapers and TV in this "era of information"? Do the foreign policy elites share the same perceptions about the region and Islam with the general public, and how do they deal with the more emotional side of viewing Islam in Europe and North America?

FOREIGN POLICY AND THE COLD WAR TRADITION

Foreign policy tends to be based on two pillars: interests and perceptions. "Interests" does include obvious factors like economic resources or strategic location, but it also entails domestic considerations. Diverting attention from social problems at home to some foreign conflict has been tried time and again and may illustrate this point. The problem with "interests" is that they are far less clear a concept than often assumed: political parties, "interest groups" or companies may very well have quite different views about their countries foreign policy interests. "What is good for General Motors is good for America!" - This definition may sound plausible for GM executives, but perhaps not for Chrysler, AmTrack, MacDonalds or even the UAW. "Interests" are not a clear-cut concept, to be defined with mathematical precision. It always includes judgement of preference over alternatives. And it includes judgement on values and priorities.

This brings up the second starting point of any foreign policy: "perceptions". Foreign policy deals with "foreign" people, foreign governments and political actors. It implies dealing with other cultures, traditions, religions and values. Our perception of "the other" necessarily is being shaped by our perception of ourselves, of our own identity. Feelings of inferiority or superiority, of cultural distinctiveness, or of insecurity do shape the way foreign policy is conducted. The United States will deal with the British government differently than with the Egyptian, Saudi or Kenyan Governments. And nobody in Managua, Islamabad or Harare would seriously expect to be treated on equal footing with Washington. Obviously, there is a link between culture and power involved here: different cultures can hardly treat each other in a balanced way, as long as their (economic, military, political and ideological) power is extremely unbalanced. Foreign relations involve interaction between players with very differing power and weakness. They happen in the context of history, with its traditions and experiences of war, domination, colonialism, slavery, and the struggles against them. And these experiences of unequal relationships have undercut any ability to perceive "the other" as equal. Perception is colored by a sense of ones own superiority, by suspicion, paternalism, ethno-centrism, arrogance, mental blockades, aggressiveness or a feeling of frustration and inferiority. Equality is rare, either in the reality of power relations (and "interests"), or in the mutual perception.

Therefore, dealing with foreign policy includes the paradoxical situation that in theory (and international law) all States and Governments are equal, while in reality both their material and ideological power are not. Ignoring this fact of life cannot produce a sound base for foreign policy analyses. At the same time, foreign policy processes are not something "objective", like mechanical transformations from "interests" into "policies". They are based on judgements and perceptions, coloring both ones own "interests", and the view of the opponent. Foreign policy (and foreign policy analyses) has to both take into account the realities and their perceptions. The obvious problem is that human beings can never see realities without at the same time interpreting them.

This may seem obvious, but it is not. During the Cold War, for instance, the "Soviet Threat" had been consistently overestimated. The quantity of military hardware was consciously and unconsciously exaggerated, and the quality and fighting power of Soviet weapons overrated. A nearly bankrupt Soviet Union was perceived as an overwhelming enemy, and often portrayed as militarily superior to the

Western forces. Also, political intentions of Moscow have been misperceived quite impressively: long after the Soviet Union had turned into a conservative power struggling to survive, Western analysts and politicians still pretended to be frightened by Soviet designs of World conquest.

One example of many is a statement of former U.S. Secretary of Defense Caspar Weinberger. He expressed this viewpoint quite clearly at a conference he arranged on the subject of low-intensity conflict in early 1986: "Today's world is in a state of war. It is not a world war, although it is taking place throughout the world. It is not a war between fully mobilized armies, although it is not less destructive... Today one in every four countries in the world is at war. In practically every case, the face of these wars is hidden behind a mask. And in practically every case, the Soviet Union and those who do the work for it are hiding behind this mask."

OVERSTATING THREATS

It is difficult to decide to which degree these nociperception were real or just political statements to achieve specific goals – like boosting the defense budget, or use anticommunism as a disciplinary factor in domestic politics. But it seems evident that over time the overrated expression of the Soviet Threat became the common wisdom, and was taken seriously without going through the pain of checking the facts. In this case the perception – or the pretense of perception – of reality was more important than reality itself. Policies were for decades based on fiction, on an assumption that Moscow was about to conquer the World and just waited for the West letting down its guard. (This argument does not imply to view the Soviet Union or its policies in a positive light. It is quite sufficient to assume that the "threat" was unrealistically exaggerated.) The result of this misperception was an incredible waste of tax money for excessive and useless military spending, and a higher level of tension in international relations. There have been countless other cases of perceptions misrepresenting realities and thereby distorting policy formulation. Often the question is not whether these distortions happen, but whether they take place by mistake or by design.

Two US intelligence experts have recently discussed this problem, publishing an article in the US Naval Institute Proceedings. They start from the assumption that US policy and its armed forces need a realistic assessment of current and future threats. In their view a wrong analysis of possible adversaries cannot be useful to foreign policy and military policy makers.

They "suggest more nuanced political assessments of hostile states, especially when looking at long-range trends. Good analysis means moving beyond the simplistic characterizations of the Cold War. It is no longer enough to count the number of rockets in the Moscow May Day parade, and thereby initiate calculations toward some figure that explains our own requirements. The sheer size of the Soviet forces may have justified such methods in the past. There is little to justify confining our analysis to such methods today."

One of their main arguments is dealing with the general level of foreign policy dangers after the end of the Cold War. Many analysts and politicians have stated that after the Soviet Union's demise the World has become even more dangerous to the United States and the West. Hirschfeld and Carus strongly criticize this view: "Repeated claims that the post-Cold War world has become more dangerous for the United States are hard to justify. It is absurd to compare the remaining dangers to threats we faced during the Cold War. Today, no country is capable of posing a threat comparable to that of the former Soviet Union. Major threats that might require application of significant military force are hard to find now. Claims about the growing numbers of internal conflicts and more ethnic strife are almost as hard to sustain. Internal wars and ethnic conflicts are not increasing in number or intensity; they just have become more visible, now that our anxieties about the danger of global war have receded."

The end of the Cold War has been a watershed of international relations. Its main characteristic was the breakdown of the Soviet Union, which had led to triumphalist tendencies in Western foreign policy circles. The famous phrase of a "New World Order" proclaimed by President Bush in 1990, Fukuyama's funny idea of an "End of History", or Anthony Lake's foreign policy concept of "Enlargement" have been expressions of this feeling. Since the author has dealt with these ideological phenomena already in a different context, we may skip them here. But two aspects should not be overlooked in this context: One, politically the feelings about a New World Order - no matter who expressed them – has strongly been connected to the Middle East. The Second Gulf War of 1990/91 had been the opening shot of the postwar order: it brought the US and the still existing USSR into an alliance against Iraq, and it demonstrated US hegemony in the Gulf area and beyond.

Two, the feeling of triumph and control soon gave way to a sense of insecurity. Often, analysts or politicians began to talk about a "New World Disorder", emphasizing instability, and a lack of orientation about the future development of global politics.

Both trends were based on reality: the West had in fact won the Cold War and could feel as its victor; but it also discovered very soon, that this did not translate into being in control of the whole world. The disaster in Somalia, the political stability of Saddam Hussein's regime in Iraq and the stubborn sabotage of the Middle Eastern peace process by Prime Minister Netanyahu were illustrative.

With the end of the Cold War the foreign policy orientation of the West was open to discussion. The dissolution of the Soviet Union had taken away its one overwhelming adversary, and made obsolete the overall foreign policy strategy and the legitimacy of most of the foreign policy, intelligence, and military apparatuses. Foreign and military policy had lost its ideological foundation. This fact was made more complex because the huge bureaucratic and logistic infrastructures did still exist: all the defense ministries, intelligence agencies, armed forces and foreign offices with their respective budgets are still in place. Well-funded bureaucracies hardly ever consider themselves useless. They tend to either pretend that nothing fundamental has changed, or that some new reason for its existence has taken the place of the old one. The second approach will also produce a measure of internal "reform", to demonstrate its flexibility and willingness to adjust to new realities. But the general approach will be to interpret the changes of circumstances in the light and context of "old thinking". Bureaucracies do not reform easily. But even if they are changing, the tendency very often is to preserve as much as possible from old times, and from the previous bureaucratic mentality.

NEW THREATS

Therefore it is not surprising that even after the end of the Cold War foreign policy thinking has not started from scratch, but is still heavily influenced by its former assumptions. Obviously, the Soviet Union today cannot figure as a dangerous threat to the West, since it does not exist any longer. But instead of feeling secure, many foreign policy analysts even today manage to feel threatened as badly as they felt before. The difference is that today not one overwhelming enemy creates this professed feeling of insecurity, but instability itself, and some minor powers that at best play a third rate role on the global stage. "Rogue" or "outlaw states" now have to pose as enemies, connected to specific topics of concern. "The Middle Eastern "rogue" states threaten us by maintaining programs for weapons of mass destruction, sponsoring terrorism, often targeted specifically at Americans, and by their hostility toward and active opposition to our political and social systems and those of our friends and allies." Gati, Tobi T.; Assessing Current and Projected Threats To U.S. National Security; Statement by Assistant Secretary of State for Intelligence and Research, Toby T. Gati, before the Senete Sele.

This category of countries includes Iraq, Iran, Libya, Sudan, North Korea, and Cuba, four out of seven located in the Middle East or with Muslim background. The concerns include migration, drugs, terrorism, and instability. Both lists are not of cast iron character, but quite flexible, with additional countries and concerns to be added as political need requires.

It should not be forgotten, that both the lists of enemy countries and threats had been quite similar in the final phase of the Cold War: formerly, the countries involved had been perceived mostly as "Soviet surrogates" or allies of Moscow. Today they are interpreted as threats in their own right. Also the topical threats are less than new: the emphases of terrorism and drugs ("drug war") as foreign policy dangers for instance have been quite lively during the 1980s already. Also "instability" as a foreign policy threat is anything but new, just that it has been promoted in importance. Having said that, it should also be emphasised that some of these actually do concerns matter in reality, and not only ideologically. Terrorism is real, not fiction. And it is a danger, which should not be ignored. The same thing applies to some of the countries named above (and quite a few not kept on the list of bad guys): North Korea is not exactly a pleasant place to live in or to deal with. And the same very much applies to the Iraqi regime. But the conceptual question here is not, whether the World has turned into paradise after the collapse of the Soviet Union, or whether it still has many unpleasant or undesirable aspects. It is, whether these problems or trouble threats constitute a serious danger to the West and should be put center stage in its foreign policy analysis - or whether they (and others) may pose problems and difficulties, that can be dealt with on a case by case base. The basic distinction is between a realistic threat assessment and an obsession.

At this juncture we are dealing with several aspects of conceptual importance. First, the need of pragmatically dealing with foreign policy problems when and if they arise, second, the possibility and desirability of formulating an integrated foreign policy concept for the West. And third, the utilization and instrumentalisation of these two points for other purposes, like providing ideological hegemony, fat defense budgets, or justification for specific policies.

The problem of analysis is that these three aspects of foreign policy formulation are difficult to separate, and in many ways are linked to the intentions of political players, not hard facts. And intentions in politics often are hidden or kept out of sight.

Also: in the last paragraphs we have discussed foreign policy formulation in the context of a bureaucratic setting. We have tried to emphasize the tendency of big bureaucracies to keep intact as much of its mentality, ideology, procedures and structures as long as possible. But it would not be sufficient to interpret the amount of "old thinking" after the end of the Cold War mainly by pointing to bureaucratic rigidity. It is important to understand that usefulness of foreign policy concepts is not just a function of their realism, intellectual creativity or seriousness. It depends on results, not on coherence. In politics wrong or funny concepts can potentially produce better "results" than intellectually more reasonable alternatives. Success in foreign policy is hardly linked to academic brilliance, to moral integrity or being "reasonable". Wrong perceptions and shaky analyses can, under specific circumstances, produce success. When the United States invaded the tiny island of Grenada in October 1983, it perceived Grenada as a serious threat to US security. Obviously, this was not just an exaggeration, but baseless. Still, this self-invented threat triggered a military reaction of Washington, which in turn strengthened US dominance in the Caribbean Basin. There are countless similar cases where wrong assumptions have paid off. At this point of discussion it cannot be ruled out, that "old thinking" in foreign policy terms after the end of the Cold War may be illogical, intellectually flawed, even absurd – but still be useful in terms of results. Today the West, and especially the United States, doubtlessly is the dominating global players in World politics. They are not seriously threatened because of a complete lack of political, economic and military counter-powers. But still, pretending to feel threatened and behaving accordingly may still be a useful strategy. It could legitimize policies that were illegitimate otherwise. And the most effective way to pretend something is to actually believe in the pretension.

THE GREEN PERIL

The end of the Cold War considerably strengthened the foreign policy position of the West in international relations, since its main antagonist had disappeared. But at the same time it had created several problems of ideology and legitimacy: One, the Cold War had partly defined Western political identity, in the framework of anticommunism. The West could easily perceive itself as democratic, freedom-oriented and liberal, by contrasting itself with the opponent and its Stalinist or repressive practices. The East-West-Conflict was interpreted as a struggle between Freedom and Repression, Democracy and Dictatorship, Capitalism (or market economics) and Command Economy, and the West could feel confident to be on the right side of history. Being Western meant being democratic, liberal, and all the other things that the West liked to be, and its fighting Communism provided the proof. With the end of Communism, the West lost part of its political identity. Instead of being able to define itself in contrast to the Soviet Union, it now was forced to develop a stronger positive identity.

Second, the Western policy at the same time lost part of its legitimacy. When formerly Western powers had supported doubtful governments or dictatorships in the Third World, it could always argue this to be a lesser evil compared to a communist threat (Jeane Kirkpatrick had presented a prominent example of this rationale) and also its tremendous military expenditures and the build-up of the 1980s could be legitimized similarly. But after the end of Communism, these convenient justifications lost credibility, and support for repressive regimes or human rights abuses became much harder to explain.

It was exactly at this juncture that many foreign policy analysts or politicians discovered the new "Islamic threat". A few months after the second Gulf War, a Newsweek article remarked matter-of-factly: "The Atlantic Alliance still has not found a threat to replace that of the Soviet Union and the Warsaw Pact." But this was to chance very soon. Less than a year later the Far Eastern Economic Review wrote: "Back when the Soviet Union was the "Evil Empire," Islamic forces in Soviet Central Asia and its southern neighbours, notably Afghanistan and Pakistan, were seen by many US policymakers as potentially useful allies against the big communist enemy. This was despite the Western image of Islam as an irrational and unpredictable element in world politics - an image reinforced by the 1970s' oil embargoes and US hostage crisis in Teheran. Now that the Evil Empire is no more, however, the US may adopt a less friendly stance towards Islam at the peripheries of the former Soviet Union."

This observation was quite accurate. But the change was even stronger: a relevant section of the Western foreign policy community advocated not only a "less friendly stance towards Islam", but outright confrontation. Many observers perceived Islam as "the new Communism", as an officer at Führungsakademie·der Bundeswehr (the German National War Academy in Hamburg) put it to the author. Others in Europe and North America agree, among them Amos Perlmutter: "Islamic fundamentalism is an aggressive revolutionary movement as militant and violent as the Bolshevik, Fascist, and Nazi movements of the past," according to him. It is "authoritarian, anti-democratic, anti-secular," and cannot be reconciled with the "Christian-secular universe". Its goal is the establishment of a "totalitarian Islamic state" in the Middle East, he argued, suggesting that the United States should make sure the movement is "stifled at birth."

These kinds of perceptions obviously attempt to keep the basic structure of Cold War thinking alive, by substituting Islam for Communism and often Iran for the Soviet Union. The "totalitarian, anti-Western, militant revolutionary, oppressive, dictatorial, anti-freedom oriented" Islamic culture and religion takes the place of Marxism-Leninism. The lack of a credible organizational or state center of the new threat is interpreted not as a weakness, but strength: this new threat is more difficult to predict, less clear, instead more underneath the level of open state policies.

The former journalist with the Jerusalem Post, Leon Hadar, comments on this political tendency in US foreign policy: "Now that the Cold War is becoming a memory, America's foreign policy establishment has begun searching for new enemies. Possible new villains include "instability" in Europe – ranging from German resurgence to new Russian imperialism – the "vanishing" ozone layer, nuclear proliferation, and narco-terrorism. Topping the list of potential new global bogeymen, however, are the Yellow Peril, the alleged threat to American economic security emanating from East Asia, and the so-called Green Peril (green is the color of Islam). That peril is symbolized by the Middle Eastern Moslem fundamentalist ... a Khomeini-like creature, armed with a radical ideology, equipped with nuclear weapons, and intent on launching a violent jihad against Western civilization."

This observation proved to be remarkably precise. It was exactly one year later that Samuel Huntington published his famous article in Foreign Affairs, on a "Clash of Civilizations". He declared a "Confucian-Islamic connection that has emerged to challenge Western interests, values, and power" and predicts: "a central focus of conflict for the immediate future will be between the West and several Islamic-Confucian states."

Huntington's "Confucian-Islamic connection" obviously is a combination of Hadar's Yellow and Green perils. It is well known and it has been demonstrated elsewhere that his theory is historically, analytically and academically shallow. Here it is sufficient to just remind us of his political conclusion: "to limit the expansion of the military strength of Confucian and Islamic states; to moderate the reduction of Western military capabilities and maintain military superiority in East and Southwest Asia; to exploit differences and conflicts among Confucian and Islamic states; to support in other civilizations groups sympathetic to Western values and interests; ..." In a nutshell this means "to maintain the economic and military power necessary to protect its interests in relation to these civilizations." The obvious purpose of Huntington's contribution was not analytical, but to distinguish friend from foe in the Post-Cold War era. It was to define a new enemy after the Soviet Union and its Communism had disintegrated. In this regard it was quite successful, no matter how weak the intellectual foundation of his approach may have been. And Huntington was not the first or only one to point towards the Middle East for the Next Threat to Western powers and interests. A report already published in May 1990 by the Center for Strategic and International Studies (CSIS), argues that, with the decline of the Soviet military threat to Europe, the potential for American involvement in the "dangerous form of conventional combat" in mid-intensity conflicts (MICs) in the Middle East and Moslem southwest Asia "will provide a key justification for military budgets during the 1990's and will establish most of the threats against which U.S. forces are sized, trained and equipped."

"To provide a key justification for military budgets" - and for a foreign policy that is required by this goal: this has been and still is one of the major functions of the Islamic Threat. Hadar explains how it has developed: "The creation of a peril usually starts with mysterious "sources" and unnamed officials who leak information, float trial balloons, and warn about the coming threat. Those sources reflect debates and discussions taking place within government. Their information is then augmented by colorful intelligence reports that finger exotic and conspiratorial terrorists and military advisers. Journalists then search for the named and other villains. The media end up finding corroboration from foreign sources who form an informal coalition with the sources in the U.S. government and help the press uncover further information substantiating the threat coming from the new bad guys.

In addition, think tanks studies and op-ed pieces add momentum to the official spin. Their publication is followed by congressional hearings, policy conferences, and public press briefings. A governmental policy debate ensues, producing studies, working papers, and eventually doctrines and policies that become part of the media's spin. The new villain is now ready to be integrated into the popular culture to help to mobilize public support for a new crusade. In the case of the Green Peril, that process has been under way for several months."

It should be noted that Hadar's description is of quite general character. It applies not just to the perception of Islam and the Middle East, but generally describes how big political debates and paradigms are initiated in the United States. Also, this pattern does not apply to most European countries, as far as Islam is concerned. In many parts of Europe, like France, Germany and Spain, a negative perception of Islam has not been engineered by political elites, but has grown from below, with a big sector of the media reinforcing it. We will get back to this later.

Also, Hadar seems to underestimate the divergence of views in the US policy elite: creation of the "green peril" has never been a project of all or most of the foreign policy mainstream, but some of its sectors have tried to resist it.

ISLAM AND GOVERNMENT POLITICS

Quite a different discourse can be observed in most foreign policy circles. Hadar's Green Peril is one of the important lines of argument, a more pragmatic assessment of threats and Islam the other. James Phillips, working with the Heritage Foundation, a conservative Think-Tank in Washington, is presenting a good illustration of the first viewpoint. He writes specifically about the dangers of "Revolutionary Islam in Algeria", but what he identifies as "undermining U.S. interest by posing a threat" is quite typical for his school of thought generally. From his perspective, six key points are under attack or dangers developing:

1. *Pro-Western Arab Secular Regimes*: Besides providing all kinds of practical assistance to Islamist allover the Middle East (like weapons and training), a victorious Islamist movement in Algeria "will embolden other Islamic revolutionaries, providing a psychological boost to those who will see it as a vindication of Islamism and a harbinger of things to come in their own countries."

Mostly threatened states are Algeria's neighbors Morocco and Tunisia.

2. *International Terrorism*: "Islamic Algeria, like Iran, Sudan, and Afghanistan before it, is likely to become a haven and base for Islamist terrorist groups."
3. *Arab-Israeli Peace Negotiations*: "Algeria's Islamists vehemently reject any compromise with Israel and would cooperate with Iran, Sudan, and Palestinian Islamists to block a permanent settlement."
4. *Non proliferation*: "A nuclear-armed revolutionary Islamic Algeria, just 200 miles from Europe's southern shores, is a chilling possibility that would pose a critical threat to NATO allies, regional friends, and American forces in the Mediterranean basin. Moreover, an Islamist regime in Algiers might consider sharing nuclear technology or materials with Iran, Sudan, or radical Islamic terrorist groups."
5. *Western Access to Energy*: "Islamic revolutionaries will be prone to subversive and terrorist activities that are likely to disrupt the operations of the pipeline through Morocco or the Transmed pipeline bringing Algerian gas to Italy via Tunisia. Support for international terrorism also could trigger international economic sanctions that would disrupt the flow of Algerian gas to Western markets. Algerian support for Saudi Islamists, who provided FIS with considerable financial support, would increase the risk of destabilization in Saudi Arabia, which in turn could disrupt the flow of Saudi oil exports and push up world oil prices."
6. *Human Rights*: "If the Islamists seize power, Algeria's human rights situation is sure to worsen as they seek vengeance on the supporters of the current regime and struggle for power among themselves."

Phillips summarizes his own arguments in a few lines: "The triumph of Muslim militancy in Algeria, at a minimum, would embolden Islamists elsewhere in the Islamic world to redouble their revolutionary efforts, increase subversive pressures on pro-Western secular regimes, and encourage further opposition to the Arab-Israeli peace negotiations. In the worst case scenario, a radical Islamic Algeria could become another Iran- a base for actively exporting anti-Western revolution, terrorism, and anarchy".

This is an interesting set of arguments. His more specific six points of danger have relatively little to do with religion. They almost completely deal with Western political and economic interests, like losing political allies in the Arab world and energy resources. Most of these points can be questioned: the Arab-Israeli peace process is not mostly threatened by religious opposition, but by Prime Minister Netanyahu's intransigence. Or, they ignore that any regime in Algeria or any other oil-producing country in the Middle East will be forced to keep selling oil to the West, as a matter of economic and political survival. Or, the quite secular reasons for internal instability in most Middle Eastern countries are ignored, like incompetence, corruption of and repression by the respective governments, and mass poverty. It is very convenient to put all the blame just on somebody else's doorstep. But still, this criticism apart, his main points of threats are of a secular character. His intellectual and political achievement is, to focus them all into one, more general enemy: Islamism. The structure of the argument implies that there are no questions to raise in regard to Western interests or former Western policies, there is hardly anything to analyse in regard to reasons of instability in the Middle East. For Phillips it is a plain matter of us against them, of our – unquestioned legitimate – interests being under attack by some bad guys.

In his conclusion, which are quoted above, things get another interesting twist: Islamist are being portrayed as "militant", "revolutionary", "subversive", "radical" and "terrorist" – all terms that where used time and again in regard to former Soviet policies and Third World liberation movements allied (or not allied) to it. The history of the Soviet Union and Communism should have told us that even an "evil empire" is not just evil, but many more things. By reducing the complexities of dealing with Moscow or with Islamism to a simplistic Us-versus-Them antagonism, we lose the ability to even understand our real relationship to our adversaries. In many cases the protagonists of an Islamic Threat try to keep their polar worldview of a struggle between Good and Evil, between Us and them intact, and only switch enemies. In its final form the result is to interpret the World in Huntington's terminology: "The West against the Rest".

Many foreign policy makers and more sober analysts consider much of this alarmist thinking as of little use. Blowing Middle Eastern dangers out of all proportions would provide a shallow base for Western foreign policy, if taken seriously. Hirschfeld and Carus are examples of this skepticism.

"Uncertainty dominates the current environment, in sharp contrast to the clearer challenges of yesterday. We do not know whom we may fight years from now, and there are few unambiguous threats of any magnitude. As a result, we frequently generate inadequate and uncom-pelling evidence in an attempt to find threats, or to assert that enemies, adversaries, or competitors exist, or will exist."

Speaking as intelligence experts, they have more criticism, which is not put forward from a "liberal", but from a purely professional military perspective.

"Exaggerating today's threats to U.S. national security, by creatively highlighting ways the forces of other states pose dangers for U.S. forces, does the nation and the military services a profound disservice. ... By exaggerating today's threats ... we distract attention from what truly matters, and delay and ultimately short-change the allocation of resources needed to develop the future capabilities that we really will need. Over the longer term, we also undermine the credibility of the intelligence product, the intelligence community, and ultimately the justification for the defense program. Finally, there is no long-range benefit in conforming today's forces into the comforting outlines of some formerly familiar threat pattern, simply because we can imagine no other. Growing ever larger and heavier, in anticipation of fighting forces like those of yesterday's enemies, foreshadows the fate of Goliath of Gath."

To a big degree the Foreign Ministries in the major Western capitals agree with the need of realism. Key government officials, including foreign ministers or the Presidents of the United States and Germany, have criticized the Green Peril and the Clash of Civilizations. These confrontational approaches are often seen as too ideological, and quite unpractical. Chancellor Helmut Kohl, who seems to be not altogether free from anti-Muslim prejudges, still stresses the commonality with Islam when a proper opportunity arises: "If we are to secure a good future for our continent, it is also important that the three major monotheistic world religions - Judaism, Christianity and Islam - reflect on their common roots and values and allow themselves to be led by the spirit of charity and brotherly love."

Such statements might present a somewhat narrow view by reducing Islam to religion, but still they do not work well with positions which prefer an anti-Islamic campaign. Peter Hartmann, Ass. Secretary ("Staats-sekretär") in the German Foreign Office would agree with his chancellor. In December 1997 he opined that it would be wrong "to present new enemy perceptions or even a 'war of civilizations'", and that instead "a dialogue between the big cultures should be supported – a task which may not be new, but perhaps is more urgent than many others."

The problem with these kinds of statements is not to support a confrontational "The West against the Rest"-scenario, which they clearly are not. Instead it is, that precious little has been actually done to organize such a dialogue, instead of only proposing it. And exercises like the "critical dialogue" with Iran of Mr. Kinkel have been hardly more than a legitimizing cover for business-as-usual economic relations.

Officials in the European Union or the German Foreign Office often may not like Iran and Iraq. But they very well remember that Iraq's Saddam Hussein has never fit the bill of an Islamic Fundamentalist, while many more religious regimes (like Saudi Arabia or Morocco, along with many more secular Arab or non-Arab Muslim countries, like the Islamic Republic of Pakistan) joined the anti-Iraqi alliance that Washington had put together in 1990/91.

It cannot be denied that some of the anti-Islamic sentiment has crept into Western government circles. Two examples: when President Bush passed on his office to President Clinton, anti-fundamentalist rhetoric increased. The background was the very close relationship the first Clinton-Administration kept with Israel, while Israel played the fundamentalist card to drum up support when after the Gulf War and after Oslo the PLO did not work as a credible threat any longer. Another case has been the German Chancellor Kohl characterizing the European Union as a "Christian Club" as a justification to keep Turkey out. In both and other cases it cannot be decided whether Kohl or the Clinton-Administration actually believed in their own rhetoric, or whether they just used it as a political tool. Also discussions with several German Foreign Office officials confirm that there is a minority position quietly sympathizing with the Green Peril perspective, but the majority of officials object to it. Generally speaking, there even exists a broad "pro-Arab" sentiment, which again is balanced by a "pro-Israeli" one (especially at the very top), which draws its main strength from its moral base resulting from the Holocaust.

Western foreign policy towards the Middle East is shaped by down to earth considerations like economic interests and migration, and much less by cultural or religious considerations. An important recent example of defining Western - in this case US - interests in the Middle East was the statement of Lieutenant General Patrick M. Hughes, as Director of the Defense Intelligence Agency (DIA) presented to the Senate Armed Services Committee in February 1997. He enumerated what he perceives as key threats for the future: population growth, humanitarian needs, resource scarcity, and weapons proliferation, rejection of Western culture, terrorism, drug trade, and "critical uncertainties".

The one aspect that might include notions of an Islamic Threat obviously is the "rejection of Western culture". But when Hughes explains his point, he is quite secular and Islam is not even mentioned.

"The abrupt end of the Cold War, the rapid spread of western values, ideals, and institutions, and the dramatic personal, societal, and global changes underway as a result of the global village phenomenon and broad technology proliferation, are changing fundamental concepts, beliefs, and allegiances in many areas of the world. Those peoples, groups, and governments who are unable to cope with or unwilling to embrace these changes frequently resent the dominant role played by the United States in the international security environment, and attempt to undermine US and western influence and interests. Two aspects of this condition are particularly noteworthy. First, although there is not at present an ideology that is both inimical to our interests and widely appealing, one could conceivably arise under the rhetoric of providing a counterpoint to western culture. Second, the perception of western political, economic, and especially military "dominance" means that many of our enemies will choose asymmetric means to attack our interests – that is, pursuing courses of action that attempt to take advantage of their perceived strengths while exploiting our perceived weaknesses. At the "strategic" level, this probably means seeking to avoid direct military confrontation with US forces; at the operational and tactical levels it means seeking ways of "leveling the playing field" if forced to engage the US military."

From this it is quite obvious that Hughes, as DIA-Director, is afraid of any ideology that might argue against US dominance. Therefore, Islam would not be of concern because it is Islamic, but only if and when it is questioning US foreign and military policy by criticizing its dominating strength. Also when presenting his summary, Islam does not figure at all: "On one hand, for at least the next decade, the threats facing the United States will be of a decreased order of magnitude and we will not likely see a global "peer competitor" within 20 years.

On the other hand, the world remains a very dangerous and complex place and there is every reason to expect US military requirements at about the same level of the past several years: the explosive mix of social, demographic, and economic conditions – extant and through the foreseeable future – will mean a continued high demand for peace and humanitarian operations. Consequently, there is likely to be a continuing requirement for US forces to engage in these demanding activities.

Several key regional states- particularly North Korea and Iraq- retain the capability to threaten US interests with conventional offensives. This condition demands constant US vigilance and the retention of demonstrable war fighting capabilities. A number of transnational threats – terrorism, weapons proliferation, drug trafficking – continue to plague the international environment and threaten US citizens, forces, property, and interests. Russia and China retain strategic nuclear forces capable of threatening the US homeland. Moreover, these pivotal states are both undergoing what are likely to be protracted, fundamental changes with uncertain outcomes and consequences. Both have the potential to emerge as large-scale regional threats to US interests beyond the next decade.

The changing nature of future warfare- the application of new technologies and innovative doctrinal concepts to "conventional" military operations, and the development of new forms of asymmetric warfare-poses a constant challenge to US forces."

All of this already applies without any government or powerful interest groups trying to create the perception of an Islamic Threat for political reasons. Therefore we can concentrate on some of the resulting questions: why, for instance, is an important part of the media and public perception of Islam so highly emotional? And why are phenomena of religious fanaticism in the Christian or Jewish context so often being seen with less alarmism, compared to the same in an Islamic environment?

One of the reasons is that Islam is foreign, something alien. Perceiving "The Other" as threatening reassures "Us" to be someone better. And criticizing foreign fanaticism and irrationality relieves us from frightening symptoms of the same diseases in our own societies. Burning down of abortion clinics or the Oklahoma Bombing like violence against immigrants in Germany therefore can be perceived as simple crimes or aberrations, while similar acts of terrorism in a Middle Eastern context will often be interpreted as somehow inherent in Islamic culture and politics. Or, to take another example, it is quite striking how the same people who want to keep women out of the labor market in Europe suddenly enjoy protesting women's discrimination in the Middle East. These kinds of double standards are definitely not a result of political campaigns or of media reporting, but of a psychological need of individuals and societies. That biased reporting regularly reinforces them is obvious. It can be concluded that a big part of negative perception of Islam has preciously little to do with anything Islamic. Andrea Lueg has given an important example how more general sentiments feed into the perception of a Green Peril:

"The anti-Islamic image of the enemy is part of a more extensive fear of the Third World. Dangers and threats which are more often of a social, political or cultural nature rather than a military one also seem to come from the poor South. The Third World as a whole, not just the Islamic Middle East, is seen as a place of instability, insecurity, of tribal and civil wars, incomprehensible violence, disease and countless other evils. These regions of misery and unrest stand in contrast to the apparently well- and clearly-ordered West. The affluence in the West stands out against the reality of need in the developing countries, and is to be psychologically (and if need be materially) defended. The fear of the Third World is in a certain sense a fear of poverty, a fear of being infected again by its evils. This is another reason why migration from Islamic countries is perceived to be so threatening: the Third World is coming to us, forming bridgeheads in our cities. Perhaps these islands will also bring their misery to us?"

It is difficult to ignore that any Red Menace or Green Peril has not just to do with the opposing side, but often even more with an insecure self-definition. Lueg continues: "One of the preconditions of this fear lies in the fact that the West is no longer as sure of its achievements as it would like to be. This does not only apply to the rational, enlightened and secular character of Western societies, which is constantly being called into question by racism, fundamentalist bishops or 'tribal' and religious wars as in former Yugoslavia or Northern Ireland. It is also applicable to the really important civilising value of the West: material wealth. Today, even this is, at least, unsure: even the middle classes could soon face financial ruin.

The Western standard of living - our wealth - is being threatened, and this is another reason why fear of poverty is an important factor. This poverty is represented by the Third World, whose religion, as the West perceives it, is Islam. Other religions such as Hinduism are perhaps culturally and geographically too distant. Fear of Islam is also an ideological-religious version of the fear of the future. This is then associated with and highlighted by truly destabilising, threatening or costly developments, such as environmental catastrophes, large scale migration and the influx of refugees, as well as by the increase and radicalization of political or politico-religious movements."

SELECTED MECHANISMS OF BIASED PERCEPTIONS

1. *Comparing un-comparable categories*: The "West often is compared to Islam", that is a geographic (or political) area to a religion. Instead Europe and the Middle East, or Islam and Christianity should be compared.
2. *Presenting fundamentalist argumentation and definitions as "Islam"*: Often western observers take fundamentalist positions and present them as defining Islam. They quote fundamentalist leaders to point to a true Islam, ignoring that most Muslims take quite different viewpoints.
3. *Religious interpretation of secular policies*: Declarations of Middle Eastern politicians and religious leaders are being taken at face value. Religious terminology is automatically perceivedasan expression of religion, the

instrumentalisation of religious terms for political and other purposes are being ignored.

4. *Assuming what should be proven*: Instead of analyzing the importance of religion in the Middle Eastern discourse, it is being assumed as crucial. From this assumption it is concluded that politics is being of a religious character.
5. *Confusing Islam as a religion with Islamic culture and tradition*: Middle Eastern societies are often culturally influenced by Islam. Islam has become an important part of popular culture. Many seemingly religious manifestations have more to do with culture and tradition, than with religion.
6. *Non-historic interpretation of Islam*: Recent events are not being analyzed in their historic context, since they supposedly are of "religious" character and therefore can be explained from the Koran and the Sunnah. The historical conditions and developments of current phenomena are being substituted by referring to holy texts.
7. *Neglecting analyses of political and economic interests*: Problems and conflicts in the current Middle East will often be reduced to "religion", instead of analyzing olitical and economic interests behind them. Again, this is being done by reducing "Islam" to the Koran and statements of religious experts.
8. *Cultural arrogance*: From Western dominance in regard to economic and military power often a cultural superiority of the West is concluded.
9. *Using double standards*: Things the West considers legitimate for itself are being perceived as off-limits to Muslim societies, e.g. weapons of mass destruction, which are supposedly useful for peace and stability when in Western hands, but dangerous otherwise.
10. *Perceiving politics in purely psychological terms*: What in the West might be termed "power-politics" or "real-politic" in a Middle Eastern context will be often termed "insanity", "irrationality", "aggressively". Instead of analyzing conflicts of interests observers will use psychological categories.

6

Foreign Policy of Islamic Media

INTRODUCTION

In regard to the perception of Islam and the Middle East there is an obvious gap between many of the mass media and the foreign policy elite are thinking. It varies over time and from country to country, for instance in Europe the gap seems to be deeper than in the United States, but exists everywhere. Two questions arise from here: Is this fact relevant or just a coincidence, and how do the media and politics influence each other? The importance of the media-politics link is easy to establish. The US Army Field Manual "Information Operations" put it plainly in this way: "As we have come to recognize and depend on air superiority as a key condition for military success, information dominance has taken on a similar importance for military operations".

Knowing the overwhelming importance of air power in recent US military doctrine, this statement is quite remarkable. And "information dominance" is a concept closely connected to the mass media.

"The role of the news media will continue to expand. The number of news organizations and their means to gather, process, and disseminate information is increasing exponentially. ... Clearly, the effect of written, and, more importantly, visual information displayed by US and international news organizations directly and rapidly influenced the nature of US and international policy objectives and our use of military force in Rwanda, Somalia, and in the former Yugoslavian republic".

The media do influence "the nature of US and international policy objectives", that is the political goals of military operations, which implies, they influence foreign policy goals. In some cases of major importance the whole policies have been driven nearly exclusively by media and public opinion considerations, like the intervention in Somalia. In this specific case, the US Department of State, the Pentagon, and the CIA objected to a US military intervention because of hardly any gain to US national interest or security despite high potential risk. President George Bush, because of dramatic TV footage starting in summer of 1991, decided to go ahead anyway, to secure his "place in history".

In this case the reporting triggered a complete set of policies, including military intervention. Also even military and political planning today is heavily influenced by the need, to "sell" specific activities: for instance, the air attacks on Libya in 1986 or the US- troops landing at the beaches of Somalia where planned to happen during US prime time TV hours. The Marines in Mogadishu did not use the harbor to enter the country but the inconvenient beach - because it looked much better on television. Media reporting can also heavily influence the results of policies, like the Field Manual "Public Affairs Operations" concedes. Media coverage can be pivotal to the success of the operation and in achieving national strategic goals.

This was first discovered as a result of the Vietnam War: it was not lost in the jungles of Southeast Asia, but at the "home front". Pictures of stoned or dying US troops or of the victims of the US massacre at My Lai helped ending the war: the US public just got tired with the killing and being killed of nice college kids in the swamps. Other examples were the reporting of the incompetence of the US invasion of the tiny island of Grenada in 1983: the US troops afflicted more damage onto themselves, than the hardly existing "enemy" did. This was perceived as embarrassing for US policy and the military. And one of the latest prominent cases were the TV footage from Somalia, where angry crowds pulled dead US soldiers through the streets of Mogadishu, embarrassing the supposedly "humanitarian" intervention. Despite very minor losses, the US forces had to be withdrawn - the media forced the hands of the politicians: first into sending troops, then to get them out fast.

These quotes and examples show that media reporting - at least in specific cases - can and does exercise political power by influencing decision-makers and policy implementation. They also show that the foreign policy and military apparatus is quite aware of this fact, and tries to instrumentalise the media for its own purposes. From its viewpoint it burns down to the question whether to be driven by media and public opinion, or to manage them. Politicians and military officers obviously prefer the second option. A highly effective example was the way the US military completely controlled the reporting in regard to the second Gulf War, 1990/91. No journalist was allowed close to the battlefield, no journalist had a chance to independent research on the ground. TV reporters were only allowed using material from the famous "media pool", which was completely managed and controlled by the US Army and to some degree, by the Saudi government. This author was twice denied visas to Saudi Arabia with the argument that the Saudi government was not interested in more media people. Journalists who managed to get in were fed ready made information and tapes, showing a "clean" war, with "video game" footage, high-tech weapons systems, and - no victims. Journalists were kept far away from the frontlines and real fighting, and got a meager diet of what the military wanted to present to the public. To make matters worse: censorship was everywhere, not just in Saddam's Baghdad but also afflicted on the media by the US-military and the Saudi Government. One major German daily, Frankfurter Rundschau, before, during and shortly after the

Gulf War put a short note on its front-page on a daily base: "Military Censorship / Reporting from the Gulf is done under conditions of heavy censorship. Correspondents and photographers covering the war are restricted by military censors. The US, Great Britain and France apply censorship, as Iraq does, which has expelled nearly all foreign journalists. Israel and Turkey have introduced censorship, too. Censored because of military considerations are especially all reports about war operations and its victims".

This daily note to readers to please distrust the own paper's reporting because of the impossibility to do an unbiased, fair and professional job, was at least honest. But the problem was that being aware of the problem did not solve it. The media were completely depending on information provided to them by one of the fighting parties – who handed out pathetic but precious, small pieces of "information". And the criteria for providing the informational handouts were not truth or realism, nor journalistic considerations, but the desire to support the war effort. No other information was available. No new media catastrophe like Somali was to be allowed, and control and censorship of the media was the instrument to keep this from happening.

A few of European war correspondents after the war brought up the question whether there ever had been a war at all. The frightening answer was, they had no way to prove it. Only the military press officers had told them about this war, but they themselves had never seen it. Being kept in Dakhran/Saudi Arabia, they were hundreds of kilometers from the battlefield and only saw Pentagon propaganda video clips, plus military press briefings. The results were, that military terminology crept into the reporting, that the official line of the US Army dominated it, and that even the very few people close to the shooting (mainly CNN in Baghdad, because it had reached a special deal with the Iraqi government) did more to create sentiment and emotion than factual information. John Holliman, for example, covering an air attack on Baghdad live, excitedly exclaimed: "It looks like a Fourth of July display at the Washington Monument ... We just heard – whoa! Holy cow! That was a large air burst that we saw!"

It is difficult to call this independent journalism, when the live coverage of a war is being presented as an entertainment show, and is linked to a patriotic symbol, like the Fourth of July. Victims were rarely a matter of reporting. And Iraqi victims hardly figured at all. The propaganda role of the media went to nearly absurd proportions. One important US news magazine featured a cover story: "How US (High-Tech) Weapons Save Lives". Weapons and war in this context did not any longer symbolize death, but life.

A German newspaper editor observing his eight-year-old son watching TV coverage of the war was surprised to discover that most of his compassion was concentrated on a dying, oil infested bird stranded on the Gulf beach. Again, human suffering never appeared "real" on the screen; it was just an abstract possibility. A few exceptions existed: for example Israeli citizens with gas masks in Tel Aviv were a common view (not Iraqis in Baghdad, though), and the Kurdish refugees fleeing Saddam's troops in Northern Iraq after the war had ended made quite emotional footage. But obviously in both cases it was Saddam who was responsible, not the own side of the war. Suffering afflicted to human beings by the enemy was good reporting, suffering caused by the US and Gulf War Alliance was taboo.

The censorship was only one cause of this bias, but many media did not need censorship at all: what they perceived as "patriotism" was at least as effective: self-censorship and jingoism was a moral duty to many journalists and publishers. The media in these cases played two roles that overlapped conveniently: one, they provided a service to Government by distributing and even embellishing their official lines of propaganda; and two, they themselves profited from doing this by increasing their circulation, the number of their viewers and listeners, and their customers booking commercials. The "Tagesschau", the most prominent evening news show in German TV (which journalistically still was more serious than many competitors) had a huge boost in numbers of viewers and at one point reached some 40 percent of all households in the country. And CNN could afford to quadruple its prices for commercials at prime time, because demand rose sharply. The Gulf war was big business, and in commercial terms it would have been harmful to produce "controversial" - that is critical coverage.

Up to now we have pointed to censorship, opportunism and jingoism, plus commercial self-interest as main causes of biased and unprofessional reporting in the Gulf war. These factors did and do exist in the Western media, and they should not be ignored. But the problem is that often analysts or observers in the Middle East stop here and integrate them into juicy conspiracy theories. This may be understandable, but it still is wrong. All these factors do exist, but they do not provide the whole picture. First of all, there always are journalists who try to break this habit of reporting what the powers that want to be reported, or who try to avoid being censored. This may happen out of desire to do an ethical and professional job, or out of self-interest. During the War one CBS TV crew tried to break the strict rules of the official "media pool" and went out on their own to the Saudi desert to research. They somehow got lost for weeks and did not succeed. Also a discussion among journalists after the war about the problems encountered was a strong indication of frustration with the experience of being instrumentalised.

But the conspiracy theories also ignore a crucial factor contributing to shallow, biased and opportunist reporting: the work environment in the media in general, and the lack of knowledge about the Middle East by most reporters and journalists. Two examples may demonstrate the point.

Shortly before Iraq invaded Kuwait in 1990 this author after his return from Baghdad discussed writing an article about Iraq with a top-weekly. The editor was enthusiastic: Iraq seemed to be a potentially important country, "but we don't know anything about it." This was quite remarkable, since during the first Gulf war (1980-88) already some 1.5

million Iraqis and Iranians had been killed, and one would assume a major paper to have done some homework on Iraq over the last decade. It had not. When Iraqi forces occupied Kuwait a short while later, the same editor called to cancel the article. It was too important and too urgent now, and the weekly wanted to put a team of some twenty people on the job (who all "did not know anything about Iraq", as was explained before) to write a long cover story. The result was pathetic: lots of shallow material, half-truths, hearsay, and outdated information. For weeks the standard remained as bad, and then it slowly improved: the people involved had finally educated themselves and learnt quite a few things about Iraq.

A second example: again, the same author was asked by a major Western European TV network to participate in preparing a special show on the beginning of the Gulf war. The meeting included some 15 people, from technicians up to the top foreign department bosses. No matters of substance or politics were discussed, only technicalities, nobody present knew anything about Iraq, Kuwait, or the Middle East - and hardly anybody perceived this as a problem. Only one participant just before the end of the meeting exclaimed: "Oh, we still have not discussed the content of the show!" But there was no time left to do this. Broadcast the next day, this "special report" was a wild mix of news bites that did not make any sense. Most participants of the meeting recognized the failure - after it had been screened.

The point with these examples is that "conspiracies" or even censorship were not necessary to produce bad journalism. It was quite sufficient to work in an environment where content and substance are secondary and definitely less important than timeliness and speed. The need - and this need is real, not self-invented - to produce a long cover story or special report in just a few hours or days, coupled with little competence in the specific topic of reporting makes serious and professional reporting or analysis impossible. If people are working under heavy pressure to provide extremely fast voluminous information and background on topics they know very little about, it would be unreasonable to expect high quality.

Under this kind of pressure journalists will necessarily tend to stick close to the "common wisdom", since this will minimize risk and if they confront a common wisdom or Government line observers and journalists will be criticized. They will only do this, if they are sure about their matter, and about their own position. But since they cannot easily develop a serious understanding of most topics – like Iraq - (since they will have to report on Somalia tomorrow, Rwanda next week, and many other topics waiting in line), it is very difficult to do in-depth or critical, investigative journalism. The easy way is to substitute clichés and emotionalism for facts and information, since they will sell, they are easier and cheaper to produce, and they do not require loots of time and research. Sticking to off-the-shelf judgements, preexisting sentiments and perceiving other cultures as threatening while the own one as benevolent may be bad journalism – but it is very practical. Again: it does not require lots of conspiracies to end up with those results; often the unbearable pressure of the market and one's own working conditions will be quite sufficient. One of the problems obviously is that this mechanism plays very well into the hands of people who consciously attempt to "manage" the media for their own political reasons.

The ways mass media effect policies can be very diverse. The spectrum ranges from disclosing specific single facts and information that might be embarrassing or supportive of one side in a policy debate, to shaping general sentiments or frameworks of reference. Obviously, the mass media are crucial to define the perceptions of foreign countries, foreign governments and cultures. This role on the other hand does not give them complete freedom to shape perceptions of the public (and many politicians) at their own discretion. They themselves are strongly influenced by ideas, viewpoints and interests from the general public of which they are a part; and by many subtle and less subtle attempts to set their agenda and guide their reporting from the political class. And since –

at least mainstream oriented - journalists and politicians (plus entertainers, athletes, actors, etc.) are linked in a symbiotic relationship of mutual dependence, there is no way to separate them cleanly from political and commercial influences. This link is of importance for how Islam is perceived in the West. It is crucial for Hadar's model of establishing a Green Peril in public discourse, but also for public prejudges creeping into the policy elite. The relationship between the media and politics is an ongoing battle of mutual influencing each other, of sometimes one side clearly dominating the other, sometimes quietly cooperating, and sometime openly clashing over hegemony. It is far from stable, and analytically it is a moving target.

Generally speaking the Islamic threat in the West does exist as a sentiment and as a policy tool. But is does hardly ever drive foreign policy decision making, since it is mostly relevant to the domestic policy arena. The Green Peril is useful to produce colorful and entertaining news in TV and print media, and it can be utilized to drum up support for a foreign policy that has been decided for because of quite different reasons. Decision makers sometimes may share a weak version of anti-Muslim ideology, but they are driven by more practical and more specific factors: in Europe by a desire to cut off immigration from Turkey and the Maghreb to protect the labor market in times of high unemployment; by the strategic consideration to control the Gulf area; by enmity towards specific countries or political actors; by an interest to guarantee stability to friendly regimes; and by similar considerations. These practical interests will make it impossible to deal with the Middle East and Islam in a highly ideological fashion. Muslims and their governments very often are strongly in the Western camp, and it would be quite foolish waging ideological wars against them.

THE NEWS MEDIA IS MORE CAREFUL OF ITS REPORTING

"We have seen a good change in the coverage in the past six years since CAIR was formed," notes Hooper in an interview from his office in Washington, D.C.

"Now journalists are much more reluctant to label everyone as a fundamentalist, everyone as an extremist and make gross generalizations about Islam and the Muslim community. It's still not there but they're beginning to differentiate between individuals and Islam or individual acts and Islam and groups. They're becoming more aware of the nature of the Muslim community worldwide and don't always perceive it as monolithic." However, these distinctions are not being made often enough, despite the fact that most journalists do not make similar generalizations of other religious groups.

"The old example we always give is the IRA (Irish Republican Army) in Northern Ireland," says Hooper. "When they blow up something, no one blames the Catholics and if somebody said it was the Catholic church that was at fault they'd go, 'that's ridiculous' because they know what Catholicism is. But when somebody does some violent act in the name of Islam, they say, well, maybe it is Islam because they don't have a context in which to put that individual act."

ISLAM NO LONGER PERCEIVED AS MONOLITHIC OR ONLY ARAB

Hooper notes that another change is the understanding amongst more journalists and media professionals that Islam is not an Arab religion, but an ethnically diverse one with local roots.

"As long as Islam was perceived as this foreign, exotic religion, it was very difficult," he says. But now I think reporters are recognizing that Islam is indigenous to North America."

The 1992-95 war in Bosnia and the genocide in Kosova in 1999 also played a role in shattering the myth of a monolithic Muslim world.

"I think it shocked people to realize that there are blond, blue-eyed Muslims and European Muslims...and that Muslims can be victims as well as perpetrators," says Hooper.

MUSLIMS CREATING THEIR OWN MEDIA

Muslims today, though, are not just fighting stereo-types, outside looking in. They are increasingly taking the media into their own hands, knowing full well that sitting on the sidelines is ineffective.

A number of Muslim magazines, if not most, are connected to Islamic institutions. Islamic Horizons, for instance, is a publication of the Islamic Society of North America (ISNA). The Message is a publication of the Islamic Circle of North America (ICNA). Other publications are connected to local mosques and Muslim Students' Associations. Others still are independent. They range from quarterly, to monthly to weekly. So far, no one has reached the target of being a daily publication. But the need for Muslim publications cannot be ignored.

"Mainstream media cannot address all the issues for all communities equally," says Mustafa of the Muslim Journal. "Therefore, each one has to have its own vehicle to make sure that those issues and those ideals that are important to them are always presented in this proper context. It's no less the case for Muslims." "It is our obligation to present Muslims and the good works that they are doing," she adds.

The 25-year-old weekly newspaper was born out of the experience of African-Americans who left the Nation of Islam following the death of leader Elijah Muhammad in 1975 and accepted true Islam.

The publication, Mustafa explains, became a vehicle for Islamic education for many of these new Muslims and focused on their aspirations and concerns. Today, the paper is one of the most well-established publications in Muslim America and its focus has broadened to the Muslim community in America and the world, not just the African-American Muslim community.

But the Muslim Journal is not a mere public relations organ for the Muslim community. "Of course there are controversies, there are sad moments in the lives of any community and we are there to report on those events and ideas also. We cover the gamut," she says in an interview with Sound Vision and RadioIslam.com from her home in Illinois.

THE CHRISTIAN SCIENCE MONITOR: A MODEL FOR DEVELOPMENT

Mustafa says to one publication that she sets as a standard is the U.S.-based weekly newspaper *The Christian Science Monitor*. "Although it's Christian-based in its faith, in its reporting...religion is not the over current," she explains.

"They are where the media needs to be. Usually [in] remote areas, areas in conflict and we would assume, that based on their religious faith, that their obligation is to be accurate and to be fair. So therefore, we want to have the resources and the outreach and the courage as we would see in a newspaper like the Christian Science Monitor to be a paper from Muslims, about Muslims but also out in the world to report on events as they are happening and to give an accurate report"

THE DANGER OF HAVING MUSLIMS IN THE MEDIA

Some Muslims have felt that the solution to the problem of Muslims and the media is by having more Muslims enter the fields of journalism and communication. But Hooper takes this views very carefully.

"You need to be careful," he warns. "It's like you're always sending African-American reporters to cover the inner city. You know you don't want that person just to be some token and representative of a particular religion or ethnic group"

EDUCATION OF JOURNALISTS IS THE KEY

But even with the presence of Muslim media and Muslims in the mainstream media, stereotypes and prejudice persist. This is where, according to Hooper, Muslims need to actively work to educate journalists.

"When CAIR started it was recognized that there was a great need for some vehicle to educate the media about Islam and the Muslim community," he says.

"I think prior to that time there was really no restraint on the media. They could say whatever they wanted and a few people would challenge them but there was no organized way to challenge stereotypes and bias in the media. CAIR's success, Alhamdu lillah (Praise be to God), has been [in] having a systematic approach to education of the media." But this needs to be a continuous process.

"There's still people who know nothing about Islam and still have to write stories or edit stories about it and it's up to us in many ways, to educate these people," notes Hooper.

OKLAHOMA CITY BOMBING, 1995: AN EYE-OPENER FOR JOURNALISTS

If any event changed the relationship between Muslims and the media, it was the April 1995 bombing of the Alfred P. Murrah building in Oklahoma City, the worst terrorist attack on U.S. soil in American history. Hooper describes it as a "watershed event".

"When Muslims were first accused of it and there were several days of anti-Muslim hysteria and when it so quickly became apparent that it was not a Muslim who did it, it was kind of a slap in the face to many journalists who realized their bias when it was not apparent to them before," he says.

In the hours after the bombing, fingers pointed almost automatically to Muslims. It was later discovered that anti-government white supremacists were responsible for the attack which led to the death of over 160 people, including children.

MUSLIMS ARE MORE ASSERTIVE TODAY

The days of Muslims ranting and doing nothing about media bias and prejudice against Islam and Muslims are still here, but more Muslims are willing to challenge these perceptions.

"Even something as small as a letter to the editor is sometimes revolutionary," notes Hooper. "That people, particularly those who came from overseas, where if you wrote a letter to the editor you got a knock on the door at midnight and got hauled off to jail, to get somebody from that environment to write a letter to the editor about anything is quite revolutionary." Muslim assertiveness has paid off.

"Just as every other religious and ethnic group defends its image, Muslims are beginning to defend their image and that makes an impact on the reporters who don't want to be accused of inaccuracy or bias," says Hooper.

THE ENTERTAINMENT INDUSTRY: BIGOTRY'S LAST BASTION

If there is one area where portrayal of Muslims has not seen an improvement, it's in Hollywood. "That is the last bastion of anti-Muslim bigotry, the entertainment industry," notes Hooper.

"They haven't changed; in fact they may have gotten worse over the years. That's our next big hurdle for the Muslim community is to fight these stereotypes coming out of Hollywood."

Films like the fall 1999 movie The Siege and more recently, Rules of Engagement, continued to portray Muslims as bloodthirsty, backwards terrorists. Both movies drew protests from Muslims, especially in the U.S.

About one-third of the 1.2 billion Muslims in the world currently live in countries where there is a non-Muslim majority; of this one-third, a sizable number live in North America and Europe.

The presence of Muslims in the West is problematic to say the least. Muslims in the West have had to grapple with the fundamental issues of identity, citizenry and minority rights on a variety of different levels (the local, the national) and in a variety of different spheres (the social, the economic, the political). As a community and as individuals, Muslims living in Western countries are often socially marginalized, politically disenfranchised and popularly vilified.

The first Muslim "communities" (if they can even be described as that) in the West were comprised of mostly immigrant working-class laborers who came in search of economic opportunities and with the idea that they would eventually return to their home countries once they had "made it" financially.

Did little to motivate them to participate in or interact with the nations to which they had emigrated. Even if they had chosen to participate politically or socially in the formal institutions of their host states, they were ill equipped to do so due to their generally low levels of education and lack of fluency in the host language. It was therefore up to the children and grandchildren of these first Muslim immigrants, living in the West by "permanent choice" as it were, to think critically about their place as Muslims in a Western society and attempt to come to terms with that society's dominant institutions, customs and values. As Muslim communities become increasingly established and organized, and as more immigrants acquire citizenship and their progeny depend upon the social positions and interests and objectives of those who produce them."

This study analyzes eight video programs and animated pictures geared to Muslim children between the ages of 2 and 9 that were made within the last 10 years. The videos are compared and contrasted in an effort to find recurring themes and images as well as pinpoint an underlying hegemonic articulation of Islamic ideals and traditions that is imperative to American-Muslim identity construction. This paper addresses the motivations behind the production of Islamic media as well as their substantive content. In addition, the underlying tensions found in these productions between the different "concentric" circles of identity that Muslims in America occupy (Texan-American-Pakistani-Sunni-Muslim for example) as well as the tensions between the different worlds (Islamic vs. Western) they have to negotiate on a daily basis are addressed.

Finally, I engage the paradigm of Orientalism (as articulated by Edward Said) and show its applicability to Islamic media production in America. "Halal" TV? In a poll conducted by US News and World Report in 1996, 81 percent of Americans surveyed felt that television contributes to the perceived decline in family values.

Another poll undertaken by Gallup in 1991 showed that 62% of Americans believe that television does not represent their values. These concerns are echoed by Muslims in America who worry about the effects of the daily consumption of television has on their children and families.

However, while most non-Muslim critics of television merely want to "clean up" TV by removing offensive sexual and violent scenes or ensuring that such scenes are not aired at a time when children are likely to be watching, "the perceived moral laxity [of American culture] has promoted many Muslim parents to search for alternative schoolings and social activities for their children."

One of these alternatives is creating a type of "Islamized" television, whereby media is produced by Muslims, for Muslims and given an explicit Islamic content. There are two primary motivations for this "Islamization" impetus. First, Muslim parents have a very real fear that their children, through the influence of daily interaction with non-Muslim peers and through the influence of the secular Western education they receive in public schools, will grow up either to reject Islam or be ignorant of Islamic values.

Parents see Islamic media as a way of providing children a fun and educational Muslim alternative to the (non-Muslim) fun they have with their friends and the (non-Muslim) education they receive in school.

They become second, third and fourth generation "Muslim Westerners" rather than newly arrived immigrants, their power not only to create more space for themselves in the social, political and economic spheres but also to fundamentally change the nature of that space, will grow. Central to the Muslim experience in the West is the challenge of retaining an Islamic (religious and cultural) identity in a predominantly non-Islamic society. The seemingly entrenched secular legacy of Western liberal democracies poses special problems for Muslims who view Islam not only as a religion, but also as "a way of life."

They conceive the function of religion as providing a type of blueprint for how to live not only spiritually, but also socially, economically and politically. Muslims in the West have formulated different responses to this challenge, ranging from total assimilation into the hegemonic culture of the white, nominally Christian majority, to complete rejection and isolation from mainstream society. An important segment of the Muslim community, however, has adopted a midway approach. Many in its ranks seek to publicly affirm their Islamic identity within the Western context and through interaction with it. Some Muslims have attempted to use communication technology in the form of media production to this aim. To this end, they have produced "Islamic media" in the form of magazines, newsletters and more recently, videos, audiotapes, DVDs and CDs. This paper will address the phenomenon of Islamic media production for children in a Western country that has an important (and in a post 9-11 context rather controversial) Muslim presence—the United States.

This phenomenon is symptomatic of the desire on the part of the Muslim community in America to ensure that the coming generations of Muslims do not get lost in the so-called American "melting pot" which strives for the homogenization and assimilation of all minorities and immigrants into the hegemonic culture, as defined and practiced by the white, Christian majority. Analyzing Islamic media production is important in that it has the potential of shedding added light on the dialectics of identity construction/consolidation/ redefinition of Muslims in the West and their resistance to pressures to conform or recast that identity within the dominant (and for them alien) sociocultural modes. I will thus argue that Islamic media production for Muslim children in America represents an important factor in the inter-subjective process of identity construction and Islamic socialization. These productions represent to a significant extent the (idealized) way Muslims in America see themselves and would like to be seen by others.

Furthermore, these productions represent the way in which Muslims see others (i.e. non-Muslim Americans). As these productions were made not merely for entertainment purposes, but with a strong and overt "educational" agenda in mind, we can safely assume that they are deliberately and consciously seeking to build a particular vision of reality and construct a particular Islamic identity (the "right" Islamic identity). They do this by continuously presenting and consistently reiterating several dominant (and ultimately dominating) images and themes, leading to the construction of a very stylized and exclusive image of The Muslim Community, History, Woman, Family and Values. Therefore, as Linda Steet put it in her discussion of the representation of Arabs in National Geographic, it is fundamental to ask what are "the conscious choices made in structures of representation". In order to better understand the underlying ideology of those who generate these structures since they "constitute versions of reality in ways which belonging to all ethnic groups."

However, another study has shown that television can be also used to counteract these very tendencies. For example, research done on Sesame Street, a popular television educational show for young children which presents minority groups in a non-stereotyped fashion, demonstrated that minority children who viewed the show gained markedly in terms of self-esteem and ethnic/cultural pride.

The Islamic media productions seek to do what Sesame Street has done but with a very specific target audience in mind—Muslim children. Since even "positive" mainstream educational programs such as Sesame Street typically do not feature Muslim characters, Islamic media thus fills an important representational gap. It speaks to the concerns one Mexican-American media researcher raised: "Where, I wondered, was someone on TV who looked like me? Where were my family and friends? Who were Cinderella and Snow

White to me? I liked them, but they didn't look like the folks I knew."

The producer of Adam's World states that "children's audiences of this video will see other Muslim kids in action, doing Islamic things like praying, reading Qur'an, etc." In this way, Islamic media instills pride in Muslim children of their Islamic identity, thus transforming it from a source of embarrassment to a source of empowerment.

The Dominant Themes Several recurring themes appear to be the dominant substance of Islamic media productions and aid in Muslim identity construction in America. They are: the diversity/unity of Muslims, the greatness of Islamic civilization and history, the centrality of God and the Prophet, the functional role of women and the veil, the importance of the family, and finally, the makeup of "Islamic values." The themes constitute the essential pillars of Islamic media, around which secondary themes are woven.

MUSLIM 'MELTING POT' OR MUSLIM 'SALAD BOWL'

According to the producers of Adam's World, the children featured in the series represent over 40 different ethnicities. This is readily visible in each episode, which features children who look South Asian, Arab, East Asian or African-American. However, while it is important to look at what is visually/textually present, it is equally important to look at what is absent, for, as one author puts it: "The unsaid, the already said, the presupposed, is of particular importance in ideological analysis, in that ideologies are generally embedded within the implicit meaning of a text rather than being explicit."

There is a marked absence of "white" children in both the Adam's World Series and other children's films about "contemporary" Muslims such as Muslim Scouts. We can only speculate as to the reason white children are not portrayed. To take a rather mundane possible reason, perhaps the absence of white children is due to the fact that the overwhelming majority of Muslims in America are not white and that the images are therefore only striving to be faithful to demographic reality. In addition, it may be that the producers recognize that their primary consumers and buyers will not be the parents of white children, but rather the parents of non-white children and are therefore trying to cater to consumer tastes and demands as befitting any for-profit endeavors. A far more interesting reason, however, to explain the lack of white children is small way, I hope that shows like Adam's World can create a much more wholesome experience for children. If an Islamic children's series can become a viable alternative, then we will have played an important role in laying a better foundation. " Thus, it is important to note that Islamic media productions are seeking to combat the effects of un-Islamic media by appropriating the very tools of these media. Furthermore, in addition to the motivation of counteracting the assimilating tendencies of mainstream television through its reflection of the hegemonic culture and norms, Muslims have a second motive for supporting Islamic media production that is intimately linked to the way Muslims themselves have been depicted in mainstream American popular culture. Jack Shaheen of Southern Illinois University has dedicated much of his time to documenting the image of Arabs and Muslims in American popular culture as it is shown on television, as well as in films, books and the press.

His conclusions serve as evidence for the proposition that the West views the Arab-Muslim world as an alien "Other," embodying negative characteristics such as unfettered violence, anti-democratism and irrational hatred. Indeed, the TV serials he surveyed "show all Arabs, Muslims, and Arab-Americans as being at war with the United States."

If we take the United States as embodying the ideals of democracy, liberty and peace for Americans, this means that Arabs and Muslims are at war with these ideals and therefore condone tyranny and violence. In other words, "Hollywood's Arab Muslims threaten our freedom, economy and culture." Arabs and Muslims remain fair game for media stereotypes and racism, while it is no longer politically correct to present other ethnicities (who historically have also been subjected too much of the same stereotyping such as the Jews and the Chinese) in such a negative light. With the end of the Cold War this tendency has only increased as the West lost the convenient ideological "Other" it had in Communism and began looking to other movements and entities against which to construct its own identity. Increasingly it appears that a replacement for the "Evil Empire" has been found in the "Evil Islamist." Shaheen's focus on images in the media is not arbitrary. He recognized that "by influencing public norms, perceptions, expectations, hopes, fears, desires and angst about diversity, the mass media play a powerful role in the social construction of knowledge about race, ethnicity, religion, gender, culture, sexual orientation and other aspects of diversity." Two Members of minority groups are particularly susceptible to this media power of knowledge construction. Indeed, children from minority and low socio-economic backgrounds are more prone than white, middle-class children to having their conceptions of reality shaped by the small screen as they are more likely to believe that the world portrayed on television faithfully mirrors the "real" world.

This is because US television presents a predominately Anglo-Saxon and middle class world and "portrayals of a social milieu unlike the child's own... [Will] they have greater power to shape the child's view of that milieu?"

Muslims as a minority are therefore understandably justified in being sensitive to the potential effects negative representations of Islam (with a simultaneous positive representation of other religions/groups) could have on the self-perception of their children. In a general study conducted on the effects of the media on social behavior in children, it became clear that members of racial minorities are projected as poor and powerless by US television, leading to these images becoming "internalized" by children Islamic Media for Muslim-American Children and the Politics of Identity Construction Yasmin Moll become virtually indistinguishable from each other. Again the message is we are all Muslims who believe in the same things. Indeed, a song of the series goes: "Muslims are never far apart / we are always together in the heart." By portraying the American Muslim characters as part of a larger global umma, these productions construct a Muslim identity that is internationally collectivized. This leads to the concerns of Muslims abroad becoming the concerns of Muslims at home, in America, illustrating the Prophetic saying that "the umma is one body, if one part is ill the whole body feels it." An interesting segment in an Adam's World episode entitled "Take Me to the Ka'aba" shows a picture of Al-Aqsa mosque in occupied East Jerusalem being surrounded by Israeli soldiers. The narrator says: "We hope one day Muslims will be able to go there."

Although he never explains why most Muslims are not able to go there now, the implied message is that the situation of Islamic holy sites in Jerusalem concerns all Muslims, not just Palestinian Muslims. Muslims are understandably sensitive to the potential effects these types of representations could have on the self-perception of their children. Concern for the fate of all Muslims collectively is also expressed in other productions. For example, in Muslim Scouts one of the boy scouts says: "The umma was once strong. Insh'allah it will be strong again."

A Glorious Past The glory of Islamic history and civilization is another dominant theme in Islamic media production. One animated film, Sultan Muhammad II: Fatih, is entirely devoted to this theme. The film tells the story of the Islamic conquest (called "liberation" in the film) of Constantinople in 1453 by the Ottoman sultan Muhammad II. This event is important in both Muslim and Western popular imagination, with the Muslims viewing it as one of the crowning achievements of Muslim leaders and the West viewing it as an example of an Islamic menace seeking to subjugate Christendom.

The film stresses that while the Muslims were technologically superior to the Byzantines, the reason behind their successful conquest of Constantinople was not military might alone, but also due to the fact that God was on their side. In a particularly dramatic scene, the Ottoman army is seen rushing to the gates of Constantinople to the cries of "Allahu Akbar" as the Qur'an is recited in the background. The film ends with the Sultan renaming Constantinople "Istanbul, city of Islam, where science, art, religion and scholarship flourished." Muslims often feel marginalized in the American educational curriculum, which in their opinion does not give enough (or even accurate) attention to Islamic history.

In fact, "Muslim children in public schools across America are educated to believe they have no place in the scope of world history and that Islam has made no significant contributions to world history." In the first volume of the Muslim Scouts series, the Muslim American boy scouts are given a tour of Al-Azhar University in Cairo and told about its role in producing some of the greatest scholars of history. The boys are astonished and one of them sighs, "I wish I learned some Muslim history in school," underlining the feelings of Muslims about American education. In a way, these media productions are seeking to fill that gap by making animated films for children about Muslim history for educational consumption. This is intimately related to the role these media play in identity construction. By producing films that show historic Muslim "heroes" or to posit that Islamic media seeks to "other" white culture.

As already discussed, these productions were made, to a large extent, to counteract the non-Islamic influences Muslim children are exposed to in daily life. These influences often come from non-Muslim peers, educators, and celebrities who come from the majoritarian white background. Thus, by leaving out the very people who the Muslim child either directly or indirectly sees most, these productions are implicitly saying that these people (to be more blunt, these whites) are "different" from us and not to be emulated. This shows how the construction of a Muslim identity through these media is a selective and exclusive business, a business that decides for children who is and who is not a part of their greater collective identity. In any case, the ethnically diverse Muslims portrayed in these productions are a direct reflection of the diversity of the Muslim community in America. Muslim immigrants in America come from a myriad of different countries and regions.

The existence of such diversity within the Muslim community challenges Muslims "to attempt to build the bridges within the Muslim communities necessary to spare the Muslim Americans the racial divides that presently split the other Abrahamic religions into multiple ethnic/racial islands." Islamic media attempts to do just that by featuring Muslim children who, despite their differing origins, all play, pray and have adventures happily together. This is well illustrated in the Muslim Scouts series which shows a close band of four young Muslim boys of varying ethnicities who go around the world (the Muslim world, that is) "fighting injustice." The theme of the diversity and unity of the American Muslim community is carried over in representations of the larger Islamic umma.

In Adam's World, there is a recurring segment in each episode where Adam travels with the aid of a "transvisualiser" (a nifty space age travel machine taken from the Star trek series) to different Muslim countries like Turkey, Egypt, Jordan, and Malaysia. Adam then proceeds to showcase the food, history, customs and language of these countries. However, what is always stressed is the fact that despite cultural, historical or linguistic variations, the inhabitants of these countries are all Muslim and that is what counts—in fact, that is all that needs to be retained and nothing else. For example, when talking about architecture in Muslim countries, it is always the mosques that are featured and more "secular" buildings such as palaces, bridges or national monuments are ignored. This highlights for the children viewers that the single most important common denominator is religion: Islam.

The same theme is also found in the Muslim Scouts series which, as I noted earlier, features a group of American-Muslim boy scouts who travel to Turkey, Egypt and several countries in sub-Saharan Africa doing good works in the hope of earning the "umma badge". In their travels, they meet other young Muslim boys from various countries, all speaking with different accents and possessing different physical characteristics. The film, however, repeatedly shows these young boys engaging in communal prayer, where they see a far more interesting reason, however, to explain the lack of white children is to posit that Islamic media seeks to "other" white culture.

God-centered knowledge in the Islamic worldview is based on the realization that God created everything."

These media serve to contrast implicitly the God-centered Islamic world-view with the Man or Self-centered Western world view through their constant allusions to the divine. For example, animated films or programs for children typically feature a hero who has to overcome some sort of obstacle and usually does so through a process of self-will and self-confidence, where the mantra is "I can do this if I believe in myself." In Muslim programs, however, the obstacle is overcome with the help and mercy of God, and the mantra is, "I can do this if I believe God will help me." The Prophet as the earthly voice of the Divine also figures prominently in Islamic media, and his Sunnah is frequently alluded to.

He is described in one Adam's World episode as "the most successful person in the world" and various behaviors are applauded by showing that they conform to the behavior of the Prophet. Thus, when Adam talks about the need for people to have sabr, or patience, he does so by quoting a Hadith which shows that the Prophet valued patience. Adam the Muslim Muppet is far from being perfect. He has many faults such as being forgetful, a procrastinator and short-tempered. He always manages to correct these faults, however, by remembering the Prophet and asking himself whether or not the Prophet would approve of his behavior.

In this manner, it becomes evident that the real hero of the show is not Adam, but rather the Prophet himself. Adam acts as the connection for children to the Prophet, a mechanism for making the Prophet relevant to their lives and attractive to their minds. In sum, Islamic media constructs two essential aspects of Muslim identity: taqwa (God-consciousness) and a high regard for the Prophetic example. This fosters a sense of religiosity in Muslim children and makes religion the defining pillar of their identity. The Right Type of Woman in all of the animated films and programs I viewed, without exception, women either play no role at all in them (meaning they are not physically present) or, if they are given a role, it is secondary and supporting. They are not the "heroes" who save the day. In fact, all of the protagonists of these films (from Adam the Muslim Muppet, to the Muslim boy scouts, to Salam, to Sultan Muhammad) are males.

Only one episode of Adam's World speaks explicitly of women and it does so in the context of a Prophetic Hadith which says that "Paradise lies at the mother's feet." The episode then goes on to show various snapshots (or, in the popular jargon, "Kodak moments") of mothers with their children. By legitimating or allowing their presence only in their function as mothers and by giving them value and voice only in relation to that function, women are effectively marginalized and instrumentalized in these productions. This is indicative of the place of women within the traditional patriarchal family. This carries over to the Muslim community, where women's roles are largely functionally defined in relation to men and within a familial context, meaning women are seen as mothers, sisters or wives. This is especially true for the first generation of immigrants, who brought with them the conservative, parochial notions of their home countries regarding what it means to be a woman in society.

In this conceptualization, women are given the responsibility of upholding Islamic values through the upbringing of their children according to "the straight path," thus collapsing the constructs of womanhood, religious piety and child-rearing. The domestic space becomes the space of woman by highlighting past Muslim scholarship, this media is giving Muslim children a valorized conception of the role their "ancestors" or fellow Muslims played in world history. This promotes a positive conception of the self by association. For example, in an episode of Adam's World, the narrator tells us: "Almost one thousand years ago, Muslim scientists studied the fossils of sea creatures so whenever you see an old animal, remember; Muslims studied them a long time ago." Yet another episode describes Muslim Spain (Andalusia) as "a leader in sciences, math, arts, Hadith and many other things." In a way, this is telling Muslim children to remember that Muslims are, well, smart too. The need to make such an assertion can be understood in light of the modern day scientific achievements of the West and the near monopoly on scientific innovation and knowledge production it enjoys; the superiority of the West in these areas puts Muslims on the defensive, causing them to assert that they too once (and still can) contributed to knowledge production.

Allah and His Messenger God is very much a central and prominent actor in Islamic media productions for children. In fact, it would not be inaccurate to say that He is the unrepresented (and unrepresentable) ultimate hero of these productions. A useful way of analyzing the role God plays in these productions is to see what attributes of God are stressed and why. In Salam's Journey, an animated film inspired by Surat Al Feel in the Qur'an, a young Muslim boy, Salam, finds himself in several rather precarious situations. In each situation, he puts his faith in God saying "Ya Allah please help" and God does not let him down. The story of Salam is juxtaposed against the story of the people of Mecca who put their faith in God to defeat the army of Abraha, an evil king bent on destroying the Ka'aba.

Clearly, the God of Salam's Journey is a Protector, a Being who will not let down His believing and faithful creatures. This film thus stresses the Islamic worldview in which man is in no way self-sufficient, but is in dire need of divine help to be successful. This world-view is also expressed in Muslim Scouts, where the motto of the boy scouts is "put your trust in Allah and do your best." In one scene, one of the scouts saves another from the hands of poachers who were going to leave him in the jungle to be eaten by wild animals. The scout saved is not appropriately grateful, leading his savior to exclaim, "Doesn't he mean to say 'thank you for saving my life'?!" At this point, their Muslim mentor interrupts, admonishing firmly "Don't say that! Only Allah saves!" In two different episodes of Adam's World, "Happy to be a Muslim" and "The Humble Muslim", the stress is on God the Creator. Children sing "The world is so beautiful/Who could have made it except for Allah?" and "Look around you and you will see all of the beautiful creatures/Nothing is greater than Allah, Lord of the Universe/ That is why Muslims say Allahu Akbar."

These theological views are expressed while teaching children something about nature. Thus, while the viewers learn several important facts about say, the ocean, and what is ultimately stressed is how this is God's creation and a living testimony to His existence and wonder. Why this stress? The answer becomes apparent when one reads that some Muslims find that "the most serious conflict between the secular and the Islamic curriculum is that the secular curriculum is not going to the mosque or praying at home. The productions stress respect and obedience to parents as proper Islamic behavior. Indeed, for some Muslims "the strong assertion in the Oneness of God and His Worship is linked, as one of its inherent conditions, with respect for and good behavior towards one's parents to obey one's parents, to be good to them, is the best way to be good with God."

This idea is underlined in an almost comical way in Salam's Journey. In one scene, the kidnapped Salam wants to leave to find his pet elephant, knowing that that will make his parents search to find him more difficult. However, an elderly Bedouin admonishes him that "your duty is to your parents first," not to your pet. In addition, the productions stress parents as a source of wisdom and guidance for children. In Salam's Journey, Salam tells us that "my father taught me that Allah will look after me and I trust him." This is in keeping with the attitude prevalent or evident in the Muslim discussion of the vital role the family plays in forming loyalty and adherence to Islam among children, by leading through example, providing an "Islamic environment" at home and socializing children into Islamic norms and values.

The family is consequently seen as the last bastion of hope for providing Muslim children with a firm grounding in Islamic teachings. On an Islamic web page, a Muslim-American writer makes the argument that "we as responsible parents need to ensure that our children do not absorb un-Islamic practices" through their viewing of television since "all children's programs produced by non-Muslims will contain elements which may not be acceptable to Islamic teachings."

By incorporating the family in its story lines, Muslim media productions for children are hoping to instill in children from an early age a respect for their parents and thus by extension a respect for the Muslim identity these parents represent and in some cases openly advocate. Heroes and Villains The declared aim of all of these productions is to teach children in a creative and engaging way "Islamic values" while promoting a positive image of Muslims.

It is therefore essential to take a closer look at what values are advanced by these programs and how they figure in the construction of a "positive" Muslim identity for children. The values preached on the animated films and shows could in fact be on any mainstream educational program such as Sesame Street. The admonishments to children to be clean, kind, patient, helpful, generous, etc. are not original or specific to Islamic media. However, what is original is the fact that these admonishments are Islamized, where they are presented as being integral to being a "good Muslim" not just a good kid. Values are rationalized islamically. For example, in Muslim Scouts in Africa children are told to not abuse nature and animals because "animals are Muslims too…let's watch what we do to the creation of Islam." The narrator goes on to say that a spider once helped the Prophet and Abu Bakr (the first caliph and companion of the Prophet) "be safe." This values are presented as being integral to being a "good Muslim" not just a good kid par excellence. This sexual division of labor is perhaps best illustrated by recalling a scene from Salam's Journey which depicts Abu Salam working in the field while Umm Salam prepares his dinner. The closing credits of an episode of Adam's World recommends a work by Abou

'Alaa Maududi, the founder of Jamat-i-Islami, a Pakistani Islamic revivalist movement that has a strong following in the United States and a man who possesses rather conservative views on the societal role of women. For example, he writes that "the real task of women is to look after the family."

This means first and foremost to "create an Islamic atmosphere in your homes in such a way that your children can see a living vision of Islam and assimilate it by direct experience…children should be acquainted with the message of Allah's unity and the meaning of prayer and their lives saturated by Islam."

Maududi would also no doubt feel that this "living vision of Islam" finds a manifestation in the hijab, or Muslim headscarf. When women, and most of the pre-pubescent girls, are shown in these productions they are portrayed wearing the hijab. There is a consensus among Muslim scholars (with a few important, mostly feminine, voices of dissent) that the hijab is not just permissible (and thus in the realm of personal choice) but obligatory.

However, while the majority of Muslim women would in fact agree with this consensus in principle, a substantial number of them still choose not to wear the hijab for various reasons:

1. These unveiled women have no place, however, in Islamic children's media. These productions construct an image of the Muslim woman that takes as a necessary ingredient that she be a hijabi/mohajaba.
2. This construction is idealized and artificial to the extent that finds no problem in directly contradicting (or ignoring) reality. For example, in the first volume of the Muslim Scouts series, there is a scene on an Egypt-Air flight which features a veiled air stewardess, even though Egypt-Air does not employ veiled women to serve on board its carriers. The veil is a much-maligned article of clothing in the West. In the Western popular imagination it is seen as an instrument of male oppression and dominance and a potent symbol of the alleged anti-modernism of Islam. The hostile reactions of Westerners

to the veils take the veil out of the domain of personal choice or belief and firmly places it in the domain of public opinion and therefore subject to public judgment and action.

In this way, "taking off the headscarf was seen as a sign of integration, whereas wearing the scarf was a sign that integration was somehow being hampered." However, for the Muslim producers of Islamic media, having the veil figure prominently in their productions could perhaps be legitimately construed as a sign of resistance to these pressures to integrate and a message to children to regard their veiled mothers, sisters, friends etc. as embodying the "norm." In sum, the image of the Muslim woman in these productions that is constructed is patriarchal and exclusive. It is patriarchal in that it relegates women to a secondary place *vis a vis* men and it is exclusive in that it allows only veiled adult women to appear and be part of the stylized Muslim identity. "Say not 'Fie' unto them" (Qur'an 17:23) the family is a recurring image in Islamic media production. Families (consisting usually of a mother, father and one male child) are depicted doing "Muslim" things together like Islamic Media for Muslim-American Children and the Politics of Idenitity Construction Yasmin Moll Allah."

By presenting Islam as providing all the cures to the social problems engendered by Western culture and lifestyle, the role of Muslims in America is valorized and given new meaning. They are now not merely immigrants in search of a better life, but believers of the most perfect of faiths who are speaking truth to power. As Al-Faruqi puts it, "the Islamic vision provides the immigrant with the criterion with which to understand, judge and seek to transform the unfortunate realities of North America." The Muslim immigrant or citizen need no longer look to the economically and technologically superior West for acceptance and approval, but can instead stand in judgment of it. It is he who defines the West not the reverse. In this there is much power—the power to name, define, judge and ultimately enjoin specific actions; as Edward Said puts it "to have knowledge of such a thing is to dominate it, to have authority over it."

TENSIONS BETWEEN OVERLAPPING IDENTITIES

It is clear that there are underlying tensions between Islamic identity and Western culture and between the different types of ethnic "Muslim" cultures in America. As one author attending a 1991 Islamic Society of North America (ISNA) meeting summarized: One of the most frequently raised issues was that of ethnic divisions and their threat to Muslim unity and therefore to the mission of spreading Islam in North America. But an even greater fear was of assimilation into a non-Muslim melting pot and a consequent loss of identity and values. Muslims are asking how they are going to be able to retain their valued ethnic and cultural heritage, while developing a strong Muslim environment that will protect them from the perceived destructive and immoral aspects of the dominant secular culture of North American life.

These tensions illustrate the difficulty of constructing a coherent and universal Muslim identity in a context that is as pluralistic and complex as the United States. These tensions also reveal that Muslim identity in the West is a work in progress, a construction that has yet to be completed and is in a constant state of being and becoming. Muslims and America: A Love-Hate Relationship? A central question in this dialectic is whether Muslims are "members of the umma whose orders they are completely bound by or rather true citizens of the state in which they live, bound, as all other citizens, by its constitution and laws? What are they first: Muslim or British, French, German or Spanish?"

The approaches used by Muslims in the West to reconcile their religious and cultural heritage with that of the West's cannot be neatly categorized or summarized. For the sake of analysis, however, one can delineate three general approaches that have been adopted by various individuals and groups. The first approach is of complete assimilation by the Muslim minority into the dominant culture. This assimilation meant rejecting the culture, religion and even language of their countries of origin. For example, a study showed that 70% of Beurs, or second generation French-born Maghribis, felt a closer link to France than to the original countries of their parents.

This seeming assimilation has been "greeted with relief by the French who saw [them] as a rejection Islamization of values is essential to providing Muslim children with an Islamic, rather than secular, rationalization for why certain values/behaviors are good and others are not. The aim is to teach children values that emphasize their religious underpinnings thereby consolidating a religious identity. Intimately connected to the "Islamization" of values, is the construction of a binary opposition between the Muslim Self and the non-Muslim other in Islamic media productions as a way of creating a Muslim identity for children. The existence of an "Other" seems to be necessary in the process of self-identification. As Edward Said puts it, "the construction of identity...involves the construction of opposites." While Said was concerned with representations of the Orient by Westerners, this discourse of "otherness" can also be applied to how the Muslim world (and even the Muslim community in the West) views the West. As Abubaker Al-Shingiety makes clear, "the otherness of Islam and Muslims has two functions. It acts as a dynamic of identification, by default, for the American. At the same time it is appropriated by the Muslim as a form of self-identification." An interesting example of binary oppositions at work is found in Sultan Muhammad II: Fatih. The film paints two diametrically opposed images of the Muslims and the Byzantine Christians. On the one hand, we have the Byzantine emperor Constantine II and his minions portrayed as effeminate (the Emperor sports earrings, is facially hairless and is seen filing his nails), corrupt and unjust. On the other hand, Sultan Muhammad is the epitome of masculinity (he possesses a muscular build, sports a rich beard and is seen laying down stones to build a fortress), has an uncompromising integrity and irre-proachable sense of justice. These laudable qualities of the Sultan are portrayed to stem directly from his faith in Islam and belief in God (in his own words: "our justice comes from our faith in Islam").

This "villainization" of non-Muslims is evident in other productions as well. To take another example, the Muslim Scouts series features the American Muslim boy-scouts combating various "evil-doers," be they terrorists, thieves or poachers. Aside from their engagement in illegal activities, what these bad guys all have in common is that they are not Muslim. Not only are they not Muslim, but their behavior is portrayed as being inherently un-Islamic. They engage in activities Muslims in this series simply would not do because they are Muslim and indeed, Muslims actively try to stop them. By doing this, the Muslim scouts are following the Qur'aniç injunction to "enjoin right conduct and forbid indecency." This same idea is picked up in the Adam's World Series where the un-Islamic behavior practiced by non-Muslim gamblers, superstars or unclean persons is explained by the various Muslim adult guests that appear on the show as being wrong and as therefore something Muslims wouldn't and shouldn't do. For example, the aptly named episode "The Humble Muslim" shows Adam becoming a little too arrogant when he thinks he has a fan-club. In acting out his "delusions of grandeur" he sheds his skullcap and jalabiya in favor of a Beatles' hairstyle and an Elvis inspired shirt. In sum, when Adam stops acting like a Muslim (i.e. stops being humble) he stops looking like one, too. Perhaps a quote from Salam's Journey best captures the very explicit normative meanings attached to being Muslim (being good) and being non-Muslims (being bad). Salam asks a stranger, "How do I know you won't hurt me [like the evil, non-Muslim pirates did]?" The man simply answers: "I believe in threatened the very identity, independence and way of life of Muslims."

In other cases, however, Islamic media seems to adopt a more midway course in that the Western background of the children is not ignored, but incorporated into the media. The clearest example of this is the Muslim Scouts series which takes a thoroughly American social institution for young boys, the Boy Scouts, and grafts it with an Islamic identity. It is an example of those Muslims "who want to maintain [their] group identity based on religion but also want to give full allegiance to society."

The first volume of Muslim Scouts features the Muslim American scouts away at camp with other Muslim scouts from different parts of the world. The boys sit in a circle and introduce themselves variously as Ahmed from Kuwait, Mohamed from Palestine etc. When it is the turn of the American Muslim scouts they introduce themselves as Zakaria Al-Kadi from Los Angeles, Faisal Mohieddin from Texas and Jamal Abdullah from New York. Clearly the film aims to stress the American birthplace of these young Muslims rather than their ethnic/national origin, which is never alluded to throughout the series. Later in the film, the scouts take a boat trip in the Marmara Sea in Istanbul and are told by a Turkish guide about a campaign underway to "clean it up." Immediately one of the boys says "We should do something like that and clean up Central Park." Thus, the boys are portrayed thinking about what they as Muslims can do to help their country, the United States.

At the same time, while stressing the American context of the target audience, the series also attempts to draw linkages to the wider Islamic umma by showing the boys traveling to different Muslim countries and working with scouts to "make a difference" as they put it. In a way such Islamic media are aiming to build safe, "sanitized" bridges between Islamic and Western cultures so that Muslim minority children are not assimilated or conversely alienated. Muslims in America: An Ethnic-Free Islam? While differences between Muslims and non-Muslims are emphasized, differences within the Muslim community are de-emphasized in Islamic media. As discussed in the previous section on the theme of diversity and unity, the Muslims of America are a diverse community. Muslims are very aware of this fact and in some cases view it as a source of weakness.

As one author writes, "some Muslims find the development of the ethnic mosque an objectionable and unhealthy development, part of the Americanization process which has historically divided the various immigrants into their constituent parts." Muslim organizations such as Islamic

Society of North America (ISNA) and Islamic Circle of North America (ICNA) were formed in part to counter this ethnicisation by seeking to "bring together much more ethnically diverse groups of Muslims for common action and mutual strengthening." It is telling to note that ICNA is one of the main collaborators in Islamic media, helping to produce Adam's World. Their mission to bring together diverse Muslims is seen in the series, where ethnic affiliations are never explicitly mentioned (except in relation to Muslims outside of the US) and where Muslims are presented as being just that—Muslims and nothing else. This is done primarily through an emphasis on the common ibada, worship of Muslims, the five pillars of Islam to which all Muslims universally adhere. In one episode Adam confides that he likes going to the mosque "because it makes me feel like a part of something so many others of ethnic signs and Islam and embracing Western liberal values." On the opposite pole, one finds an isolationist approach.

Muslims who adhere to this approach attempt to keep contact with the greater Western society to a minimum. For them "Islam in the West serves as constant source of identity available to a person who lost his national orientation." Thus, they seek to keep that identity as "pure" and undiluted as possible by effectively building boundaries that render their communities inaccessible from the outside, by "ghettoizing" as Tariq Ramadan puts it. They argue that developing deep ties to Western society will only serve to "contaminate" their community with values and ideas that are in direct contradiction with their own religion and culture.

In the middle of this continuum between assimilation and isolationism, one can find a growing trend among Muslim communities that emphasizes retention of their Islamic identity while at the same time positing that identity within the larger framework Western society and political institutions. The younger, Western-born Muslims who "have moved to openly carve a place for themselves within [Western] intellectual and social spheres" best represent this trend. What differentiates the members of this group from the assimilationist group is that they have self-consciously and deliberately chosen to participate in society as European or American-Muslims and not merely as unhyphenated Europeans/Americans. Indeed, "they are opting for an open public presence in which they will be able to demonstrate their understanding of what it means to be [Western] and Muslim" and perhaps creating in the process a new "Western Islamic culture," free of any contradictions and comfortable with itself. It is not clear where Islamic media productions would place themselves within this continuum.

At times, it seems closer to the isolationist position in that it seeks to develop an Islamic media "enclave" for children via communication technology to protect their Muslim identity from being influenced by un-Islamic western values and culture. I would argue that the animated films of Salam's Journey, Sultan Muhammad II: Fatih and even the Adam's World series is isolationist in outlook.

Nowhere in these films do we find a "synthesis" of Islamic and Western cultures. Rather, what we see is traditional, historical and ritualistic Islam being simplified and presented to Muslim children born in America. The only western aspect of this is the fact that the presentation is in English. In some cases, these productions take an explicit stance by highlighting the difficulty of being Muslim in a non-Muslim society. In the very first Adam's World episode, "Let's Pray," a segment is filmed in an Islamic school classroom of girls (all veiled, including the teacher) where the students express the difficulty of performing salat or prayer during school time. One of them complains: "I go to public school, so I have classes during Friday prayer; what should I do? I feel bad not being able to pray." One of her class mates readily responds: "You should go to Muslim school, where we can all pray." The teacher reinforces this comment authoritatively: "In a non-Muslim society, it is difficult for Muslim children to offer juma'ah [Friday] prayer." She adds that the child should ask the school administrators to allow her to pray during school time, reminding her that "we pray to please Allah, not people."

Thus, these media would seem to agree with Maududi,

who felt that "Westernization saying "Allah you are peace and you bestow peace." To take another example of the negation of Orientalist discourse (this time regarding the "irrationality" of Islam), an entire episode of Adam's World, "Born to Learn," is devoted to illustrating for children that seeking knowledge is an intrinsic Muslim quality.

Reversing Orientalism: It is interesting to see that in opposing the negative qualities imposed by Orientalism on Muslims, Islamic media takes these very qualities and reverses them to apply to the Occident. For example, the Orientalist paradigm posited a "feminized" (read weak) Orient and a "masculinized" (read strong) Occident.

As discussed this binary opposition is taken up by the Faith film but with an important reversal: Islam (in the person of the Sultan) is masculinized and Christianity (in the person of the Emperor) is feminized. In this reversal of roles, Islamic media portrays Muslim values, behaviors, and identity as superior to those of non-Muslims. As Sadiq al 'Azm puts it: Given the decline of the West at the end of the twentieth century the Orient is supposed to rise under the leadership of [Islam] and under the banner of its mission civilatrice to guide humanity out of a state of decadence to which Western leadership has brought it. For, the 'western essence' produced such unmistakable signs of decadence as: 'mechanism, Darwinism, Freudianism, Marxism, Malthusianism, secularism, realism, positivism, existentialism, phenomenalism, pragmatism, Machiavellism, liberalism and imperialism', all of which are worldly doctrines manifesting 'a purely materialist essence.'

Appropriating Orientalism : However, while negating or reversing the major tenets of the Orientalist paradigm, Islamic media simultaneously and paradoxically appropriates some of its thinking. Indeed: The analyses, beliefs and ideas produced by the Islamanic [sic] trend in defense of its central thesis simply reproduce the whole discredited apparatus of classical Orientalist doctrine concerning the difference between East and West, Islam and Europe. This reiteration...is only reversed to favour Islam and the East in its implicit and explicit value judgments. There are several examples one could draw on to illustrate this. First, Orientalism viewed the Islamic world and the Muslim peoples as "monolithic"—an undifferentiated mass of believers. Islamic media also seeks to present a vision of the Islamic world that is "monolithic" in that it stresses that all Muslims (or "good Muslims" rather) in the end think, believe and act in the same things and in the same way despite their diverse histories, languages, customs, etc.

These other components of identity are marginalized and trivialized by the religious component in Islamic media productions. Second, Orientalist characterization of Muslims as being "warrior-like" is in one instance appropriated and endowed with a positive, rather than negative connotation. For example, the image constructed of Ottoman Muslims in Faith might as well be share." As Tariq Ramadan notes, "Islamic worship has a double dimension, individual and collective. In striving to attain excellence in the practise of their religion, Muslims are immediately called upon to face the community dimension of the Islamic way of life." Other Islamic media productions also ignore ethnicity. The ethnicity of the four boys of Muslim Scouts is never discussed and even Salam in Salam's Journey does not have a clear ethnic identity. While the world of Adam the Muslim Muppet and others seems to be an ethnic free zone, the reality is not so uncomplicated, however. As one author puts it, "Muslims have always held up a unified umma as their ideal. But this is easier to do when individual Muslim societies stay put in their national and ethnic regions.

When significant populations are set in motion, as is happening with large-scale migration, Muslims come face to face with their actual differences beneath the transcending levels of creed, cults and romantic myth." Other Muslims, however, have expressed a more idealistic outlook arguing that "American Islam is a purer form of Islam than is practiced in some Islamic countries, because of the absence of cultural amplifications." Orientalism and Islamic Media "The asymmetric relationship between a self-defined West and a western defined Other (Islam, non-West)" has been discussed almost ad nauseam by scholars since the publication of Edward Said's seminal study Orientalism. This study showed how the Orient was imagined by the West in a way that reduced it to set of essential, unchanging and ultimately constructed "fundamental" characteristics.

It is interesting to see how this paradigm of Orientalism can be applicable in a discussion of Islamic media. One has to note some of the important points that show how an Orientalist discourse has been negated, reversed and even appropriated by Islamic media.

Negating Orientalism: In promoting a positive view of Muslim identity, Islamic media productions are reversing the negative Orientalist conception of Muslims/Islam/the Orient. The Islamic world has long been for the West the representation of a religious and civilizational Enemy. The Crusades of the 11th and 12th centuries where Western European Christians journeyed to the Middle East with the aim of "reclaiming" the Holy Land set off the beginning of hostile polemics by both sides and a struggle for power and domination which continued in the modern era in the form of European colonization of Muslim lands, then Western attempts at economic and military hegemony in the region. Out of these historical experiences emerged a regime of representation of the religion of Islam that is frighteningly negative and highly inaccurate, sensationalizing the religion into one of unfettered violence, decadent sexuality and, worst of all, an uncompromising irrationality. Islamic media, by contrast, seeks to show that Muslims are peace-loving, virtuous and seekers of knowledge par excellence. For example, in Sultan Muhammad II: Faith, we are told that the Ottomans "obeyed the orders of [their] true religion and offered you [the Byzantine Christians] peace;" in a later scene the Sultan invokes God.

7

Ownership Diversity in Islamic Media

INTRODUCTION

Across the 15 largest Muslim media systems, ownership patterns vary in interesting ways. In many Western countries, there is less and less diversity in the ownership of media assets because these assets are being concentrated among fewer and fewer corporate actors. In some Muslim countries, media assets are also concentrated, but among state actors such as ministries of communications, government secretariats, or publically traded companies in which state agencies still hold controlling shares. In other Muslim countries, there is modest competition among the state and private owners of television stations, radio stations, mobile phone service providers, newspapers, and internet service providers.

METHODOLOGY

Before embarking on the exploration of media ownership in the 15 countries with the largest Muslim populations, we first had to reach a general consensus on the meaning of diversity. At its most basic level, we determined that diversity would be defined by ownership diversity. It would consist of a balance between state-owned and privately funded television, newspapers, and mobile phone carriers. Private ownership would then be divided into foreign and local investors. Expanding on this definition, we also reached the conclusion that diversity entailed a certain level of freedom in terms of the expression of political diversity, which we determined by observing political party ownership of media sources, case studies on arrests and topics censored. In some cases, newspapers and networks are owned by specific political parties and politicians. Ayna TV in Afghanistan is owned by Gen. Abdul Rashid Dostum and it is used to push his agenda. Censorship may be a result of pressure from the government/monarchy or other political groups such as warlords and opposition groups; topics include discussion of the Western Sahara in Morroco, labeling the "Armenian conflict" genocide in Turkey, and criticism of the Saudi Arabian government.

Media systems in the Muslim world have undergone major changes in recent years. Major economic, military, and political change has greatly affected the media landscape in the largest nations of the Muslim world. United States military involvement in Iraq and Afghanistan has completely restructured media from previous regimes. Destructive military operations in Iraq and Afghanistan, as well as Sudanese genocide and civil war have created conditions where international firms have seen a clean slate for developing communications technologies. Political turmoil surrounding elections in Pakistan has resulted in enhanced restrictions on all forms of media. In nations such as Iran and Saudi Arabia the government has maintained its stranglehold on media. Even as new technologies grant more citizens' access to alternative forms of expression other technologies have been used to tighten the grip totalitarian regimes hold on their media systems.

There are plenty of examples of positive improvements in Muslim nations in media, communication, and infor-mation technologies. The Turkish government has made great strides in loosening restrictions on media in accordance with EU standards, while continued economic progress has spurred major growth in information technology. In India international investment has spearheaded major growth in private and competitive media markets. In North Africa Egypt, Morocco, and Algeria have seen positive improvements in media freedom and availability with the rise of new information technologies. Direct government support to media and communications systems in Uzbekistan has lead to major improvements in the Central Asian nation. Since landmark elections in 2004 Indonesia has seen a rise in availability and diversity of media sources while progress in Nigeria following their elections in 2007 has been much slower.

Finally, we assessed the extent of cross ownership by media conglomerates—whether state-owned, privately operated, or publicly traded. We created a four point scale to contrast countries where there are no media conglomerates from countries where there are one or more conglomerates owning multiple media outlets. At the top of this index are countries with many media conglomerates, many instances of cross-ownership, or a high degree of concentration of all media assets in one conglomeration. States with several instances of media conglomeration, intermediate levels of cross-ownership, or a moderate degree of media concentration were listed in the middle of the index. Countries that have only a few media conglomerates, with only a few instances of cross-ownership, are at the bottom of this index. Some countries have no media conglomerates, and neither the state nor privately held firms nor publicly traded companies have significant control over media outlets.

INDONESIA - MEDIA PROFILE

Politics has played a huge role in the state of Indonesia's media system today. General Suharto was in control from 1965-1998 and he dictated much of the policies in Indonesia as well as the media. Finally, post-Suharto Indonesia is slowly making the transition to democratization and the state held its first direct presidential elections in 2004. Media is still in a state of transition to liberalization and a freer press. Before 1998, media was highly supervised by the Ministry of Information and it held the reigns over a lot of the domestic media in the country. Currently, there are numerous commercial networks in Indonesia that are in direct competition with the publicly owned Televisi Republik Indonesia (TVRI). There are also few publicly owned stations within certain provinces of Indonesia. Internet is really taking off in Indonesia with approximately 20 million users. Television broadcasters and radio stations are not allowed to relay live programs received from global stations. Indonesia's media system is under close watch by the United States' Human Rights Watch, and recent observations conclude that journalists still are not receiving the freedoms to pass judgment on public figures. Many journalists in Indonesia feel as though a lack of technology and sufficient equipment is hurting the system as a whole. The media is lacking important assets that could create much growth and expansion.

Overall, Indonesia has a somewhat diverse media ownership pattern. In terms of ISPs, there is a wide variety of Internet providers throughout the country and it is quite diverse. Newspaper ownership is only somewhat diverse, because there are still some restrictions against Indonesian journalists. Although diversity has greatly improved as Indonesia grows as a newly democratized state, press freedoms and ownership are still developing. Television ownership is diverse, as there are numerous commercial networks in direct competition with the publicly owned station TVRI. Radio stations in Indonesia are somewhat regulated by the government, so they are restricted to what they are allowed to broadcast, but there is still some independence within the privately owned stations, making radio somewhat diverse.

PAKISTAN - MEDIA PROFILE

When Musharraf came into power, he enforced new policies to liberalize print media and broadcasting. In 2007, a resistance campaign went into effect against Musharraf and media policies became stricter. Private radio and television stations grew stronger and their expansion ultimately brought down over 50 years of Pakistan's domination of broadcasting. The state-owned Pakistan Television Corporation is finally up against some competition of over 40 private satellite television stations; however, there are currently no terrestrial television stations. Although Pakistan and India tend to clash in media wars, Pakistanis still watch a lot of international satellite channels such as India's Zee TV and Star TV. There are about 100 private FM radio station licenses yet these private stations are not allowed to broadcast the news. Some of the private stations in tribal regions such as the North-West Frontier Province have sectarian separations. The government has quite an influence on press freedoms. For example, its law on blasphemy has held journalists back from reporting many stories. In comparison to South Asia in general however, Pakistan has one of the most blunt and opinionated print media systems. As far as Internet use goes, around 4 million users were online in 2007 (Internet Service Providers Association). There are only several small political bloggers thus far, and the government still has some control over websites.

Overall, Pakistan has a relatively diverse media ownership pattern. In terms of ISP ownership, Pakistan has over 50 private providers of Internet service, therefore diversity is very high. The press system is somewhat diverse; although the press is quite opinionated in comparison to other South Asian countries, there are still many laws and restrictions against journalists in Pakistan. In terms of cell phone ownership, there is insufficient information to judge the diversity in ownership. Radio ownership is somewhat diverse, because although there are over 100 privately owned stations, there are strict limitations on what they are allowed to broadcast. TV station ownership is quite diverse, as there are over 40 private satellite stations and one large state owned corporation. In general all of these stations are in fair competition with one another.

INDIA - MEDIA PROFILE

Before the 1990s, India's media systems saw very little diversity. It wasn't until 1992 when the country's TV monopoly broke apart, bringing in many new privately-owned stations. Star Plus is one of the most watched stations, and it comes to no surprise that it is owned by the mega media company, News Corporation. Entertainment television is very successful yet the news broadcasts are more popular, most likely because many of the stations run for 24-hours and they are constantly being updated. The publicly owned Doordarshan reaches approximately 400 million viewers in India, and overall the country's cable TV market is one of the biggest in the world. India's press system, generally read by the middle class, is also very diverse as there are numerous circulations and titles. Internet use in India has grown as well, with over 42 million users online in 2007. The Indian blogging community has grown extensively over the past few years. At the beginning of the 20th century, Indian radio frequencies have widely opened up to FM and AM broadcasters. Service is generally limited to urban areas. Many of the metropolitan cities have private FM channels that air popular music. They still are not allowed to broadcast the news; however, All India Radio (formerly known as Akashwani) broadcasts the news all over India. Overall, there has been a constant tension between India and Pakistan's media systems, and sometimes they even ban their broadcasting in the other state.

Overall, India has a very diverse media ownership pattern. In terms of ISP ownership, India's first ISPs were ERNet and NICNet; both of which were regulated by government restrictions. They were still doing quite well in providing fundamental services and access to the public. In the '90s India's ISP system had a lot of restrictions to who could have access to information; however, today the Internet in India is very open to the public, access is not a problem, and the ISPs are private. The press system in India is very diverse with numerous privately-owned newspapers. Just in 2001, India had 45,974 newspapers, published in over 100 languages. India's cell phone service providers are very diverse now. Today, 140 million Indians have phone service from various providers around the country. India has a large variety of radio stations to choose from, with privately and publicly owned FM and AM broadcasters; however, since there are still some restrictions on who is allowed to report the news to the public, the country's radio ownership is somewhat diverse. Overall, India's TV station ownership is diverse, with several privately owned stations and one huge publicly owned station, Doordarshan.

BANGLADESH - MEDIA PROFILE

With a population of approximately 160 million people and a huge percentage of that population living on less than a dollar a day, media in Bangladesh is incredibly constrained by infrastructure, poverty, and population. Major television and newspaper outlets are centered in the capital Dhaka and limited to other major cities. Deep poverty and widespread illiteracy tremendously limit the reach of Bangladeshi media into rural areas of the country with radio being the most widely used. A major segment of broadcast and print media is focused on foreigners within the country and Bengali immigrant populations living abroad in the Persian Gulf states, Australia, and the United Kingdom. State run broadcaster BTV has been on the air since 1964 but the state-held monopoly on television broadcasting wasn't lifted until 1998. Like other developing nations, the advent of satellite technology and the prevalence of inter-national broadcasting spurred growth in private Bangladeshi satellite broadcasters such as Channel I and NTV.

Political and economic hardship within Bangladesh has created an environment where journalists are frequently the focus of attacks from political parties and religious groups. Frequent harassment and government influence are common as the Reporters Without Borders Press Freedom Index ranked Bangladesh 134th out of 169 countries. The wide range of private Bangladeshi Newspapers such as the Daily *Ittefaq*, founded in 1953, have a history of being very outspoken yet despite protections of press freedom in the constitutions members of the media frequently find themselves under fire. Media in Bangladesh has a strong base but has been severely limited by difficult economic, political, and demographic problems that face the country as a whole.

Media in Bangladesh operates in a somewhat diverse environment. Television stations had been limited by monopoly to a single state broadcaster before 1998. Since restrictions on private ownership have been lifted private satellite broadcasters have gained market share for a somewhat diverse environment within Bangladesh. Newspapers in Bangladesh operate in a very diverse environment with widespread competition between privately owned firms, however there continues to be heavy involvement of party politics within print media as papers tend to follow partisan lines heavily in their reporting. The mobile phone industry is somewhat diverse with a few major foreign owned carriers providing the majority of service. There is not enough information regarding ISPs or Radio broadcasters.

An examination of media systems in Bangladesh shows low density of state organs in the media and intermediate levels of conglomeration of private firms. Television concentration is moderate, with a small state broadcaster BTV competing with numerous private channels. There is moderate density of ownership in newspapers as function with political influence and private competition. Mobile phone carriers are more heavily concentrated with Norway based Grameen Phone controlling 50% of the market.

EGYPT - MEDIA PROFILE

There is a major contrast in Egyptian media between state owned and privately owned television and newspapers. Egyptian media consumption is marked by high levels of illiteracy and poverty that foster a culture of social media where cafes often function as the source of satellite television for entire neighborhoods. State run Egyptian television has been established since 1960 with the Egypt Radio Television Union controlling eight terrestrial channels throughout the country. The rise of satellite broadcasting, along with the elimination of the state run monopoly in 2001 has created a large widely popular television industry in Egypt. Privately owned Dream TV and Al-Mihwar utilized some of the first television transmitting satellites in the Arab world and have become major regional broadcasters throughout the Middle East.

Egyptian newspapers are some of the oldest in the Muslim world. Al-Ahram was established in 1828 and is the oldest Arabic language newspaper in the world. Despite its credentials Al-Ahram remains state owned and operated through the Ministry of Information and along with Al-Jumhuriyah form the backbone of nationalized pro-government print media. There are widely circulated national dailies that support opposition political parties, and privately owned papers attempting to provide unbiased news, yet they are continually limited by laws that limit criticism of the government. With continual struggle for free private expression in Egyptian media and common place restrictions on information deemed damaging or critical of the government Reporters Without Borders rated Egypt 146th out of 169 countries in their media freedom index.

Egyptian media in general operates in a somewhat diverse environment. Ownership of television stations is sharply divided between the older terrestrial channels run by the government and the newer privately owned satellite channels. Despite competition between state-run and private television stations in a somewhat diverse market, restrictive laws and regulations still limit the autonomy of broadcasters. Egyptian newspapers are some of the oldest in the Middle East yet are only somewhat diverse as many are run through Egyptian government ministries or face strict government restrictions. Egyptian mobile phones are a very diverse industry with direct competition between private firms based in Europe, elsewhere in the Arab world, and a privately owned Egyptian carrier. There is not enough information to make accurate judgments of diversity in radio or internet providers, however all forms of broadcast in Egypt face similar restrictions.

State control and influence throughout Egyptian media has been diminishing in the past decade. Egypt has moderate conglomeration with its state-owned media and low concentration in the public sector. Television stations are moderately concentrated with state stations' ERTU terrestrial broadcasting competing with a few private satellite operators such as Dream TV. Newspapers are moderately concentrated with government issued dailies and restrictions on content. Mobile phone providers have a low concentration, with major foreign companies competing with private domestic power Orascom.

TURKEY - MEDIA PROFILE

Turkish media is shaped by two dramatically different elements of modern Turkish culture. Television stations and newspapers in Turkey today are caught between old oppressive censorship laws and the new found openness of Turkish politics as the government attempts to join the European Union. Within the past decade, government restrictions on freedom of speech and freedom of the press have lifted somewhat in response to European guidelines. Despite this, Turkey is still only rated number 101 out of 169 countries in the 2007 Reporters without Borders Media Freedom Index. The government has recently loosened restrictions on previous crimes such as publishing or broadcasting in the minority language of Kurdish. However, ambiguous laws such as those that prohibit insulting Turkish identity are still used to intimidate, censor, or imprison journalists, authors, and publishers. Recent relaxations, however, have not lead to a completely independent media system as business and political affiliations within print and broadcast media are common.

In the past ten years major segments of state owned media and telecommunications firms were auctioned off and privatized in accordance with EU regulations. Loosened business ties to the government have resulted in increased competition and economic diversity in media markets. Despite increased government privatization and attempts at economic competition in broadcast and print media, a few large corporations control a significant number of media outlets. The Dogan Group owns STAR TV and Kanal D, two major national broadcasters as well as Hurriyet and Milliyet, two of the nation's most popular mass circulation daily newspapers. Turkey is in a period of transition as external political and economic forces continue to shape the media landscape.

Overall the Turkish media system is one of the most diverse among the largest states in the Muslim world. Ownership of television stations has been almost completely private and very diverse since the state monopoly ended in 1990 with the exception of a public broadcasting channel the government continues to run. Private ownership is almost universal in print media as well with a very diverse market; however there is some density in that ownership as some of the major papers and channels are run by the same corporations. Print and broadcast media in Turkey must limit discussion of certain political topics or face prosecution by the government, but for the most part Turkish media operates in a competitive and diverse environment. The Turkish mobile phone industry is very diverse as a few privately owned firms compete in the national market. Information on ISPs in Turkey is difficult to track as there are too many private servers and providers to cover. There is not enough information to judge diversity in radio ownership as the volume of regional broadcasters is too high.

Turkish media is an almost exclusively private competitive market with low levels of state control but higher levels of centralized conglomeration among corporations. Turkish television is moderately concentrated with one of the countries last remaining state run outlets in TRT and an arm of Turkey's largest media group Dogan Holding in Star TV and Kanal D to complement its other private channels. Turkish newspapers are moderately concentrated in private conglomerates with Dogan Holding subsidiaries Hurriyet and Milliyet, two of the countries largest dailies, competing in an otherwise diverse market. In mobile phone companies a few domestic and international companies make up a small moderately dense market.

NIGERIA - MEDIA PROFILE

Nigeria is among the more diverse media climates in the Muslim world, with a mixture of both state and privately owned news and media outlets. While rating at 131 out of 169 in the Reporters without Borders 2007 Press Freedom

Index, Nigeria still maintains a larger diversity of media ownership than some other Muslim Countries. For example, in the mobile telephone arena, the three most widely used carriers are all privately owned and two of the three (MTN and Celtel) are based in places other than Nigeria (South Africa and Kuwait, respectively). In terms of newspaper and television station ownership, however, the state maintains a much higher level of control. According to the African Media Development Initiative (a study conducted by the BBC in 2006), print media in Nigeria is following "a promising trend towards newspapers operating independent of the government, made possible by the decreasing reliance on government subscriptions and adverts, and by the deregulation reforms of the present administration". While Nigeria was the first sub-Saharan African country to privatize its broadcasting stations, the government owned National Television authority still maintains control of a large portion of the broadcast media. However, the private sector of television broadcasting is following a positive trajectory and the private stations are expanding their influence to a large degree. The print media in Nigeria is largely state-run, peppered with a few privately owned newspapers, but still highly regulated by the government. Three of the most widely accessed radio stations in Nigeria operate under a corporate ownership structure, which offers a wide variety of perspectives, however, the most accessible radio station remains under government control. Nigeria boasts a large and diverse ownership structure in the broadcast media sector, but still maintains vast government control of print media.

Overall, Nigeria has a very diverse media ownership pattern relative to the other countries in this study. While internet use in Nigeria is low, ISPs are able to operate under a very diverse system; under the Nigerian Communications Act of 2003, the Nigerian Communications Commission liberalized ISP licensing. Newspapers are largely privately owned, interspersed with several government owned press, which makes for a very diverse and lively press in Nigeria. All three of the top mobile phone providers are based in foreign countries, none being controlled by the Nigerian government, which provides a very diverse environment in terms of mobile phone ownership. In terms of radio stations, the most readily available is Radio Nigeria, operated by the state controlled Federal Radio Corporation of Nigeria. However, there are also several privately owned radio stations, allowing Nigerians a wide range of choices and offering a very diverse range of radio sources. While the Nigerian Television Authority operates on a large scale over broadcasting, Nigerians have a very diverse range of other privately owned stations as well.

The state maintains a medium level of media conglomeration in Nigeria. It owns several television stations, radio stations, and newspapers, but not the majority. Privately owned media outlets have started to overcome government owned ones. In one case, DAAR communications owns African Independent Television (AIT) one of the more popular television broadcasting services, as well as the Raypower radio station, and an ISP. In comparison to the other countries in this study, this penetration of the private sector into media conglomeration is medium.

IRAN - MEDIA PROFILE

Iran boasts one of the least diverse media climates, in terms of ownership, in the Muslim world. Cell phones, newspapers, and television stations are nearly all entirely run by the state. In the Reporters without Borders 2007 Press Freedom Index, Iran ranked a dismal 166 out of 169. Under the current religious leadership of Ayatollah Khamenei and political leadership of President Ahmadine-jad, the media has been effectively controlled, in its entirety, by the Islamic state. However, Iran does have a history of government-controlled media; the television stations have never been privatized and are controlled under the monopoly of the Islamic Republic of Iran Broadcasting service. Newspaper ownership is also largely controlled by the state. According to the BBC country profile of Iran, the newspapers of the country are controlled by either the state run IRIB or IRNA (Islamic Republic News

Agency). In this respect, the mass distributed media in Iran is almost entirely dictated through the mouthpiece of the government, leaving little room for dissent or oppositional viewpoints; the operations of several independent newspapers were suspended for promoting an antigovernment stance. The only opportunity for obtaining foreign television or news is through satellite television, although owning a satellite dish is illegal. Beyond the press, the government also maintains a monopoly over the cellular telephone industry, with the government owned Telecommunication Company of Iran owning all of the telecommunications and cell phone networks in the country. Radio in Iran, aligning with the previous media outlets explored, is also entirely run by the IRIB. The Internet has become the most diverse outlet of Iranian media. Even though all ISPs must register through the Data Communications Company of Iran, the introduction of the private market has stood as an anomaly in a media system otherwise functioning under the monopoly of the Iranian government. Overall, the government's control over the media in Iran is all encompassing, including all aspects of popular media and telecommunications sectors.

Overall, Iran's media ownership pattern lacks diversity. ISP ownership has some diversity, but all providers must register with and are effectively controlled by the government. Newspapers lack ownership diversity because the major press outlets are state-run and there have been efforts to prevent privately run newspapers from printing material that suggests reform or speaks against the administration. In terms of cell phone providers, Iran lacks diversity as the providers all operate under the Telecommunications Company of Iran. The TCI also has a monopoly over radio broadcasting in Iran, which renders this media outlet not diverse as well. Similarly, the TCI maintains control over television broadcasting, limiting the possibilities of a diverse broadcasting system as well.

Iran's media system is under a high government monopoly. The state runs all of the media outlets in the country, besides Internet Service Providers. However, all the

ISPs must register with the Telecommunications Company of Iran before providing service, allowing the Iranian government to impose strict regulations on content and censorship. Satellite television is also not controlled by the Iranian government, but the ban on owning a satellite compromises the ability of antigovernment information to enter the country.

ALGERIA - MEDIA PROFILE

Algeria maintains one of the more prominent levels of media diversity in the Muslim world. While some aspects of Algerian media are government run, others are entirely privatized, making for a diverse ownership structure. Rated at 123 out of 169 in the Reporters without Borders 2007 Press Freedom Index, Algeria is continuing on a positive trajectory to an even more diverse media ownership structure. In terms of mobile phone operators, of the three main companies, one (Mobilis) is state-owned and the other two (Djeezy and Nedjma) belong to a foreign corporate ownership structure, Djeezy being a subsidiary of Orascom Egypt, and Nedjma a subsidiary of Kuwaiti based Wataniya. Television in Algeria is entirely controlled by the state-run ENTV (Enterprise Nationale de Television); however, French satellite television channels are also accessible to those with a satellite dish and allow for diversity in the types and opinions of news programs watched. According to Menassat, around 60% of households in Algeria have access to a satellite dish, which has initiated a relative decline in the viewer ship of Algerian national television stations. Radio is also entirely run by the state. The print media in Algeria is mostly private and would therefore seem to be free to offer a wide diversity of opinions on politics as well as express dissent and distaste with the administration. However, all four of the printing presses used for newspaper distribution, as well as the actual paper that the newspapers are printed on, are owned by the government. The Internet poses an interesting solution to this; in 1999, with its privatization, more newspapers began to post their controversial material online. Overall, Algeria's media ownership structure offers more diversity in some sectors than in others, but still maintains a high standing in overall ownership diversity.

Overall, Algeria has a somewhat diverse media ownership pattern in comparison to the other countries in this study. Some ISPs in Algeria are owned privately, but most are subsidiaries or partners of the state-run Algerie Telecom. Despite private ownership, all ISPs must register with the Ministry of Post and Telecommunications which monitors the sites accessed, making ISP ownership in Algeria somewhat diverse. The press, however, is vibrant with many privately owned newspapers that create a very diverse ownership structure. Two of the three top mobile phone providers are privately owned, also demonstrating a very diverse ownership pattern. However, the radio is almost entirely controlled by the government, rendering a lack of diversity in the ownership structure of this aspect of the media. Also, the state runs the major television stations through ENTV. However, satellite television operated through BRTV in France offers some diversity in the ownership structure of broadcast media.

State media conglomeration is high in Algeria, with the government maintaining control over all of the national television and radio stations. While the government does not directly control the press, it retains ownership over the four printing presses, making it increasingly difficult for newspapers to print anti-government articles. In terms of private media conglomerates, Orascom Telecom, based in Egypt, owns a mobile phone company as well as an Internet Service Provider in Algeria, rendering the private media monopoly low in the country.

MOROCCO - MEDIA PROFILE

Moroccans have access to approximately 2,000 domestic and foreign publications. However, readership is low due to low literacy levels. The press is usually in French or Arabic. Some of Morocco's press is at least partially government owned, while others are privately owned. Though much progress has been made over the years and censorship was banned in domestic publications in 1977, journalists practice self-censorship heavily. Sensitive and censored topics include the Western Sahara, the monarchy, Islam and corruption. Recently, the Western Sahara, rise of Islam and human rights corruptions has been reported more frequently. The topic journalists are most prosecuted for is criticism of the royal family. Consequences include heavy prison sentences and fines.

Two French-language newspapers have suffered legal action recently. TelQuel was ordered to pay libel damages of 500,000 dirhams ($73,570) to the head of a community association in February 2007. Later that month, Abou Jamai, managing editor of Le Journal Hebdomadaire, and journalist Fahd Iraqi paid 3.1 million dirhams ($417,480) in damages for libel to the European Strategic Intelligence and Security Center, an organization that specializes in researching and consulting in terrorism-related matters. Publications are usually in French or Arabic. Censorship and government ownership is less intense in newspapers than television. RTM and 2M, the two major television networks in Morocco. They are both state-owned. Radio-Television Marocaine (RTM) is a state-owned television and radio station. Medi 1, the other radio station in Morocco, is privately owned. Cellular phones are owned by a French company, a Portuguese company, the royal family, and portions are privately owned. With over 40 Internet Service Providers (ISPs), there is diversity.

Overall, Morrocan media has made many strides. While newspapers are a mixture of state-owned, partially state-owned, and privately-owned, there are still some forbidden topics. Morrocan television networks are fully state-owned and mobile phones and ISPs are fairly diverse in ownership. Reporters without Borders rank Morocco 106 out of 169 in its 2007 worldwide Press Freedom Index.

SAUDI - MEDIA PROFILE

Saudi Arabia is home to 26 million citizens, an array of newspapers and one television station. Arabic is the primary language of media outlets. However, a small amount of news media is in English. Media in Saudi Arabia is considered one of the most heavily censored media markets in the Middle East. The Broadcasting Service of the Kingdom of Saudi Arabia

(BSKSA), a government organization, oversees all media. While Saudi newspapers are privately owned, the Saudi government must approve all publishers and editors. A member of the Saudi royal family or someone close to the family closely monitors each newspaper. BBC lists seven major daily newspapers. Most of these papers were started in the 1960s and 1970s.

There is one major television news network, which operates four channels and is owned by the Saudi government. Because of these tight controls, most Saudis get other information from foreign news and the internet. Any criticism of the government, royal family or Islamic religious practices is strictly prohibited in the Saudi media. A specific case includes journalist Fawaz Turki, of the government daily Arab News. Turki was fired for writing about the atrocities perpetrated by Indonesia, the country with the highest Muslim population by percentage. The atrocities took place during Indonesia's 1975-1999 occupation of East Timor. Saudi media has recently begun to report on more controversial topics such as women's rights, terrorism and political, economic and educational reform. There are 130 media publications supported in Saudi Arabia.

Saudi media is quite tightly controlled by the BSKSA. Television networks are completely state-owned and while newspapers are privately owned, they are closely monitored and thus still heavily censored. Internet websites are often blocked by the Saudi government, but internet service providers are generally privately owned. Government media conglomeration is high because the BKSA oversees all and the Saudi government owns all television networks. Private conglomeration is low as there is little cross ownership besides the government. Saudi Arabia ranks 148 out of 169 on the Reporters without Borders Press Freedom Index.

AFGHANISTAN - MEDIA PROFILE

Afghanistan has experienced tremendous growth in its recent years as the Post-Taliban reform period has inspired 400 new publications. Under the Taliban regime, Afghan media was incredibly restricted and influenced by Taliban ideologies. Television was seen as immoral and therefore, banned. Although, journalists today are under some threat from warlords, conservative religious leaders and the government, great strides have been made. Many foreign groups own the new media. The Moby Capital Partners own Tolo TV and Lemar TV. There are eight major television networks, only one of which is state-owned (Afghanistan National Television). Privately owned television stations are the first to be criticized by religious conservatives. Ayna TV is owned by Gen. Abdul Rashid Dostum and is considered propaganda. Much of the television material is foreign such as Indian music and Western-style formats. Television is particularly popular in urban cities amongst young people under the age of 30. These television networks all began in the mid 2000s. There are over 50 radio stations. Internet access is still rare and computer literacy rates are not high. There is still much development needed in this area. The country's five newspapers, which were established in the 1960s and 1970s, on the other hand, are still heavily state-owned. Afghan Wireless is the cellular phone provider in Afghanistan and is privately owned. Afghanistan is mixed in terms of media diversity. Television stations are very diverse, while mobile phone providers are diverse and newspapers are not. Government media conglomeration is medium because newspapers are still state-owned, but nothing else is. Corporate conglomeration is low because few private owners own more than one form of media. Reporters without Borders rank Afghanistan at 142 out of 169 in the 2007 Worldwide Press Freedom Index.

SUDAN - MEDIA PROFILE

Media in Sudan has been hard pressed to find an outlet to spread throughout the country without limitations. Television and radio are almost completely dominated by the control of the Sudanese government. The majority of the broadcast programs are highly regulated by the govern-ment to ensure that only official state views are transmitted to Sudanese citizens.

Local television is controlled completely by the Sudanese government, and operates two channels. Sudan TV has a permanent military censor to ensure that news reflects official state views. In the semi-autonomous South of the country, the Sudan People's Liberation Movement operates Juba TV, which enjoys more broadcasting liberties for broadcasting material, advocated by the region's president. However, satellite dishes have become increasingly common among affluent citizens who can use them to watch international channels from across the Middle East to Europe.

Local radio is also government controlled to ensure that government perspectives are upheld via news and cultural programs. Sudan National Radio Corporation, the government-run radio broadcaster, relays national and regional programs in multiple languages. Music stations have earned some leeway with the government, allowing stations such as the Khartoum-based Mango FM to be privately owned. In the southern region, several stations are supported; including UN established Miraya FM and government supported Radio Juba. It is also from the south region where opposition parties broadcast their political views on shortwave to the rest of the country.

Print media is allowed more freedom than the previously mentioned media. Much of the press was restricted following the political coup that took place in 1989, but print media has made a comeback in its liberties since then. Many press establishments are privately owned, providing them more independence to publish views other than those of the state. Newspapers such as Al-Ra'y al-Amm and Al-Ayam are privately owned and popular throughout the nation. There are also several daily local papers, including Al-Khartoum in the north region and the Juba Post in the south. Though the press enjoys more freedom than their partners in Sudanese media, the state still utilizes their control to influence what is published.

Internet usage is extremely limited throughout the country, but the penetration rate has increased significantly from nearly zero in 2000 to about 7% in 2007. Internet is largely regulated and provided by half-private half-state owned Sudatel. Cell phone technology has flourished under the investment of foreign companies. Kuwait MTC is the country's largest provider, with South Africa MTN and Sudatel.

Overall, Sudan's media system ownership is somewhat diverse. ISP ownership is not diverse, being solely provided by Sudatel which has government investments. Print media ownership is diverse. Restrictions have been loosened over the last 19 years with the emergence of several private papers alongside state media, but these are still kept in check by government sources. Cell phone companies operating in the region are largely foreign, but very diverse. The state only controls a small piece of the cell phone market. Radio is diverse, through both private music stations operating alongside state stations and opposition parties from the south broadcasting pirate signals countrywide. Though local television is completely state-owned, ownership is now diverse with the popularized use of satellite TV which circumvents this barrier.

IRAQ - MEDIA PROFILE

Iraqi media organizations have been constantly changing since the overthrow of Saddam Hussein and the following U.S. occupation. Near the end of Hussein's regime, media was tightly controlled and regulated with a small selection of media available to the Iraqi people. With the regime now toppled, a series of independent media outlets, both foreign and domestic, have set up shop.

The TV stations initially established by the U.S. government are now part of the Iraqi Public Broadcasting Service (IPBS), which funds state media operations. Iraq's main station is Al-Iraqiya, which is government owned and publically funded. Privately owned stations have also moved in to compete under the new Iraqi establishment. Dubai based Al-Sharqiya broadcasts through local stations and via satellite. Channels from the autonomous territories of Kurdistan are also received throughout the country. Satellite TV is watched by a majority of Iraqi viewers, allowing them to access Arab stations such as Al-Jazeera and western stations such as the BBC.

The IPBS also maintains several radio stations, including Republic of Iraq Radio and Radio Basra. More important, however, is the emergence of local private radio stations. Voice of Iraq broadcasts over AM frequencies, while Hot FM and Radio Dilja provide talk shows and music to Baghdad residents over high-quality FM frequencies. Foreign broadcasters are also looking to stake a claim in the Iraqi market, including the BBC and Paris-based Radio Monte Carlo, ensuring the eventual presence of foreign capital.

A variety of publications have surfaced since the fall of Hussein. Al-Sabah is the state-run publication sponsored by the Iraqi Media Network. Aside from this, however, there are numerous publications operating independently of the state, including some foreign investment. Based in London, Al-Zaman is printed in major cities with English and Arabic sections. There are also local daily publications, including Al-Mada and Al-Mashriq in Baghdad and Al-Manarah in Basra.

Internet usage is severely limited in Iraq. There is only a 0.1% penetration rate in the country. However, usage is on the rise due to increased satellite broadband access and Internet cafés. Cell phone access was devastated by the war, but is now being rebuilt under the investment of various foreign companies. The country has been divided into three equal parts for service, distributed to Kurdish group Asia Cell, Egypt's Orascom, and Kuwait MTC.

Overall, the new Iraqi media ownership pattern is very diverse. As it is still under development after the war, data on ISP diversity is still insufficient to judge. Print media ownership is very diverse, with both state-owned and private papers in publication in the cities. Cell phone provider ownership is diverse with a multitude of foreign companies prepared to invest. However, there is no word of a local operator as of yet. Radio station ownership is also diverse. Though the state still maintains its prominent stations, new private entertainment stations have emerged. Television station ownership is diverse as well. The state operates the large stations locally, but international stations are becoming readily available through satellite television.

UZBEKISTAN - MEDIA PROFILE

Despite a constitutional ban on censorship, the Uzbeki-stani government continues to maintain tight control over the country's media. Many have criticized the government for being eager to silence opposition to its views. Self-censorship is a common practice; a law issued in 2007 holds media organizations accountable for their view and its effect upon broadcast. Regardless of government control, private endeavors still manage to make their way in the country.

The largest organization in Uzbekistani media is the state-operated National Television and Radio Company of Uzbekistan (NTRC), which operates the two major TV and radio networks. Alongside the NTRC TV channels, there are various privately owned stations that operate locally in their respective regions. These include MTRK in Andijan, Bagdad TV in Fergana and Bekabad TV in Tashkent. Foreign channels are also available to viewers in addition to the local stations.

The NTRC holds dominance over national radio as well, operating a variety of channels including youth-oriented Yoshlar. Aside from the national channels, private stations operate in local regions. Some of these include Radio Grand, the first private radio station in Tashkent, and Radio Sezam FM which operates in the Syrdarya region. Though privately owned, they are not nearly as influential as the NTRC. Acknowledging the government supervision, news programs continue to be self-censored to maintain govern-ment views.

Like other forms of media in Uzbekistan, the press is largely controlled by the government. In some cases, federals own publications and in others they endorse private agencies with pro-government agendas. The state prints a number of dailies, including Khalq Sozi and Ozbekistan Ozovi. They also print Russian-language dailies such as Narodnoye Slovo and

Pravda Vostoka. Fidokor, though not owned by the state, is supported publically because of its pro-government perspective. Self-censorship is a widely-used practice; the Committee to Protect Journalists reports that many Uzbekistani citizens rely on foreign news sources such as the BBC for their news. These channels are available on the widely-accessible national cable TV networks.

Internet has struggled to become established in the country, but Internet penetration has increased significantly in the last 7 years by 6.6%. This growth comes largely from the government's decision to prioritize ICT in the national budget and a $30 million loan from the United States. Cell phone service is dominated by large Russian providers due to dependency on Russian fiber-optics. Due to prioritization of ICT development by the government however, cell phone markets will become competitive in a relatively short amount of time.

Overall, Uzbekistan's media diversity pattern is not diverse. There is not enough information to determine the diversity of ISP ownership because of its limited penetration. The print media system is not diverse either. If publications are not produced by the government directly, the private companies are mostly coerced to be pro-govern-ment. The cell phone market is not diverse. A majority of providers are Russia-based and will continue to be so until Uzbekistan is able to free their fiber-optic connections to Russian hubs. Radio network ownership is diverse with state radio and local private radio co-existing. However, state radio is most likely much more influential than local private stations which only provide to limited areas. The television system is diverse, mainly due to the usage of satellite TV to receive international channels. Aside from these however, channels provided locally are all state-owned.

8

Structural Obstacles in Islamic Media

INTRODUCTION

Since the advent of Islam, as the final and all-compass-sing Message to mankind up to the moment, its adversaries left no opportunity to thwart it and curb its followers. Right from day one, they did their level best to kill it in the bud using different ways.

With the pro-reform factions' victory to elect Mohammad Khatami as the new president in 1997, the civil society debate has also gained considerable currency in Iranian politics and intellectual discourse. In addition to his institutional support, other activists and intellectuals have also contributed to the clarification of civil society objectives in Iran. The present work refers to media duties and responsibilities in parts as follows:

IN RELATION TO PEOPLE

1. Being consonance and companion with the masses,
2. Fulfill and perform on the basis of people's will,
3. Posit the media in the people's route,
4. Introducing the plebs and unanimous public instead of concentrating on high officials and authorities,
5. Being at the service of the oppressed people of the world

6. Play the leadership role for people,
7. Enlighten them,
8. Work on their heart,
9. Pay attention to youth cultivation and training,
10. Do your job in order to ascribe human up growth,
11. Pay attention for training thoughtful and fruitful man,
12. Encouraging ingenious persons,
13. Understanding people's real language and knowing them as they are,
14. Realizing all strata in Training honourable style of living to people,
15. Giving hope to people,
16. Avoiding from deceiving and fooling people by deviated banners in press,
17. Strengthening people's morale,
18. Recanting to own faults,
19. Honesty in delivering news and messages,
20. Entering people to political stage and sensitizing them toward their destiny,
21. Propelling people toward knowledge and literature instead of corruption,
22. Perform authentic and genuine training
23. Improving self-believing and self-confidence
24. Improving political growth of the youth
25. Avoiding from narcotizing people, but attempt to awake them
26. Avoiding from broadcasting conspirators and deviants
27. Not to cast only the faults but also the successes
28. Not to include all the opponents as enemies except those like "Saddam".

IN RELATION TO VALUES AND ISLAM

1. Developing martyrdom thinking,
2. Restraining from deviation in a proper manner,
3. Introducing Islam properly,

4. Avoiding from violence and repress,
5. Compensation of 50 years of ruin and corruption in Pahlavi period (Shah and his father),
6. Not dragging youth toward corruption and immorality
7. Restraining from misguiding and vulgar Arts,
8. Not pursuing deviant's satisfaction, but trying to correct them,
9. Not to gather more audiences through exciting and luscious pictures,
10. Not to situate yourself as a standard media. The standard of our deeds is about Allah,
11. Checking the movies by experts before broadcasting them,
12. Avoiding indifference toward damages,
13. Purgation of Broadcasting from absurd.

IN RELATION TO POLITICS AND POLITY

1. Informing people all the problems and issues while preserving calm and peace,
2. Being at the service of the nation and Islamic system,
3. Mobilizing people for securing nation independence and freedom,
4. Restraining from schism and disparity,
5. Expressing and reflecting Islamic Republic's services and success,
6. Avoiding underestimation of Republic's services,
7. Defending the Islamic system,
8. Reflecting the revolution adventures to the outsiders
9. Informing the oppressed people of the world,
10. Illuminating the governments' deeds in depriving people,
11. Delineating people's friends from the enemies,
12. Avoiding from casting those issues harmful to unity and Islam,
13. Avoiding from scepticizing world toward Islamic Republic,

14. Beware not to help enemies direct or indirect,
15. Beware of message sensitivity, regarding its social, economic and political effects,
16. Disclosing the issues and problems to the extent not being harmful to the system,
17. Giving up the controversies harmful for unity,
18. Criticizing without any prejudice,
19. Not to grandiose the neglect problems,
20. Casting the problems with compassion like a preceptor.

IN RELATION TO ENEMIES

1. Securing freedom from East and West powers
2. Informing people about dangers and threats, such as nuclear weapons
3. Awakening world in order to arise against super-power's warmonger
4. Not broadcasting colonialist movies
5. Leading pessimism, malignancy and defamation toward superpowers
6. Reacting against enemies' media when trumping up about Islamic Republic.

ISLAMIC MEDIA AND PRESS

Imam Khomeini has proposed is far different from western pattern in general. In his approach, the non-Islamic media has its own necessities and exigencies and the same with Islamic media. That's why he has repeatedly emphasized that the press in Islamic country should be Islamic too. Moreover our standard to realize and evaluate a country as Islamic is its media and press.

Radio and TV are more than an entertainment service. They should do their task in role of a preceptor for people. So that entertainment and recreation should be set up in such a way that can help reaching the educational goals.

The presses are not legitimate to deviate from Islamic

orders for increasing their circulation. The journalists should always regard Allah's satisfaction instead of mere people in their career. They should criticize the society just for promotion of it and taking the evils from it. In fact the media manner and style of broadcasting and informing should be in a peaceful discourse context and away from violence and propagation. In his view, the journalists are society's advisors.

To him the media is responsible to train and promote people including the masses and the officials. This role is comparable to mortire act and even has been evaluated more. The main audiences of media are youth. The media should regard this stratum more than the others in their planning.

THE ENVIRONMENT

Part of the lectures was done in the first period just after the victory of revolution in 1979. In this period so many presses as dependents and organs of variety of left and right political groups who had the opportunity of using the free condition of this period, aroused and anarchistically misused this condition. The silence and repressiveness and censorship of the Shah's regime were one of the causes of this behaviour. The other part of the lectures was presented in the period of Iran-Iraq war. Under the impact of this condition we can easily observe a strong emphasis on unity and governmental strength.

The image of media personnel and organization in Imam Khomeini's view is the one has experienced long enough to be influenced in Shah's western and formal modernization. Although some of the key officials of the media were fired, but the main body of major remained.

His expressions and words about media are completely frank. He didn't want to speak in order to satisfy anybody, so the differences between Islam and western democracy are observable in the code of ethics he proposed. In other words when he spoke about media, there were no attempt to interpret Islam on the basis of western democratic exigencies.

PRESS STRUCTURAL OBSTACLES

Despite the plenty of Imam Khomeini's impact on many institutions and procedures after the Islamic Revolution, it is hard to believe the way media especially the press are going, is almost in the same direction as he has proposed. In order to figure out the press problems in Iran, we can refer to the following points:

1. They have been party influenced by Islamic and revolutionary values, but the current situation doesn't satisfy those in favour of Islamic revolution. There are still many problems in press in which have made all groups and political parties to think about a solution.
2. Despite Imam Khomeini's stress on being frank with people and be aware of deceiving people, one can observe a plenty of banners in press each trying to get its own political benefits from what is going on in the country.
3. There are many social, cultural, political, and economical problems in Iranian society in which deserve scholars' attention, but the press does not pay attention to them. Instead they pay attention to those problems regarding its effect on their own political group or party. Of course there are many journalists free of these disturbing tendencies, but their task in order to do their job well, would not be welcomed or highlighted in the press.
4. That's why the press focuses on issues politically. They propose it when they need and put it aside when they get what they were really fighting for it or threaded.
5. The unity of the society and the nations benefits are almost the last priority in press. Every newspaper acts just as the main standard of the nations benefit.
6. As Imam Khomeini emphasized that an Islamic country's press should be Islamic too. They are expected to promote the Islamic style of life in the society. But if evaluate them on this standard, we could obviously observe the vice versa trends in them. Leaving many of them to afford on their own has made the press to pay attention those issues in which would increase their circulation.

7. Both pro and cons regarding president Khatami, present a terrible image of the society because of reflecting just the weaknesses and evils of the other side. They almost do this with the world too. So the current and future society inside the nation and outside of it has been horrified through press in Iranians images.

What has restrained press from getting closer to apply these codes of ethics is structural. The Iranian press has been institutionalized in such an environment and condition that make them to be in this position. This is not to say that the press manner and behaviour has not changed since the Revolution, but it is rather saying that the press has still so many structural obstacles to be set up in Islamic position. In order to explain these obstacles we need to know the environment and conditions in which the press have grown and institutionalized within it.

1. Arise of the press in Iran was based on a kind of imitation to western pattern of journalism. The first Iranian newspaper was published about 170 years ago by Mirza Saleh Shirazi. He named it "Kaqaz Akhbar", that is word by word translation of the phrase "newspaper". This kind of confrontation to the press could be easily understood in the overall approach of Iranian society to western institutions and culture. The same similarization that happened in variety of institutions can be observed in press too.
2. The entrance of the press in Iran didn't rely on native and traditional patterns and values. It didn't make the native and traditional intellectuals such as "Rohaniat" whom are the religious leaders and advisors of Moslem society to be active on it and drag the code of ethics in journalism out of Islam and Iranian culture. In other words, there were rare attempts to define journalism on Islamic and Iranian morality and culture. This type of indifference in relation to press can be observed in other areas of institutionalization especially in art discipline as well.
3. Iranian kingdom regimes had the chance to be tyrannical

and repressive regarding geographical and political conditions and environment. That's why Iranians have always been pessimistic toward government and officials. In such conditions, the presses have a tendency to admire the government uncritically when they are pros and a tendency to be pessimistic extremely when they are cons. The former will prepare more financial aids from government and the latter will increase audiences and also being at the risk of governmental harassment.

SUSTAINABLE DEVELOPMENT OF ISLAMIC MEDIA

Sustainable development theory is part of international studies carried out after the Second World War and coincided with the establishment of the United Nations (1945). The UN named 1960s as the "decade of development" to encourage the then newly established countries and other nations to improve their socio-economic status. Gradually, the role of communication technologies became more important. The fulfillment of human needs while maintaining the quality of the social life made it urgent to be update about the changes. Economy should meet the needs of the present generation and oversee the future generations' potentials for their needs. Therefore, the role of new-tech communication systems in sustainable development remained as a challenge for all the nations, even in the 21st century.

Communication technologies boost the process of development. Existing competitive markets necessitate the knowledge that is in the hands of the developed countries with high-tech communication systems. In this article, we would briefly look at the role of Islamic mass communication systems in the prosperity of Muslim nations.

Sustainable development depends on the welfare as the corner stone of citizens' willingness to participate in the plans of their governments. However, it does not focus only on economy. Relative policies encompass some general areas of economy, society and communication.

ECONOMY

Economic and social challenges may create opportunities for development. Here we have an ambiguous concept, and a wide array of views to fall under. The concept includes sustainable and unsustainable development if we divide the developed and developing nations into northern and southern countries respectively.

Sustainability in economy is to continue to function properly without causing irreversible damage to the planet's ecosystems. This may involve providing the current needs of society while ensuring the welfare of future generations. It should minimize poverty, save the ecosystems, increase the value of a currency and reduce inflation.

Some Islamic nations, mostly in the Middle East are naturally gifted with considerable crude oil resources, so we can take oil industry, as an example, to define Islamic nations' share of natural resources; how they are limited to it and how it pushes them toward losing their opportunities of investing in other resources.

Such nations are suffering from lingering problems both economically and socially, though they are rich in natural resources and can spend as much as they extract the crude oil. The growth of GDP is necessary for sustainable development but it is not necessarily interpreted as the development itself.

The oil-oriented economy is different from the service-oriented one. The first one experiences higher risks while the latter carries on healthier. That is why oil production cannot compete with some international leading car manufacturers. Tourism is another good example of such potentials to create job opportunities, where private sector can play a major role in this area. So far, just a few Muslim countries have been active in this regard.

SOCIETY

If the growth process continues, in the long term we will see the development in many aspects of social life. In "unsustainable situations", the nature's resources are used up faster than it can be replenished. Therefore, it requires that people only use nature's resources in a way that be replaced naturally. Theoretically, it is impossible at the present speed of destruction. The long-term result would be the disappearing local environments that are no longer able to sustain human populations to any degree. Such degradation on a global scale could imply destruction for civilization.

NEW-TECH COMMUNICATION

Both society and economy play parallel roles in the healthy growth and development of the country. Is there any need for persuading the nation to save the world? Who can take this heavy role? The answer is mass communication systems.

Invention of radio, before the Second World War, and television after that horrible period of history, influenced the world more than any other agents of communication did. The newly born media had the power to cultivate decisions of the owners. Nazism, for instance, exploited the communication instruments of 1930s to declare war against humanity. The emergence of green NGOs and other humanitarian communities, mostly on the cyber space, has gathered a huge power from around the world in favor of peace and human rights. The mysterious media really frames the audiences' understanding of the place they live in. One can use the media for the sake of peace and prosperity of all the humanity or vise versa.

Muslim nations share the same Islamic rules and teachings about the economy. Media can work on this aspect and help the Islamic governments mobilize the nation to try for unity and prosperity of the entire Muslim nation in a greater scale. The media can help through informing, agenda setting, priming and framing those visions of the Islamic governments for Muslim NGOs and communities.

Continuous economic growth is necessary to create sustainable development. If we reach this point, we would find the way to make dreams of social development come true. Participating media educates a participating nation with democracy. Doing well in just one aspect of growth and leaving the rest untouched will not end in development; it just makes holes in the body of the economy. We should consider both growth and social development at the same time with the same pace. If governments pay no attention to welfare, education, health and happiness of their people and just concentrate on the growth, they will lose the human resources to carry out their plans.

We live in the age of information, and we are here to win or lose the opportunities. Those who invest in new-tech communications would control the market and conduct the business, but those who do not would get to anywhere. If Muslim nations continue on a knowledge-based growth, attracting foreign investment, they can help their dreams come true. It also depends on a variety of factors, namely social, economic and political stability.

Finally, it is with the combination of all the three elements of society, economy and mass media that a prosperous and participative Muslim nation can live happily and save the natural resources for the next generation on the green planet earth. Islamic media needs to raise standards.

9

The Role of Islamic Media

Media in the Islamic World have to play a better and more effective role in introducing the religion of Islam and in shedding more light on its teachings and values; it is necessary that it stands against the attacks targeting Islam and the attempts to distort its image, said Hassan al-Lawzi, Minister of Information in a speech.

In his speech at the opening of the symposium entitled "Islamic Press and Horizons of Media Work," al-Lawzi talked about the Islamic channel al-Eman that Yemen is to launch in a few months, which hopes to cope with the role media needs to have regarding Islam's morals and values. "The main goals of al-Eman Channel are to spread and raise awareness about the Islamic religion in what regards faith and legislation, and also to discuss how Islamic teachings are actually away from extremism and fanaticism," elucidated al-Lawzi. Al-Lawzi explained that the channel will work to present Islam as a religion of peace, and to show Islamic culture and heritage in its strengths to create an intellectual, cultural development guarded with faith.

The Minister of Information also considered the challenges that media in the Arab and Islamic World have to face in relation to other media. However he stated that "no matter how dangerous and influential other media can be, the goals can be reached once a vacant space to break in is found." Facing these challenges and overcoming them can only come from protection via presenting real and correct knowledge unleash responsible freedom, added al-Lawzi.

Al-Lawzi finally said that there is a great deal of potential among individuals in the Arab World and it is their talent that will enable them to play an important role in reflecting their identity and culture.

Judge Hamood al-Hitar, Minister of Guidance and Islamic Affairs, stressed the need to renew the religious discourse to meet the characteristics of today's era as well as today's technical revolution. Al-Hitar spoke about the great need of specialized media, comparing it to a preacher in the present calling on all Arab media to do their duty against the attacks on Islam and the distortion of this religion in Western media. "It is in the duty of all Islamic and Arab media to present and show the real image of Islam as a religion of peace and cultural tolerance," said al-Hitar.

Ahmed Abdul-Rahman al-Soyan, head of the Islamic Media Union and chief editor of the al-Montda magazine of Kingdom of Saudi Arabia, as well as organizer of this symposium said that the union is not a political or sectarian gathering but rather is an objective frame aiming at improving the profession of the press without marginalizing any parties.

Al-Soyan assured that the union is a way to cooperate with all sorts of publications and media ministries for the purpose of fruitful complementation.

Al-Soyan then called on all media to play a role that can enhance unity, which can contribute to civilization's renaissance avoiding fanaticism, avoiding the spread of sectarian or racial conflicts. "The union aims through organizing this symposium to take more care of the field of media that is seen as a means for breeding, raising awareness, education, domination and entertainment, and it also hopes to renew and advance media in general terms," said al-Soyan.

Many working papers were presented in the event. Ibrahim al-Mosri, chief editor of the Lebanese newspaper al-Aman, spoke about principles of freedom calling for respect of social and political principles. Al-Mosri said that with freedom should come with responsibility, but absolute freedom can result in chaos. He then expressed his fear for print media whose status is threatened by other sorts of media. He called for more focus to be given to Friday sermons, a sort of media that Islam has given greater importance.

Atef al-Jolani, chief editor of the al-Sabeel Newspaper from Jordan, spoke of the challenges that media encounter in the Arab World economically, administratively, technically and stylistically. He said that the present challenges should provoke us to improve the profession. Al-Jolani pointed out at the failure of Western media in Arabic in dealing with the Arab mentality and which Arab media has proved capable of dealing with, avoiding any invasion. He finally rejected the idea that one media outlet can exist on the expense of another, and assured that all media outlets of all sort can co-exist

R'aft Marwa, chief editor of the Islamic Palestine Magazine, based in Syria, talked about the reality of the media in the Arab World and its different schools. Marwa then talked about the key role of the media and the nature of the relationship between citizenry and media in Arab countries. Marwa finally called for developing and bettering legislations concerning media to respond to the developments of today's world and to allow for a wider freedom. Attendees then enriched the discussion with many views and debates on media, Islamic press and its role.

MEDIA AS THE VEHICLES FOR TERRORIST AGENDAS

In the age of information we know that we cannot do without information just as much as the media is aware of the power it has on the people. Winning over the mass media or influencing it has become a key motive for not only politicians but terrorists as well. It thus necessitates a closer examination of how far media has helped to provide "respectability" and a platform to argue in favor of their crimes.

Media today can add color to stories and spin them around to suit their agenda. They will provide information that they wish to highlight & hide vital information which they feel is not necessary for public attention. Yet, essentially we can but wonder whether their reporting is honest and their journalists are ethical.

Coming to the question of how far the media is independent and how far are journalists independent we can determine by finding out who owns the mass media - obviously the rich & powerful - those who influence society? So long as mass media is owned by a handful of rich and powerful people we cannot accept that media today is independent and without bias just as much as it would be hard to accept that journalists have the freedom to write the truth as how they see it - in truth what these journalists write if they want to keep their jobs is what their owners wish them to write. Naturally, the owners will push for ideas that benefit the system they belong to. A perfect example was the manner in which a steady flow of media propaganda was dedicated to establishing that Iraq did have weapons of mass destruction and created a scenario amongst the western world that they were minutes away from being fired upon. That the messages relayed by different media outlets on the same subjects will serve to prove that media owners will do what it takes to back the system they come from. Yet there have been instances where media employees have prevented bias and racism as seen in the pull out of a page promoting anti-Muslim in the Daily Star (2006) There are likely to be other such examples but they are few and far between.

JOURNALISTIC CULTURES AND OBJECTIVE JOURNALISM

The journalistic cultures from country to country vary. BBC, CNN, Al-Jazeera, Fox News etc compete with each other to report what they believe is the truth. Where BBC maintains its classic journalism, CNN has varied to meet the changes of the day and much of the changes can be seen when viewing both these channels. With events taking place and changing in quick succession many channels find little room for actual research as issues converge in to plenty of cross-theories. Global satellite television channels like CNN, BBC, Al-Jazeera provide news globally & are viewed by millions of people all over the world. But can we really ascertain that the reporting styles of the first two channels in particular are "objective" and shows respect for both sides of the conflict? or do their reports not enhance the clash further by contributing theories and issues that are not even related to the main issue? Have their reporting not affected negatively towards anti-Islamic sentiment in the West?

How far have they have succeeded in creating a world with better understanding - a world that unites the cultures of the West and East, that strengthens national governments and a truth that is not one sided has been a matter of much debate.

It is often alleged that mass media plays into the hands of terrorists. The media cannot satisfy all the public - there are many who feel that writing on the suicide attacks of terrorists serves to only meet terrorist agendas and do very little for the people reading or listening to the news. The debate naturally revolves around how to inform the public about terrorist acts.

Given a scenario where media refuses to publish or highlight terrorist attacks we can perhaps predict that the terrorists would fail to affect the morale of the people. Let us take the example of 9/11 - how many in the US would have known of the event if it had not been relayed on national television? The emotional reaction of the people having seen & repeatedly made to view the attack has become embedded in their minds and fear that the media instilled upon the people remains to this very day. If we travel back in time we can recall how the US media went over and over every detail of the event nonstop through weeks. Even the exact death toll has remained a speculation. In any case the people have responded favorably to the US Govt's overreactions and the people of the US think that Iraq & Afghanistan & possibly Iran are their sworn enemies. This does no one really any good & leaves a nation isolated from the truth.

We must accept that the 9/11 attack brought about a significant change in the global view on terrorism. The entire

US media even the global broadcasters like CNN are committed to the "USA Patriotic Act" giving the CIA & FBI important tools to watch over citizens. For its part the Pentagon has taken measures to have journalists accredited to cover war zones but restricted to areas demarcated by the US Govt, which also denied interviews of military personnel without escort & violations of these US rules meant detention, arrest, revocation of press credentials & expulsion from the battlefield - not much freedom of expression & what's more an opinion poll conducted after the Gulf War found that 68% of the public favored military control of news while a further 17% suggested greater control.

The BBC in contrast was merely sent an editorial guideline to their staff requesting that they carefully pick their words especially those that carries emotional attachments. However during the IRA attacks the British Government was quick to ensure that the Government's stand was effectively relayed across media though the West are often critical of how conflict is covered in other countries.

The Bush administration has been effective in unnecessarily raising the terror threat level to argue their case in Iraq & Afghanistan & sideline opposition for occasions when military attacks have resulted in mere civilian casualties in those countries. Other than reporting that Iraqi & Afghan leaders have deplored the actions of the US military on its civilians these satellite channels have refrained from actually questioning US attacks & carefully leaving out the emotional aspect that arises from the death of innocent children by the US air attacks. What the Bush administration & the media doesn't realize is that the American people are becoming alienated from what is really happening & are being blinded by a false sense of alarm that the enemies are out there waiting to attack Americans. The negative side to this is that once the truth sets in the American citizens are unlikely to feel scared - the news coverage often goes to hysterical proportions in their relaying but it didn't scare more than half of the residents from vacating Galveston despite the issuing of "death" when hurricane Ike made landfall.

Taking to consideration the 9/11 attack it was natural for news channels to provide "spot news" but now 8 years on the coverage needs to see some sort of balance. Almost three quarters of the US public supported the US invasion of Iraq & the media played an integral role in this consensus.

The Bush administration was able to mesmerize the entire country into following his "war on terror" campaign yet years on Americans are beginning to realize that there is something more to the "war" than what their President has admitted which necessitates the American media to make a shift in their pro-patriotic journalist agenda. The US armed forces - the men & women who return from Iraq are more disillusioned than they went in - plagued by the shrieks of fright many of them cannot comprehend the orders of their superiors of shooting people who are not even in armed attire on the premise that they are the "enemy" - many of these troops have even killed children & now they cannot sleep at night. Many of these troops do not know who the Al Qaeda is - who the Taliban are.

The news media has provided a perfect vehicle for terrorists to transmit their message & now the terrorists have learnt to manipulate the media as well. Terrorists themselves have become media savvy & have access to the latest technology, use latest digital video cameras & quick to release video CDs showing horrific images. There is no denying that the US state & US media have an influence on the world & sways opinions often in favor of the US or Western interests. This doesn't help to dissociate the journalists who are accused of being scourge of the truth.

The journalist's reporting terrorism has many thoughts to consider. Should terrorists be accepted as those opposing peace making it easy to report everything negatively about these terrorists or do journalists strike a chord of impartiality by giving a voice to the woes of the terrorists & why they entered terrorism but more importantly how must they keep to the editorial guidelines given - this provides them little freedom to actually write what they honestly feel about the subject.

The ownerships of media agencies play an integral role in what people are offered as newsworthy. Owners biased towards a particular political party will take pains to highlight the mistakes of its opponent. In India we can see how pro-Hindu media channels refuses to acknowledge mobilized violence.

The damaging affects of media in the climate of terror is largely since most media channels join a chorus which leads the public to assume what the media relays is correct. The same can be said of the various human rights organization which also chants similar tunes so that many tend to believe their version of human rights violations. Seeking a challenge to media coverage is the internet & radio channels but they have only succeeded in attracting the few who are able to balance the versions & arrive at a structured conclusion & not swayed by believing all that the media projects.

MEDIA IN ASIA

Countries of Asia are today experiencing a plethora of issues related to intercommunal violence, revolutionary insurgencies, separatist movements, terrorism & a volatile financial climate. Most often the media forgets its larger role of being an agent of stability, an agent to monitor Governments & an agent to serve the masses. The electronic media has depicted many horrifying tragedies – the earthquakes, the tsunami, the attack on the World Trade Center, the felling of the Bamyan Buddhas in Afghanistan & more recently to the destruction of the Marriot Hotel in Pakistan...all these events have horrified the viewers.

The media's ability to reach out to people provides the link that terrorists seek in the publicity for their atrocities. Terrorists have been successful in steering media, political debates & promoting their thoughts on public platforms & arguing their case internationally. This has to a great extent left many feeling "empathetic" towards terrorists since the media has provided the stage for the terrorists to drive their case through men & women eloquent enough to support them. Thus we can begin to understand how these violent movements have gained political power over the years - their stooges have done an excellent job & media has helped to generate a sympathy wave where Governments are seen as the enemies & not the terrorists. Governments are not denied media coverage but their manner of reaching out to the public certainly lacks the finesse that the "envoys" of terrorists are able to convey.

WHAT TERRORISTS ASPIRE?

The aim of terrorists in carrying out their heinous attacks is to get attention, thereby get recognition & aspire to achieve legitimacy for their actions. The media provides the platform to achieve these three objectives. Thus a triangle of communication is built - the terrorists, the media & the political establishments. The manner in which terrorists subtly align with the media helps them to come close to the democratic process & spearhead their motives.

The television has become the principal source or mode of information of millions the world over. The visibility factor encourages terrorists to choose locations that have relevance & significance & will guarantee prime time coverage. The 9/11 attacks provided just that & the TV channels were engaged in a frenzy to cover live pictures & commentaries of the tragedy that took place. With the limitation on time the TV channels often limit themselves to typical phrases which are repeated by other channels thus creating a synthesis in the thought processes of the viewers. Their competitive edge is provided in the manner in which they illuminate the simplest of stories & dramatize it using various techniques in audio-visual capabilities. Stories that win the media wars are those that are high in intensity, spectacular for the eyes & dictate to our emotions. This needless to say provides a dangerous pattern for it takes away the element of fact. When violence is highlighted in such manner it instills fear even among those who are unlikely to really be exposed to such events.

The media's presentation of terrorism should be one that rejects violence, empathize with the victims & their families & essentially seek to demystify the assassins. Instead what most media channels are guilty of is striking a balance between murderers & the victims which borders on justifying & accepting the terrorists as political participants with legitimate rights. This then provides the vehicle for the pro-terrorist "intelligentsia" to justify the terrorist's case further through live debates, open forums & discussions etc thus indirectly providing a very stable backstage towards what the terrorists are actually striving to achieve.

The debate over how far media & terrorism are mutually dependable has been discussed at various forums. When terrorists strike they may not want to come across the media but they do want to show off their power & the media provides this capacity & then the brief synopsis of the media's introduction of who caused the carnage suffices to provide their "brand" name across to the world at large. The terrorists even provide leakages to media that will provide them significant air time so as to further accentuate their cause.

The media has taken great pains to provide negative media coverage of those terrorist leaders that cover the interest of their respective Governments - Osama is a hated man but most of the public don't really know why he should be hated so. We were never told why the hijackers did what they did, for what they were fighting but that is because the Al Qaeda attack on the US resulted in the entire US & Western media channels taking on an anti-Al Qaeda stand which in view of its partiality has translated into an anti-Islam & anti-Muslim campaign. Similarly, the media has painted Milosevic as a murderer but that seems not the true story....our thoughts have been groomed to think in a particular fashion because of the coverage given by the media & that can be at times dangerous & bring dangerous results. The UN sessions have led to many students protesting Iran's presence - let the media have some of these students even show where Iran is located & vocalize why they are against Iran without singing the same human rights violations etc themes that are being relayed across the media.

The Western media has been particularly harsh on the Al Qaeda - it may not be without reasons but if this is the case then all terrorist outfits must be treated in similar light & all terrorists should be given the same mileage on media. This would then lead to the formation of other satellite channels which will provide easy access to networks like the Al Qaeda to gain publicity favorable to their cause so much so to even provide exclusive interviews. The Al-Jazeera channel did provide an impetus from the western media coverage the world had thus far being used to & tipped the coverage to show the other side of the American version of Afghanistan so much so that it resulted in the US "mistakenly" bombing Al-Jazeera headquarters in Kabul.

But media channels however need to realize is that terrorists are terrorists & should be called so - they cannot become "insurgents" with a "cause". Favorable media coverage towards these terrorist movements should not qualify terrorists to feel that they have a right to engage in violence.

The public should not have to juggle the Western media vs. Anti-Western media concept obviously because the two have different editorial processes. While the Western media takes an anti-Iraq, anti-Iran, anti-Afghanistan stand the opposing channels will place insurgent Iraqi's favorably & create a hostile tone towards Americans & the Allied Forces. Where does this lead the public - those of us who rely on media to provide "correct" information & not "information" they deem "correct".

THE POWER OF THE INTERNET

With terrorists dependent on media attention they spend considerable time & energy to feed channels who would promote their "cause" with a steady flow of exclusive footage - these provide the media channels their competitive edge & thus builds an indirect relationship with a terrorist movement - is it ethical? The internet provides a direct means to launch terrorist programs & affords the newest strategy for terrorists. Besides it has become a safer mode of communication. Thus we see the entry of "cyber terrorism" with the terrorists having direct control of what they say & how they say it.

Of course, let us not confuse terrorist media with media

that may indirectly prop up terrorist agenda. Terrorist media is media funded & controlled by a known terrorist organization – al Manar a television station owned & operated by Hezbollah based in Lebanon. This television station is said to use its channel to recruit suicide bombers & incite violence. Inciting violence overshadows any right for "Freedom of Expression".

What are human rights – in its most basic form human rights should be availed for every individual irrespective of race, language, sex or religion? These "universal rights" came about following the atrocities of the Two World Wars. The years preceding the two major wars saw nations in conflict, nations against nations & the unleashing of terror. The media's role in this terror scenario is when they provide the platform to stage their acts of terror an oft quoted saying is "militants thrive on the oxygen of publicity".

It is advisable for media to resist glorifying terrorists & projecting them far above than what they deserve. In Sri Lanka we recently witnessed a private media channel relay first pictures of a supposed terrorist attack on a bus in Colombo – while an explosion did take place it was not before all the passengers had disembarked. Not a single passenger was hurt though viewers of this media channel would have thought otherwise in the light of the horrifying footage of men & women being rushed to hospital. An inquiry is presently being conducted to the reasons why this channel chose to do what they did but in reality it was a violation of the human rights of individuals depending on this channel for truthful information.

Terrorists use mass media for both tactical & strategic purposes. Tactical successes comes in the release of prisoners which heightens their publicity, kidnappings, bomb threats, hijacks & even nuclear threats, while the strategic terrorism would entail assassinations, bombings in public places etc. Some terrorists enjoy accepting responsibilities for terror acts they did not even commit while some enjoy the publicity of being accused of the act through media channels. The terrorists enjoy how they are able to get across to the viewers who watch aghast at the horror that these terrorists are capable of instilling.

Today we are experiencing terrorism that transcends borders & nations - incidents originating in one country terminate in another. There are even instances where a nation not involved makes demands on nations which cannot go unheeded. Governmental patronage of certain terrorist groups results in this scenario. A CIA report declares that 40% of all transnational terrorism occurred in Western Europe or North America & of that figure 44% involved the USA. This in turn leaves little doubt the role the US has in providing that "oxygen" to terrorist movements. There are countries that provide training ground for these groups. There are men who provide the arms. There are countries that manufacture these arms & sell to the very terrorists that their men go to fight with. There are countries that depend on the sale of arms that constitute a bulk of their country's income - have media channels exposed these home truths & what of the terrorists - should they be accepted on par with Governments that are elected?

10

Changing Realities of Islamic Media

Since 11/9 and through its exclusive live coverage of the wars in Afghanistan and Iraq, Al-Jazeera has gained worldwide popularity and credibility even among Western viewers. At present, it ranks next to world-class news organizations and plays an important role in shaping Arab public opinion. As a consequence, it has been the target both of the West's acerbic criticism and of restrictive measures on behalf of Arab regimes.

Launched in November 1996, Al-Jazeera has been the culmination of Qatar's democratization process. The Qatari Emir, Sheikh Hamad bin Khalifa al-Thani, allocated to the station approximately $140 million for its first five years of broadcasting, guaranteeing editorial independence and unbiased information. Al-Jazeera succeeded the BBC World Service Arabic television, a Saudi Orbit Communications joint venture with BBC, when in April 1996 the latter was forced to close down after broadcasting a documentary on government execution policies in the Saudi Kingdom and lending voice to Saudi political dissidents.

Apart from being the first 24-hour Arab satellite news network, Al-Jazeera has turned the tables on state-controlled Arab media. Through its tackling of controversial issues and by leveling criticism at both religious and political officials, it has offered its audience alternative news reporting and challenged the official pro-governmental Arab version of events. Moreover, it was the first to conduct open debates, where dissidents and citizens from across the political spectrum express their opinions freely. Most importantly, it seems to be in touch with the "Arab street" and play a role in shaping Arab public opinion. Al-Jazeera achieved where the privately owned Saudi and Lebanese networks, launched by way of counter weighing governmental monopoly on television, had failed, that is to detach them-selves from the ruling elites and become truly independent.

The revolution that Al-Jazeera brought about in Arab mass communication became a double-edged sword for the network. Even though it has gained credibility and wide popularity among Arab viewers, it has incurred the wrath of many Arab governments and has often been accused of partiality and lack of objectivity. The criticism, coming even from guests in its programs, concerns its indulgent stance towards the Qatari government. At the GCC Summit of October 2002 the Gulf States considered taking measures against the network, which had reportedly referred to the Gulf regimes in an offensive manner. Two years later, in August 2004, the Iraqi interim government sealed the network's bureau in Baghdad on the grounds that its footage incited violence. In both cases the International Press Institute stepped in to ask for a withdrawal of the bans.

Moreover, reporters and broadcasters have been banned on occasion from Egypt, Kuwait, Jordan, Saudi Arabia and the Palestinian authority and the network's offices were shut down in Kuwait and Jordan. Algeria cut the signal when the network attempted to delve deeper into the civil war. Egypt's state media launched an anti Al-Jazeera campaign, while Tunisia, Morocco and Libya recalled their ambassadors from Qatar. For its part, the Saudi Kingdom, in an effort to acquire influence over the network, tried to reduce its ad revenues – a highly important source of income and, consequently, the vanguard of the network's independence – by urging Saudi companies to refrain from advertizing themselves on the channel.

Despite this restrictive action, its coverage of Operation Desert Fox in 1998 and of the second Palestinian Intifada in 2000 increased the network's stature among Arab audiences. Yet, the terrorist attacks of 9/11 were the turning point which lent Al-Jazeera the status of a globally renowned news network, in the same way that CNN met tremendous success during the 1991 Gulf War. The date of the US invasion of Taliban-controlled Afghanistan (October 7, 2001) is a landmark in the network's history, rendering it almost overnight a household name in the West. Al-Jazeera secured exclusive coverage of the war and broadcast exclusive videotaped messages from Osama Bin Laden. This practice has gained it labels such as "the mouthpiece of Bin Laden" or "Osama Television".

The Qatari-based network operates on the model of Western media, such as BBC and CNN, pursuing editorial impartiality and independence and becoming increasingly competitive. It is noteworthy that Al-Jazeera's staff consists of journalists previously employed, among others, in CNN, BBC and CNBC. What distinguishes Al-Jazeera from Western networks is the fact that it broadcasts Middle Eastern news from an Arab perspective. Its Muslim-centered news reporting has attracted more viewers, including many in Europe and the US who seek an alternative to the Western outlook. Indeed, according to Al-Jazeera, the number of European subscribers has doubled since the outbreak of the war in Iraq. As Al-Jazeera obtained exclusive footage from the theatre of the Afghanistan and the Iraq wars, many foreign networks (such as NBC, CBS, ABC News, Fox, French TV, the Economist, Time and the Daily Mail) tried to reach a deal with the Arab network concerning, among others, resource sharing or rebroadcasting of its crises coverage. Indeed, Al-Jazeera has signed a long-term agreement with CNN and has become a CNN World Report contributor. However, the live coverage of the wars in Afghanistan and Iraq and the broadcasting of al-Qaeda's statements have evoked the ire of the US government, which has accused the network of anti-American bias (due to its widespread use of phrases, such as "what the

US calls terrorism" referring to the 11/9 attacks or "the forces of occupation" concerning the American troops in Iraq). Washington has heavily criticized the network for airing scenes of war atrocities which are thought to be responsible for inciting insurgents to an escalation of violence.

In October 2001, Washington put pressure on the Qatari regime to impose restrictions on the satellite network. This action resulted once again in the intervention of the International Press Institute. In the same vein, in November 2005, a top-secret British government memo was leaked, according to which George W. Bush was considering bombing the Qatar headquarters of Al-Jazeera. These two incidents have raised speculations about whether the bombing of the network's offices in Kabul and Baghdad in 2002 and 2003 respectively were intentional or not. However, the network's motto is "the opinion and the other opinion" and therefore high-ranking officials, such as Condoleezza Rice, Donald Rumsfeld, Tony Blair, Colin Powell and Ariel Sharon, have been interviewed, contributing to the international credibility of the news organization. Thereby, Al-Jazeera has been characterized as the CNN of the Arab world. Apart from Al-Jazeera, there are also other news networks competing for a share of the Arabic-speaking audience. Al-Arabiya is a 24-hour news channel which was launched in March 2003 as a joint venture of Saudi-controlled pan-Arab satellite TV pioneer, Middle East Broadcasting Centre, Lebanon's Hariri Group and other investors from Saudi Arabia, Kuwait and the Gulf states.

The Dubai-based channel is becoming "the moderate alternative to Al-Jazeera" and it states that it is committed to objectivity. However, during the war in Iraq, al-Arabiya's coverage evoked Washington's irritation and, as a result, its coverage of the Iraq war was upheld for two weeks. Abu Dhabi TV, launched in 2000, follows in Al-Jazeera's footsteps as well. It is not a 24-hour news network but is still competing with Al-Jazeera and al-Arabiya in order to attract Arab viewers. The TV station has drawn attention due to its coverage of the Iraq War.

However, according to a poll conducted by the US State Department in seven Iraqi cities, it was found that during the US invasion, 37% chose al-Arabiya as their news source, Al-Jazeera followed with 26%, while the US-run Iraqi Media Network gathered only 12%. Despite the increasingly competitive race to gain the lead in Arab news reporting, Al-Jazeera is still the region's most-viewed news network and the second most watched pan Arab station. Among the approximately 40 million viewers, 175.000 are situated in the United States. According to Allied Media Corporation statistics, the largest proportion comprises of young, educated professionals and decision-makers aged 20-35, who spend about 4 hours per day watching the channel. The majorities of the viewers resides in populated urban areas and hold a high school degree. A high percentage of its viewers are reported to be Muslim, while men overwhelmingly outnumber women. Along with the statistics, what raises concern in the West is therefore the network's potential influence over Arab public opinion.

A NEW MEDIA WAR OF JIHAD

The "war on terrorism" is fought not only on the battlefields of Iraq and Afghanistan but also on the parallel microcosm of the media. The "jihadi movement" has moved the struggle to the level of information where, via the use of television and particularly the Internet, it can easily get a podium to address its audience, create a virtual ummah, spread its worldview and terrorize its enemies. Admittedly, for a movement with "medieval leanings", they have been quite successful.

"Publicity is the oxygen of terrorism", concluded Margaret Thatcher at a time when IRA violence was reaching a peak. Walter Laqueur, one of the most influential analysts of guerrilla warfare, came to this conclusion even earlier, in the early 1970's, long before we crossed the threshold of the "information age". As he put it: "The media are the terrorist's best friend. The terrorist's act by itself is nothing, publicity is all".

The critical role of the media is well understood by the Salafi groups that wage an international jihad against their perceived enemies throughout the world. The centrality of this axiom in al-Qaeda's philosophy is evident in the fact that, even before the spectacular 9/11 attacks, one of the four committees that formed its organizational structure was tasked with media and publicity. The importance of the message behind the action was stressed in a letter sent by Ayman al-Zawahiri to Abu Musab al-Zarqawi where Zawahiri said that the media represent two thirds of the battle, as well as in a speech made by Osama bin Laden in 2002 where he argued that: "The time has come to have the media take its rightful place, to carry out its required role in confronting this aggressive campaign and the open declared Crusader war by all means that can be seen, heard, and read." From this angle, the emergence of groups such as Global Islamic Media Front, the Jihad Information Brigade and Jihad Media Battalion, to name just a few, comes as no surprise.

The use of media power, of course, is by no means peculiar to al-Qaeda and like-minded groups. However, what is significant in this case is the adaptive and more or less sophisticated exploitation of the opportunities that the media offer in order to promote their goals and elucidate their worldview. The "jihadi movement" learned the lesson of Ayatollah Khomeini's use of the cassette-tape to diffuse his teachings to the point that the Islamic Revolution of 1979 was also dubbed "the cassette revolution"-, but most importantly they managed to move beyond the traditional methods of leaflets, booklets, paper magazines (i.e. GIA's magazine Al-Ansar) and audio-visual recordings that circulated in essence from hand to hand and to reach a grand audience by exploiting two phenomena of the "information era", namely satellite television and the Internet. A research conducted by Manuel Torres, Javier Jordan and Nicola Horsburgh (published in the journal "Terrorism and Political Violence") showed a concrete turn towards the two aforementioned media which the "Jihadists" prefer more and more to transmit their message. In 2001 none of the messages came out through the Internet, 9 through television and 3 through print media. In 2002 there were already signs of a change, as the Internet was used in 23 cases, television in 4 and print media in 30. In 2005 this trend became pronounced to the utmost, since the respective numbers were 2439, 10 and 0.

Satellite television was the first target and broadcaster of the "jihadi message" especially after the "big bang" of 9/11 when Osama bin Laden and al-Qaeda became the focus of global attention and any public declaration was almost certainly reported on news channels. Al-Jazeera benefited most from the ensuing deluge of public debate on terrorism, as the preferential status that al-Qaeda granted it brought the satellite channel to preeminence. Al-Jazeera was usually the first to televise al-Qaeda's communiqués and was the only channel to be granted an interview with bin Laden after the attacks. The access to the mass media underlined the power of the image in fulfilling the goals of propaganda towards either existing or potential sympathizers or towards presumed adversaries by multiplying the terror generated by a single terrorist -or not act.

While the Chechens were the first to incorporate the video camera into the equipments of a guerrilla squad, it was only after 9/11 that their example has loomed large. At the Iraqi front where the material was vast this tactic flourished. Any group that wants to build a respected profile has to release a video that depicts its activity. As a consequence, alongside the usual videos of speeches delivered, for example, by bin Laden or Zawahiri or videos with advice and instructions to future fighters, there is a growing number of recordings that show ambushes against coalition forces, roadside bombs, captured hostages and decapitations. Kidnappings and executions of foreigners was indeed the easiest way to gain immediate coverage in both Arab and international media. Besides the recent, widely-covered, video release depicting the BBC correspondent kidnapped in Gaza, Alan Johnston, who is held by a radical Islamic organization called the "Army of Islam", this tactic is waning. It was against this background that al-Qaeda established its "video arm" As-Sahab

Productions. The amount (in the first four months of 2007 it has released 35 videos, that is a rate of one video per 3,6 days) and the improving quality of its videos is at least remarkable, given the difficult conditions under which the crew has to work and the prerequisite of secrecy during shooting and editing.

However, as public "thirst" for violence reached its saturation point and perhaps as a result of an understanding between certain governments and media companies to limit their access to the media, these groups had to find other ways to impart their message. Audiences in the Middle East could still be reached via some marginal TV channels such as the Iraqi Al-Zawraa TV, (after a ban by the Iraqi government in November 2006, it broadcasts via the Arabsat Badr-3 satellite) which recently started to air a program called "Hidden Camera Jihad" that shows videos of attacks followed by a laughter track, or through direct sale of these videos in the markets of Iraq and other countries in the region.

Nevertheless, in order to keep in contact with the rest of the world, Internet had to assume the reins of the "media war". As Global Islamic Media Front (purportedly Al-Qaeda's mouthpiece) suggested: "This is the Internet that Allah has enlisted in the service of jihad and of the mujahideen, which has come to serve your interests given that half the battle of the mujahideen is being waged on the pages of the Internet, the sole outlet for mujahideen media". Ironically, the Internet is the incarnation - at least on the level of symbolism of a "virtual" ummah, even more so since the physical "scale model" of the ummah in Afghanistan was lost. Bulletin boards and chat rooms proved to be ideal in creating an atmosphere of community.

The pattern of the jihadi presence on the cyber net is infact a reflection of the movement's actual needs and organizational style. While in the 1990's, when the Jihadists formed a more hierarchical structure under the shadow of al-Qaeda, there were only a few sites of that kind, of which the most important was "alneda.com",after 9/11 the imperative to move to a more decentralized network of like-minded groups meant, in the case of the Internet, the proliferation of "jihadi cells". According to Professor Gabriel Weimann, the number of terrorist-run websites increased by 571% between 1997 and 2004.

The material distributed via the Net proliferated accordingly taking advantage of the absence of the restrictions present in the traditional mass media. In addition to various official jihadi statements, videos and monographs of ideological content, there have emerged manuscripts and on-line magazines of military and technical nature such as the "Encyclopedia of Jihad", the "Encyclopedia of Preparation" and the on-line magazine "Mu'askar al-Battar" which was published in 2004 by the al-Qaeda organization in Saudi Arabia as a complement to the "Sawt al-Jihad" magazine that dealt with doctrine issues. Also in 2004, another internet magazine appeared under the name Al-Khansa. It widened the target group by reaching to women in order to teach those married to radical Islamists how to support their husbands. Meanwhile, a rather small and modestly harmful group of hackers completed the notion of cyber war. The most notorious was Irhabi007, arrested by British authorities in 2005, who also wrote a "hacking manual for mujahideen". His example is followed by others such as the Muhajirun Brigades who aim to "attack those websites which do harm to Islam and to the Muslims".

The Jihadists do not underestimate the importance of marketing either. In 2005 a message was posted on several websites announcing a contest to design a new site for a militant group called Jaish Al-Taifa Al-Mansura in Iraq. The winner would be given the chance to fire through a computer three remote-controlled missiles at a US military base in Iraq. Likewise, in 2006 the Global Islamic Media Front created a videogame with fighters making their way through Coalition forces and eventually getting a chance to take a digital shot on George Bush.

The first reaction of counter terrorism experts was to close down these sites. However, this effort turned out to be futile as the administrators of the sites kept moving to new servers and the proliferation of similar websites didn't cease at any point. Donald Rumsfeld admitted the ineffectiveness of this policy in a speech at the Council on Foreign Relations in February 2006, saying that "the US has lagged behind the al-Qaeda network in one of the most important aspects of the war on terrorism the media war". As a result, a new approach was put forward. On the one hand, instead of trying to obliterate them, it's better to oversee what is being discussed on those sites in order to evaluate the ideological and military developments of the jihadi movement. On the other hand, their message should be countered by a persuasive retort. As Bruce Hoffman of the Georgetown University put it, "the US must help foreign governments flood the Internet with persuasively youthful Web sites presenting anti-jihadist messages yet without leaving American fingerprints". A war especially this kind of war is rarely just a matter of simple power balancing. It is also about "winning the hearts and minds" and, in that sense, it is a media war.

MEDIA FREEDOM

The influence of the Middle Eastern State on the Media has not receded over the past few years. However, the latest technological, political, economic and societal developments seem to have affected the course of press freedom in the region.

Although newspapers existed in the Middle East from the middle of the eighteenth century, they were under the total control either of the Ottoman authorities or of foreign Embassies. The first Arab newspaper, "Al-Waqae al Masreya", was printed in the 19th century in Egypt. Since then, many things have changed. Technological developments have enabled the media to expand their scope of activity there are around 200 Arab satellite TV channels. World events, like the decolonization, the end of the USA-USSR Cold War conflict, the 11/9 terrorist attacks and the US response, have influenced not only the regimes but also the populations of the Arab countries.

One thing that has not changed is the continued attempt of any regime in power to use the mass media as a tool to accomplish its goals, whether it is the integrity of the empire, the national independence, the maintenance of public order and so on.

In retrospect, the technological developments in the media sector could have had two adverse effects on the Middle East's state of affairs. They could have enabled the repressive Middle Eastern regimes to ensure their domination of Arab societies' information channels (a Middle Eastern version of London as depicted in the futuristic film "V for Vendetta"). Or, on the other hand, it could have enabled new political organizations to use the technological developments in their favour so as to mobilize the Arab populations to a rebellion or at least to demand the establishment of more representative governance (a Middle Eastern version of Eastern European revolutions). What actually happened from the beginning of the nineties was somewhere in the middle.

The media were indeed used by the political organizations that gained strength in the region. However, the voices of radicalism and extremism, stemming either from organizations like al-Qaeda or other fundamentalist organizations were much louder than the modernizing voices of the moderate political Islam.

The regimes also tried to use the media so as to preserve their dominance. Egypt had attempted to keep a strict control on the media, ever since Gamal Abdel Nasser nationalised the press after the 1952 revolution. The Baathist regimes in Iraq and Syria followed a similar course. Prior to 1990 almost all Arab radio and television channels were government monopolies. Only in Lebanon the political system fostered newspapers representing a variety of different views. In the early 1990s, Arabic satellite television networks aiming at a pan-Arab audience were established in Europe. Simultaneously, after the end of the Cold War, Egypt was pressed by the US to liberalize the press and to allow the spread of independent media. This does not mean, nevertheless, that the regime didn't attempt to stop their action by taking advantage of state monopolies, e.g. printing facilities, state advertisements etc. Especially after the Gulf War of 1991, the Gulf States had also comprehended the importance of satellite television not only in times of peace, but also in times of conflict. A major motivation for the establishment of the first Arab satellite TV networks was the fact that the coverage of the crisis by CNN was thought to convey to the Arab audiences a different picture, biased against the Arabs. Although CNN was watched by many in the Arab world, most Arabs preferred a different approach to events, closer to Arab sensitivities and interests. The most obvious example of the Arab satellite stations that were created is the state-subsidized Al-Jazeera, which enjoys the support of Qatar's government. Additionally, Muslim investors seem to invest in the large media institutions of the world so as to affect their policies via their participation in the administrative boards (e.g. Saudi Prince Al-Waleed Bin Talal holds more than 5% share in Rupert Murdoch's News Corp News Corp owns the Fox News TV channel).

Although *Al-Jazeera* is a private TV station and its officials have declared that, ideally, they would like to the network to be totally commercialized, this is not feasible. As the projected material in Al-Jazeera was considered hostile to the Middle Eastern regimes, most governments in the Middle East apart from being reluctant to grant state advertisements to Al-Jazeera used their influence and power so as to prevent their own private sector from advertising on the network. This example depicts the ability of the regimes to intimidate the private sector through indirect means, by using their financial clout.

An interesting case in point was when a liberal power encountered the difficult situations of the region and had to deal, among others, with the issue of Arab media (even under the "distorting" influence of leading an occupation force): after the successful US-led invasion of Iraq, as William A. Rugh eloquently describes, the U.S. government was dominant in the Coalition Provisional Authority (CPA) that was responsible for all aspects of governance in Iraq, including the Iraqi media, from March 2003 until June 2004. Apart from providing an example of "democratic" governance in a Middle Eastern state, the US had to improve its image in the Arab world, so as to increase the possibilities of stabilizing the region. How did the US respond in this difficult situation, where normally one would expect an occupation force to impose totalitarian measures? The American response was quite interesting. Attempting both to balance between the desire not to violate its declarations about freedom and the need to steer the post-Saddam Iraqi media into a Western course, the CPA established media outlets that would be supportive of American views. The most notable examples provided by Rugh were that of al-Iraqiya Television and of al-Sabah daily newspaper which were favoured with U.S. funding and access to information (the US had established two international broadcasting stations, Radio Sawa in 2002, an Arabic language service, and al Hurra Television).

Simultaneously, the CPA permitted the emergence of several Iraqi-controlled media all over the country' however it took action in exceptional circumstances (the CPA also tried to establish an Iraqi media regulating body, the ICMC, modelled on the American Federal Communications Commission). The US was also behind the shutting down of Al-Jazeera's offices in Iraq, on the accusation of inciting the populations to opposition against the government. From the above it can be established that the US administration initially followed a more "polite" version of state intervention in media operation than e.g. Egypt did in the post Cold War years. The US attempted to influence the Iraqi media in its favour, indirectly at first (subsidies, exclusive information etc.) but when it was judged that this was not enough, it intervened directly to shut down the dissenting media. The above example illustrates that the future prospects are not so appealing when a liberal power (although under these special circumstances) employs, among others, repressive measures in its dealings with the media.

Nevertheless, one must admit that, at this particular

instance, the growth of new market based media providers could empower more radical forces in the Middle East. As professor Shibley Telhami points out "the media looks at the world through the prism of its audience, through the prism of its consumers" and the Arab audience might be too angry at the moment to reach for the truth.

COVERAGE OF THE LEBANESE CRISIS INSIDE AND OUTSIDE LEBANON

Lebanon has a unique media environment in the region. The media is engaged in the dialogue over a number of political, economic, religious and social issues, a phenomenon unparalleled in other Middle Eastern states, in which the regimes still practice strict state censorship on their media outlets. Unlike other Arab countries, Lebanese media owners are affiliated with the various religious and political groups or sects, reflecting the political interests and divisions of the country. However, sectarianism has escalated after the June 2006 Lebanon War between Hezbollah and Israel.

Mostly sectarian, Future TV (FTV), owned by Saad Hariri, a Sunni member of parliament and the son of Rafiq Hariri, regularly airs shows and videos praising Rafiq Hariri and promoting the March 14 movement. Its news are focused on mainly Sunni Lebanese issues that do not include Southern Lebanon and are basically supportive of Saudi Arabia. On the other hand, Hezbollah-affiliated al Manar TV presents news through the prism of its own political context and orientation giving special coverage to Southern Lebanon and the Bekaa (Shia areas). It is markedly supportive of Palestine, Syria and Iran.

A media war has also erupted between Syria and Lebanon, following the February 2005 assassination of former Lebanese Prime Minister Rafiq Hariri. Not only the anti-Syrian LBC, but also the FTV channel, which attracts a large number of Syrian viewers, leveled unprecedented harsh criticism at Syria for its involvement in the assassination. The Lebanese media have played a major role in the "Cedar Revolution" and the revolts that led the Syrian forces to withdraw from the region in April 2005. However, in the months that followed media critics of the Syrian regime paid the price with their lives, as publisher Gebran Tueni and columnist Samir Qassir of al-Nahar newspapers as well as LBC-TV journalist May Chidiac were killed in car bomb attacks. The Lebanese media are very important to the Assad regime, because Syrian state television has no appeal to the Syrian public that usually tunes to Lebanese terrestrial TV in order to be informed on current events.

Disagreement in the Arab world about the Lebanon War, between the state sponsors of Hezbollah and the moderate Arab states of Saudi Arabia and Egypt, has been reflected in the Arab media too. Newspapers affiliated to the moderate regimes, accused Hezbollah for serving Syrian and Iranian aspirations in the region and for jeopardizing the interests of the Lebanese people and of the Arab states. Accusations went further to criticize the role of Iran and Syria in manipulating Hezbollah and setting off the Lebanese crisis.

In Egypt, some of the allegations directly accused Iran of manipulating the Lebanese crisis in order to drive international pressure away from its nuclear program. Abd Al-Rahim 'Ali, director of the Arab Center for the Study of Islam and Democracy in Cairo, wrote in the Egyptian government daily Al-Ahram: "When Iran saw that its nuclear dossier would soon be transferred to the Security Council, it decided to use Lebanon, along with Iraq, as a bargaining card to increase the pressure on the Americans". Egyptian columnist Hazem 'Abd Al-Rahman wrote in the same newspaper: "all Iran wants is to extend its hegemony over the eastern Arab countries, and it is trying to use Hezbollah as a Trojan horse to achieve this aim" (Al-Ahram, August 6, 2006). In the same tone, Lebanese columnist Fuad Matar wrote in Al-Sharq Al-Awsat: "Hezbollah has placed the Arabs in a questionable situation, since its operation was meant to serve Iran's interests". Muhammad 'Ali Ibrahim, chief editor of the Egyptian government daily Al-Gumhuriyya, wrote: "... the Iranian plan...seeks to destroy the Arab states from within by using Hezbollah in Lebanon and Hamas in Palestine and by swallowing Iraq... Iran wishes and plans to turn the entire Arab world into an assortment of armed militias like Hezbollah".

Saudi-affiliated newspapers, owned by or based in Saudi Arabia, also express the disagreement of their government over Hezbollah's provocative actions. Al-Riyadh newspaper published an editorial "Irresponsible wars" which called Hezbollah's war an "illusory victory". Particularly critical of Syria's involvement and role in Lebanese domestic affairs, Jamal Hashukji, former editor of the Saudi daily Al-Watan wrote about Syria: "angry, anxious, and hurting because of the loss of its hegemony over Lebanon, was interested in drawing attention away from the investigation into the assassination of Prime Minister Rafiq Al-Hariri..." Al-Watan, July 18, 2006. The Syrian regime denies those allegations and claims that it is Israel and the West that have been determined to redraw the map of the Middle East. It goes further to accuse Israel of plotting the Hariri assassination in collaboration with the US. Within this context, Syrian Minister of Expatriate Affairs Buthayna Sha'ban answered to the accusations by writing in her column in AlSharq Al-Awsat: "It is not Hezbollah which is a proxy, fighting on behalf of Syria and Iran, as some have claimed in attempt to mislead the Arabs.

Israel is the one which is fighting the Arabs and Muslims on Lebanese soil on behalf of the U.S., Britain and the entire West... In the same tone Columnist Adnan Ali wrote in the Syrian government daily Al-Thawra: "The repeated statements by U.S. Secretary of State about the birth of a new Middle East expose the intentions of those who planned this war against Lebanon and who wanted to use it as an opportunity to... create a new reality based on America's and Israel's perception of the region..." According to another article in the Syrian government daily Al-Thawra: "The war that is currently waging makes us more certain than ever that Israel and the U.S. are the forces behind the assassination of Rafiq Al-Hariri. The assassination was part of an unsuccessful attempt by the U.S. to enforce U.N. Resolution 1559. ...Israel is the only one who benefits from this resolution and from Al-Hariri's assassination". The Syrian media have also condemned as a "political vengeance" the UN Security Council resolution to establish an international tribunal for the prosecution of the suspects of the Hariri assassination, arguing that the resolution is just another instrument for the US and Israel to interfere in the Middle East and it does not reflect the policy of the other international powers. "The resolution ... is absolutely a US-Israeli one and could never be regarded as an expression of the international will," argued an editorial of the Tishrin government newspaper. The Al-Thawra government newspaper has also stated that the purpose of the resolution was "to politicize investigations in Hariri's assassination" and that it was revealing of the US intensions of a "direct and abrupt intervention" in regional affairs.

Syria's ally, Iran, who hasn't escaped criticism over its role in the Lebanese crisis, has adopted very similar arguments as Syria and its newspapers along with Syrian ones reflect the common policies of the two countries. Hard-line Tehran newspapers have been really supportive of Damascus over the Hariri investigation tribunal, accusing the US and Israel that the resolution is part of their imperialistic plans that target Syria. Jomhuri-yi Islami daily newspaper, stated in its editorial of January 3, 2006 that the assassination of Hariri was "the first phase of the project America and the Zionists had prepared to pave the way for annexing Syria and Lebanon to the imperialist plot of a Greater Middle East." Similar comments have also appeared in Resalat newspaper, accusing the United States, France and Israel of interfering in domestic Lebanese and Syrian affairs.

In conclusion, true debate over the issues galvanizing Lebanon's crisis is prohibited in the media of the Middle Eastern Arab states. On the contrary, the state of affairs in Lebanon has provided an environment which is revealing of the regional antagonisms precipitated by the political interests of the two Middle Eastern camps and their affiliates inside Lebanon who push for further division between the various political religious and sectarian groups.

INTROVERT SOCIETIES IN AFRICA: THE ISSUE OF PRESS FREEDOM

In Africa the problem of press freedom remains yet unsolved. Attacks against the press are on the rise in many countries of the Maghreb as well as in sub-Saharan Africa as journalists become more outspoken in their criticism. The struggle for free press is destined to be long, arduous and buffered by wider political forces.

In the mid-1990's Algeria was considered to be the most dangerous place in the world to practice journalism. In the 1990-92 periods the Algerian media enjoyed a freedom and vibrancy unparalleled in the Arab world. The political turmoil and the outbreak of violence widened the divide between secular and Islamist extremists. Initially, organs of the Front Islamique du Salut (FIS), such as the weeklies Al-Mounqidh and Al-Forqane, were closed down in 1992. The clampdown on news coverage gradually extended to independent Arabic publications which had been critical of the government. In addition, the Algerian authorities remained silent about the cases of "disappeared" journalists Djamel Eddine Fahassi and Aziz Bouabdallah who were abducted in 1995 and 1997 respectively by men believed to be state agents.

Despite the fact that the Algerian constitution guarantees freedom of the press, in February 2006 free expression was dealt another blow, when the cabinet passed a decree that granted immunity to perpetrators of violence during the conflict (the Algerian civil war of the mid1990s). In addition, the decree authorized imprisonment up to five years for anyone who by speech, writing or any other act used or exploited the wounds of the National Tragedy. In January 2006, the reporter Bachir Larabi of the daily independent el-Khabar was imprisoned for a month, after he was found guilty of defaming a local mayor. That same year, Mohamed Benchicou director of the Algiers-based daily newspaper Le Matin, was released from prison. Benchicou served a two-year sentence after his newspaper had virulently criticized the Algerian President Abdelaziz Bouteflika and other cabinet ministers. Another daily newspaper critical of the government, er Rai, has been out of circulation since 2003, when state-owned printers demanded payment of all bills within 48 hours.

The only country in North Africa with significant progress in press freedom is Mauritania, regardless of the fact that the government still maintains a monopoly on radio and television broadcasting. In 2005 the military council established the "National Commission in Change of the Reform of the Press and the Broadcasting". In addition, in 2006, the government created the High Authority for the Press and Broadcasting (HAPA), the first independent media regulatory body in Mauritania. The government controls two daily newspapers, while 40 newspapers are privately-owned and circulate on a regular basis nearly double the figure compared to the previous year. Further-more, newspaper owners and book publishers are exempt from all taxes on material used for production.

In sub-Saharan Africa, the situation regarding freedom of expression can be described as worrying, especially in Zimbabwe where the most recent negative developments in media manipulation and press harassment have taken place. Professional and media monitoring organizations such as the Zimbabwe Union of Journalists, the Media Monitoring Project of Zimbabwe and the local branch of the Media Institute of Southern Africa were subject to official harassment throughout 2006.

In February 2006, Gift Phiri, a freelance journalist was brutally beaten by police officers who accused him of working for foreign media outlets. The government, through Mass Media Trust Holding Company, controls several major daily newspapers, including the Chronicle and the Herald; coverage in these news outlets consists of favourable portrayals of President Robert Mugabe and his ruling party ZANU-PF (Zimbabwe African National Union-Patriotic Front) and attacks on perceived critics of the regime. Several independent weeklies such as the Standard and the Zimbabwe Independent continue to be published, although many journalists practice extensive self-censorship.

The state controlled Zimbabwe Broadcasting Corporation (ZBC) runs all broadcast media, which are seen as mouthpieces of the regime. In addition, the popular shortwave service Radio Africa, a London-based station run by exiled Zimbabweans journalists, was blocked during the 2005 parliamentary elections.

Finally in recent months, Zimbabwe was shocked by the murder of Edward Chikomba and the beating of the award winning lawyer Mtetwa. Chikomba was a veteran cameraman of the state-run ZBC. Several news reports link Chikomba's death to his alleged leaking to foreign media of footage of opposition leader Morgan Tsvangirai badly beaten after his release from police custody last month. Beatrice Mtetwa, President of the Law Society of Zimbabwe, has defended dozens of journalists and fought for press freedom, all at great personal risk. Despite the fact that South Africa's President Thabo Mbeki supports his Zimbabwean counterpart Robert Mugabe, in South Africa press freedom and freedom of expression is constitutionally guaranteed. South Africa features a vibrant press and active journalist organizations. A number of private newspapers and magazines including the Mail & Guardian, the Cape Times, and the Sunday Times are sharply critical of the government.

The state-owned South African Broadcasting Corporation (SABC) dominates broadcast media. However, the SABC is editorially independent from the government and has come under fire for displaying pro-government bias and for encouraging self-censorship. Although most South Africans receive the news via radio outlets associated with the SABC, efforts are being made in order to expand the number of radio stations through the Independent Communications Authority of South Africa (ICASA). In addition, Thabo Mbeki has been praised by several journalist organizations for his decision not to sign a controversial legislation regarding ICASA's council.

The fact remains that press freedom and free expression are at a critical low point throughout Africa. The African Union human rights agencies are gaining ground, while the establishment of an African court of human rights will also be important. If the African Union wants to shed suspicions that it is still a club of dictators, it must be prepared to give press freedom the importance it deserves.

CINEMA AS A MIRROR OF MIDDLE EASTERN SOCIETIES

Although it is difficult to speak about Middle Eastern cinema as a whole due to the particularities of the distinct cultures comprising the region, there are certain themes (neocolonial oppression, national self-determination, reli-gious fundamentalism, women's position vis-à-vis Islam) that preoccupy most of Middle Eastern filmmakers. Combined with the fact that the states have not relinquished control over the cinema, cinematographic expression is transformed into political statement.

If we accept the principle that cinema is the mirror of the society it is born in, Middle Eastern cinema is perforce a profoundly political cinema, not because the majority of Middle Eastern films deal with political issues on the contrary, political cinema as a cinematic genre is forbidden in many of these countries but because it has developed amidst regional crisis that have influenced the worldview of its creators; because its themes reflect the mysteries of the Middle Eastern way of life; because, even in the lightest mainstream Egyptian comedies, it depicts the everyday life of the habitants in this benevolent region. Mostly it is political because it has been used as an instrument of politics: by the state as a tool of propaganda; by the opposition in order to protest against national politics; by individuals as the ultimate means to express their concerns in countries where liberty of speech is rather restrained.

Certainly, cinema is not the same in all Middle Eastern countries. Indeed, we could categorize the countries on the basis of film production into three groups. First, the very productive countries: Egypt, the centre of Arab film production, which has the world's fourth-largest and third-oldest film industry; Israel, which also has a notable cinematographic history and its films are popular in the U.S. (6 times nominated for Best Foreign Language Film Academy Award, more than any other Middle Eastern country); Iran, whose cinema is quite renowned in Europe and is always present in European and International Film Festivals (one of the highlights being Abbas Kiarostami's winning the Golden Palm award in Cannes for The Time of Cherry in 1997); Lebanon, which has also succeeded in standing out though its films are mainly produced with European financing; and the Palestinian cinema which, though relatively young in comparison to Arab cinema as a whole, has gained international recognition.

The second group includes Syria, Iraq and Jordan, countries which had a noticeable film production in the past but are now in decline. Syria is the second-largest, after Egypt, television producer in the region, and has the necessary facilities, but due to the lack of public interest it has turned to film imports rather than local productions. Iraqi cinema possessed both institutional and technical infrastructure and flourished during the 1970s only to perish after the Gulf War in 1992. Finally, the third group includes Saudi Arabia and the Gulf states, whose film production is rather meagre (1-3 films in each country), mainly because of moral restrictions dictated by the strictly Islamic way of life.

The cinema of the Middle Eastern countries did not follow the same course and does not share common aesthetic characteristics. For example, the Iranian cinema is meditative, inspired by the Persian lyricism and poetic heritage, and often symbolic partly because of the strict censorship. On the other hand, Egypt's artistic cinema collated to the dominant Hollywood-style mainstream has amalgamated various cinematic trends (French poetic realism, Italian neo-realism, socialist realism, modernist German expressionism, Soviet dialectical montage) which resulted into the emergence of a distinctive realistic (and later, New Realistic) movement, expressed by prominent directors as Atef Al Tayeb, Salah Abu Seif, Youssef Chahine, Taufik Salih, Khairy Beshara and Daoud Abd El-Sayyed. Meanwhile in Syria there emerged the Alternative Cinema in 1972 as a response to the growing commercial Egyptian cinema which focused on pan-Arabic nationalism and included Palestinian and Lebanese filmmakers. Nevertheless, a common characteristic of most regional movements was their influence by the "cinema d'auteur" (the auteur theory states that one person, usually the director, bears sole responsibility for the film and that his personal views, or his "vision", can be observed in it.)

Regardless of the various regional movements, a great body of Arab cinema can be placed among the so-called Third Cinema, i.e. the cinema of the Third World. Named by the Argentinian filmmakers Fernando Solanas and Octavio Getino in accordance with the First (Hollywood) and the Second (European) Cinema, the Third Cinema decries neocolonialism and the Western or Westernized (Israel) capitalist world as well as the Hollywood model of cinema, and strives to promote solidarity among all peoples that have experienced (neo)colonialism. Examples include films by Egyptians Youssef Chahine (Cairo Station, 1958; Alexandria... Why?, 1978; Destiny, 1997) and Taufik Salih (Street of Fools, 1955; The Duped, 1972), as well as Palestinian Elia Suleiman (The Chronicle of a Disappearance, 1996; Divine Intervention, 2002). The oppressive reality of the neocolonial dominance comes dimly into sight in films as Usama Mohammad's The Box of Life (2002), which describes the life in a small Syrian village during the 1967 war with Israel and in Randa Chahal Sabag's The Kite (2003), in which a young couple, a Lebanese girl and an Israeli Arab soldier (both from the Druze religion) cannot contact on account of the barbed wire.

The subject of the Israeli occupation becomes more pungent when it comes to the Palestine issue (e.g. Michel Khleifi's Wedding in Galilee, 1987; Hany Abu-Assad's Rana's Wedding, 2002; Yousri Nasrallah's The Gate of Sun, 2004). However, Palestinian filmmakers have latterly commenced to examine the Palestinian problem from another angle. Elia

Suleiman, in Divine Intervention (2002) portrays the Palestinians as victims of the Israeli despotism, but also as victims of their own frictions. He criticises his own people directly, through the unflattering figures of the saboteur and the collaborator, and indirectly, by detecting the Palestinian stagnancy and remission. Hany Abi-Assad in Paradise Now (2005) treats the controversial phenomenon of suicide bombing missions, narrating the story of two friends who undertake a suicide mission but, in the course, have doubts about the effectiveness of such an action. The filmmaker detaches himself from the myth of the martyr and provokes a discussion about the vicious circle of violence. As far as Israel is concerned, some filmmakers renounce the encroachment of human rights in the occupied areas and propose another way for contacting the Palestinians.

In David Benchetrit's documentary Dear Father Quiet We're Shooting (2006), Israeli soldiers deny serving in Palestinian territories; Amos Gitai films Free Zone (2005) narrating the friendship between women from different cultures in Jordan (an American, an Israeli and a Palestinian), while he expresses skepticism about the issues at stake in Kippur (2002), a film on the 1973 Yom Kippur war between Syria and Israel in which he fought; and Avi Mograbi shatters the two Israeli myths, the myth of Sampson and the myth of the Massada hill in Avenge but one of my two eyes (2005), naming Sampson the first kamikaze in history and withering the praise of the collective suicide of the Zealots. The Arab filmmakers' preoccupation with the Israeli practices pertains to the general subject of national self-determination, since the Arab societies struggle to reclaim their own national identities through their contradistinction with the other, who, apart from Israeli, might be American (Nader Galal, Hello America, 2000) or European.

In Youssri Nars-rallah's The City (1999), an Egyptian immigrant in Paris suffers from amnesia (symbolizing the loss of the past, present and identity) and overcomes it only when he returns to Egypt. Other films approach the national self-determination issue by praising the heterogeneity of Arab culture; still the allusion to Jews as a part of the Arab cultural mosaic remains a taboo, although challenged in the awarded documentary Forget Baghdad: Jews and Arabs The Iraqi Connection which compares the alienation facing four Iraqi communist Jews in their homeland with that of the Arabs living in Israel.

Other films depict the various wars that have taken place in the Middle East, from the Lebanese civil war (Zaid Doueiri, West Beirut, 1998) to the Iran-Iraq War (Salah Abou Seif, Al-Qadisiyya, 1981) and the Iraq-Kuwait War (multiple directors, The Gulf War, What's next?, 1991). At the same time, films like Abbas Kiarostami's Through the Olive Trees (1994) and A Taste of Cherry (1997) provoke discussions about the vast ethnic mix of the countries that have received refugees from various Middle Eastern conflicts and offer a universal commentary on the value of human life.

Another constant theme in Middle Eastern filmography is religion and religious fundamentalism. Through their films, the cinematographers take the occasion to consider the roots of religious extremism (Youssef Chahine, Destiny, (1997); Atef Hetata, The Closed Doors, 1999) and to impugn religious intolerance (Merzak Allouache, Bab El-Oued, 1994; Yamina Bachir, Rachida, 2002). The latter film deals with religious terrorism against women, whose place in Islamic societies has also been a taboo in the Arab films for a long time. For example, Mohsen Makhmalbaf's A Time to Love (1991), depicting a love triangle between a woman and two men, was never screened in public cinemas in Iran.

However, since the 1990s, an entire genre of feminist Middle Eastern cinema has emerged and has established a strong foothold, particularly in the Islamic Republic (Marziyeh Meshikini, The Day I Became a Woman, 2000; Tahmi-neh Milani, The Hidden Half, 2001; Jafar Panahi, The Circle, 2000). In March 2007, Egypt hosted its first Woman's Film Festival, where female directors from various Islamic countries, even Saudi Arabia (Haifaa Al-Mansour), presented their fiction or documentary films regarding the position of women vis-à-vis Islam. And speaking of tumbled taboos, we should also mention the attempts to film gay and bisexual relations within the Arab society, like A Minute of Sun Less and the short films How I Love You and Diary of a Male Whore. Nevertheless, this regeneration of cinematographic manners cannot be interpreted as the beginning of a new, free, era of cinematographic creation. The state remains omnipotent as far as film production and distribution are concerned. Each country forms its own "cinema" policy in terms of its principles and aims, which ranges from absolute interdiction of cinemas (the case of Saudi Arabia) to the exploitation of cinema for the purpose of islamicizing society (the case of Iran).

In countries like Egypt and Iran, where cinematographic production is state funded, filmmakers have to endure censorship. Even in the comparatively liberal Egypt, films that dealt with the 1967 defeat were banned during Sadat's early years (e.g. Youssef Chahine's The Sparrow, 1973), and even after state censorship was eased (in the early 1990s), films that treat religious issues are subjected to meticulous examination. In fact, it is not unusual for filmmakers to have their films banned at home. Censorship is predictably stricter in the Islamic Republic of Iran, where cinema is perceived as a means of promoting the Islamic way of life.

The Iranian Constitution states that the media "are free to present all matters except those that are detrimental to the fundamental principles of Islam or the rights of the public", namely, according to the Ministry of Culture and Islamic Guidance, matters that question monotheism and submission to God, the role of Revelation (vahy) in creation and in law, and the continuity of religious leadership (emamat). Furthermore, violence and profanity are forbidden, as well as physical contact between men and women, and women in films must always wear a hejab (covering). To ensure compliance with these restrictions, the Ministry has implemented a 5-step regulation process that controls all the stages of film production. In order to evade restrictions, many filmmakers shoot their films outside Iran (like Makhmalbaf who filmed part of The Cyclist in Pakistan, A Time for Love in Turkey, and the Silence in Tajikistan) or turn to films about children as a surrogate to adult films (Jafar Panahi, The White Balloon, 1995; Majid Majidi, Children of Heaven, 1999). Yet, many Iranian masterpieces, like The Circle, Banoo and The Hidden Half have been banned by the state. Notwithstanding, the independent cinema remains the voice of the Middle East. And most important, it reflects the opinions, concerns and hopes of Middle Eastern societies, offering us a different image to that of the official proclamations. Cinema, as Amos Gitai avows, might not change the world. But it can be the means to "say to all the mechanisms that we are active, that we are not participating in their game, and that we are going to propose another reading of things".

Bibliography

Abbott, Nabia. *Aishah: The Beloved of Mohammad.* London: Al-Saqi, 1998.

Andrae, Tor. *Mohammed: The Man and His Faith.* London: George Allen & Unwin, 1936.

Armstrong, Karen. *Islam: A Short History.* New York: Modern Library, revised ed., 2002.

Asad, Muhammad. *The Message of the Qur'an.* Gibraltar: Dar al-Andalus, 1980.

Asani, Ali, et al. *Celebrating Muhammad: Images of the Prophet in Popular Muslim Poetry.* Columbia, Ashgate/Variorum, 2000.

Azam Malik, trans.). Houston, TX: The Institute of Islamic Knowledge, 1997.

Baljon, Jon M.S. *Modern Muslim Koran Interpretation (1880-1960).* Leiden: E.J. Brill, 1961.

Barlas, Asma. *"Believing Women" in Islam: Unreading Patriarchal Interpretations of the Qur'an.*

Bell, Richard. *Introduction to the Qur'an.* Edinburgh: Edinburgh University Press, 1963.

Bell, Richard. *The Qur'an Translated,* 2 Vols. Edinburgh: T. & T. Clark, 1960.

Bowker, John. *What Muslims Believe.* Oxford, UK: Onewworld, 1999.

Burton, John. *The Collection of the Quran.* Cambridge, UK: Cambridge University Press, 1977.

Cook, Michael. *Muhammad.* New York: Oxford University Press, 1983.

Cragg, Kenneth. *The Mind of the Quran: Chapters in Reflection.* London: George Allen & Unwin, CT: Yale University Press, 2002.

Dawood, N.J. *The Koran*. Harmondsworth: Penguin, 1956.

Denny, Frederick Mathewson. *An Introduction to Islam.* New York: Macmillan, 1994.

Elias, Jamal J. *Islam.* Upper Saddle River, NJ: Prentice Hall, 1999.

Esack, Farid. *Qur'an, Liberation and Pluralism.* Oxford, England: Oneworld, 1997.

Esack, Farid. *The Qur'an: A Short Introduction.* Oxford, England: Oneworld, 2002.

Gilsenan, Michael. *Recognising Islam: 'an anthropologist's introduction.* London: Croom Helm, 1982.

Hawting, G.R. et al., eds. *Approaches to the Quran.* London: Routledge, 1993.

Hodgson, Marshall G.S. *The Venture of Islam,* 3 Vols. Chicago, IL: University of Chicago International, 1983.

Izutsu, Toshihiko. *God and Man in the Koran.* Salem, NH: Ayer Co. Publ., 1980.

Jansen, J.J.G. *The Interpretation of the Koran in Modern Egypt.* Leiden: E.J. Brill, 1974.

Kahn, Muhammad Zafrulla. *Muhammad, Seal of the Prophets.* New York: Viking Press, 1981.

Khalifa, Rashad. *Quran, Hadith, and Islam.* Fremont, CA: Universal Unity, 2000.

Lings, Martin. *Muhammad: his life based on the earliest sources.* New York: Inner Traditions London: Oxford University Press, 1955.

McAuliffe, Jane Dammen, ed. *The Encyclopedia of the Qur'an,* Vol. 1. Leiden: E.J. Brill, 2001.

Mir, Mustansir. *Dictionary of Qur'anic Terms and Concepts.* New York: Garland, 1987.

Motzki, Harald, ed. *The Biography of Muhammad: The Issue of the Sources.* Leiden: E.J. Brill, 2000.,

Nasr, Seyyed Hossein. *Ideals and Realities of Islam.* London: Allen & Unwin, 1966.

Nasr, Seyyed Hossein. *Islamic Spirituality I: Foundations.* New York: Crossroad, 1987.

Nasr, Seyyed Hossein. *Islamic Spirituality II: Manifestations.* New York: Crossroad, 1991.

Nasr, Seyyed Hossein. *Muhammad: Man of God.* Chicago, IL: Kazi Publ., 1995.

Nasr, Seyyed Hossein. *The Heart of Islam: Enduring Values for Humanity.* San Francisco, CA: New York Press, 1984.

Newby, Gordon D. *A Concise Encyclopedia of Islam.* Oxford, UK: Oneworld, 2002.

Peters, F.E. *A Reader on Classical Islam.* Princeton, NJ: Princeton University Press, 1994.

Peters, Francis E. *Muhammad and the Origins of Islam.* Albany, NY: State University of New Press, 1961.

Rahman, Fazlur. *Islam.* Chicago, IL: University of Chicago Press, 2nd ed., 1979.

Rahman, Fazlur. *Major Themes of the Qur'an.* Minneapolis, MN: Bibliotheca Islamica, 1980.

Rippin, Andrew, ed. *The Qur'an: Style and Contents.* Aldershot, UK: Ashgate, 2001.

Rippin, Andrew. *Muslims: Their Religious Beliefs and Practices.* London: Routledge, 2nd ed., 2001.

Rippin, Andrew. *The Qur'an and Its Interpretive Tradition.* Aldershot, UK: Ashgate, 2002.

Robinson, Francis. *Atlas of the Islamic World since 1500.* New York: Facts on File, 1982.

Rubin, Uri, ed. *The Life of Muhammad.* Aldershot: Ashgate, 1998.

Ruthven, Malise. *Islam in the World.* New York: Oxford University Press, 2nd ed., 2000.

Schuon, Frithjof. *Islam and the Perennial Philosophy*. London: World of Islam Festival Publ. Co., SCM Press, 1996.

Sells, Michael. *Approaching the Qur'an: The Early Revelations*. Ashland, OR: White Cloud Press, Society, 1996.

Stowasser, Barbara Freyer. *Women in the Qur'an: Traditions and Interpretations*. New York: T. & T. Clark, 1939.

Tayob, Abdulkader. *Islam: A Short Introduction*. Oxford, England: Oneworld, 1999.

The Koran Interpreted. Arthur J. Arberry, trans. New York: Macmillan, 1955.

The Koran. J.M. Rodwell, trans. London: J.M. Dent & Sons, 1909 (reprint ed., 1974).

Wadud-Muhsin, Amina. *Qur'an and Woman: Reading the Sacred Text from a Woman's Perspective*.

Waines, David. *An Introduction to Islam*. Cambridge, UK: Cambridge University Press, 1995.

Watt, William Montgomery. *Muhammad at Mecca*. Oxford, UK: Clarendon Press, 1953.

Watt, William Montgomery. *Muhammad at Medina*. Oxford, UK: Clarendon Press, 1956.

Watt, William Montgomery. *What is Islam?* London: Longman, 1970.

Wild, S., ed. *The Qur'an as Text: Islamic Philosophy, Theology, and Science*. Leiden: E.J. Brill, 1997.

Williams, John Alden, ed. *The Word of Islam*. Austin, TX: University of Texas Press, 1994.

Index

F

G

H

I

J

M

N

O

P